H. BALFOUR GARDINER

'How many characteristics and qualities we who knew him can read in that profile! . . . The Puck, the Rebel . . . the loyal friend and Critic! . . .'
(Basil Sutton)

Balfour Gardiner photographed in November 1948 at
Percy Grainger's request

H. BALFOUR GARDINER

STEPHEN LLOYD

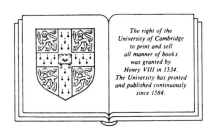

The right of the
University of Cambridge
to print and sell
all manner of books
was granted by
Henry VIII in 1534.
The University has printed
and published continuously
since 1584.

CAMBRIDGE UNIVERSITY PRESS

CAMBRIDGE

LONDON NEW YORK NEW ROCHELLE
MELBOURNE SYDNEY

PUBLISHED BY THE PRESS SYNDICATE OF THE UNIVERSITY OF CAMBRIDGE
The Pitt Building, Trumpington Street, Cambridge, United Kingdom

CAMBRIDGE UNIVERSITY PRESS
The Edinburgh Building, Cambridge CB2 2RU, UK
40 West 20th Street, New York NY 10011–4211, USA
477 Williamstown Road, Port Melbourne, VIC 3207, Australia
Ruiz de Alarcón 13, 28014 Madrid, Spain
Dock House, The Waterfront, Cape Town 8001, South Africa

http://www.cambridge.org

First published 1984
First paperback edition 2005

A catalogue record for this book is available from the British Library

Library of Congress catalogue card number: 83-14227

ISBN 0 521 25609 7 hardback
ISBN 0 521 61922 X paperback

In memory of a wonderful mother
(died 28 March 1983)

Contents

Illustrations

Foreword

When some years ago the young editor of the *Delius Society Journal* confided in me that he longed to write a book on Balfour Gardiner and his music, I was somewhat taken aback. I was impressed by the way he was bringing the journal to its highest peak of perfection, but this enthusiasm for a composer all but forgotten save for two or three pieces for light orchestra and a fine anthem seemed to me incongruous.

I had known Gardiner well through Delius. He had offered me technical advice at the start of my Delius adventure, boosted my confidence and given me whole-hearted support to its close. By then he had abandoned music altogether, maintaining firmly that a man ceases to be musical at fifty. Despite such idiosyncrasies he was unfailing in encouraging talent. His remarkable powers in criticising a score were constantly sought by composer-friends. In this I have never met his equal. The author has made it abundantly clear in dealing with his music that Gardiner gave more thought and care to the vital mechanics of musical structure, especially in writing for the orchestra, than is usual amongst composers. I knew, too, of the mental turmoil he suffered in composing – due to his searing, abortive self-criticism.

Surely this man of such charm and perception had achieved music of greater significance than that by which he was known? The surprise came for me in the revealing Gardiner Centenary Concert at St John's, Smith Square, conducted by Gardiner's great-nephew, John Eliot Gardiner. Here for the first time I heard 'A Berkshire Idyll' – finely wrought, attractive music superbly scored for orchestra – and now I understood Mr Lloyd's enthusiasm.

In ranging from 1877 to 1950 the author's careful researches disclose many hitherto unpublished details of the eager and aspiring English and German musical life of the day. The 'Frankfurt Group' – the fastidious Gardiner, rebellious Percy Grainger, romantic Cyril Scott, lyrical Roger Quilter and handsome Norman O'Neill – figure constantly from student days to full-fledged musicianship, Mr Lloyd rightly concluding, however, that the sum total of their respective works has contributed little of ultimate importance to the heritage of British music. Nevertheless they were all 'characters' of a kind sadly missing today. Gardiner and Quilter, like Bax and Vaughan Williams, were each blessed with private means whereas poor Holst was always struggling. Gardiner's private benevolence often eased his troubled way, as it did for many others, and his quiet timely intervention in patronage of the Royal Philharmonic Society can only be described as providential.

Delius, rather than Elgar, is the more prominent in these pages, being like Gardiner at heart a countryman. I love to think of the latter at Grez puffing and blowing as he lopped dead wood from the branches of trees overhanging the river at the banks of Delius's garden; or bottling the cider from nearby Recloses which for one glorious fortnight a year tasted like Pol Roger champagne!

The spirit of this endearing man has been caught in a book that one day had to be written. I am glad Mr Lloyd chose to do it himself with such sincerity and conviction.

Eric Fenby

Preface

In March 1912 a remarkable concert series of British music was launched at Queen's Hall. Although Elgar was by then well established with his two symphonies and major choral works, Vaughan Williams's early large scores like the *Sea Symphony* and *Tallis Fantasia* had not yet been heard in London, and he and a good number of young composers were seeking representation in the music capital. Largely forgotten today, these concerts brought hope to a generation of British composers, and by igniting a spark of interest in native music helped to shake off a good deal of the foreign domination that for too long had thwarted the hearing of native talent. These concerts were the undertaking of one man, the wealthy and altruistic young composer Balfour Gardiner.

It would be utterly characteristic of Balfour Gardiner to have frowned outwardly upon the idea of being chosen as the subject of a book. He was always one to avoid the limelight and shun any public recognition. The few scattered and veiled references to him in books relating to music have hardly altered this position so that today he is a little-known figure. A composer of some distinction, a conductor, an amateur architect, a pioneer forester, a philanthropist, and a champion and generous patron of British music, he numbered among his many friends men like Arnold Bax, Frederick Delius, Percy Grainger and Gustav Holst. Few of those close to him were not touched in some way by his extraordinary kindness, which was invariably tempered with astute judgment, and his memory has lived on like the Olympic flame as long as his friends and acquaintances have been alive. It is much to be regretted that those now dead who knew him well during his most active years did not (apart from Grainger in his private memoirs) put on record the debt in which they stood through his exceptional generosity.

This book is an attempt to make amends and bring to light for the first time the full story of this rare individual. I have purposely avoided the term 'biography' because this is necessarily more than the story of just one man: it is an account of many friendships (chiefly musical) during that exciting period of British music's struggle out of mediocrity to prominence, and as a documentation of one man's achievements and failures against this background, it offers an interesting sidelight on those formative years.

If, apart from friendship and unselfish benevolence, any one element can be seen to recur throughout this unfolding of his life, it is disillusionment, with the public's attitude towards British music and also with his own composing ability. In the first instance Gardiner did not stand alone, for in 1911 Delius wrote to Bantock: 'I am afraid artistic undertakings are impossible in England – The country is not yet artistically civilized – There is something hopeless about the English people in a musical and artistic way . . .' Delius was to reiterate this extreme view on more than one occasion and in time Gardiner was himself to reach a similar conclusion. Yet it was under such conditions before the First World War that he set out on a large scale to promote British music at a time when such support was most neeeded. If one of his twin foes was what he felt to be the public's general apathy towards native music, more serious was his almost destructive self-criticism. Like Tchaikovsky, whose works he greatly admired, after the excitement surrounding the birth of a composition Gardiner could often unexpectedly veer from enthusiasm, turn on his own work with a scathing dismissal and not lift a finger to promote it. Those works with which he was dissatisfied he later destroyed. There are parallels here with Duparc like whom, though for different reasons, Gardiner ultimately gave up composition, turning instead to afforestation.

If through Gardiner's critical eyes this evidenced some measure of personal failure as a composer, the obverse of the coin reveals yet another facet of his astuteness. How wisely he realised his own limitations. Even if we may think the pruning of his output too drastic, those compositions he chose to leave behind, though few in number, are of a high quality, and it is hoped that this book may help to undo the neglect that has for too long attended such fine works as *A Berkshire Idyll*, *Movement for Strings*, *April* and *Philomela*.

Many people have been kind enough to assist me in the course of my researches. My thanks are first due to those whose privilege it was to know Gardiner personally and who kindly found time to talk with me about him: Hugh Adams, Charles Andrews, Sir Robert Armstrong, Sir Thomas and the late Lady Armstrong, Richard Austin, Denis Blood, Geoffrey Bush, Reginald Cox, Hugh Cruttwell, Eric Fenby, the late Imogen Holst, Guy Warrack and Mrs Winskill.

Next, I am most grateful to the many people who have patiently answered in writing my numerous enquiries: Madame Merle d'Aubigné of Grez-sur-Loing; Gerald Barber, Headmaster of Ludgrove School; Shirley, Lady Beecham; Mrs M. Brooke of Ashampstead; the late Sir Adrian Boult; Dennis Bradbrook of East Challow; Miss Olive Burson of Childrey; Ralph Coward; Mrs Joy Finzi; the late Douglas Fox; John Griffin (who also alerted my attention to H.H. Bashford's book); Paul

Hanbury; Mrs Kirstie Milford; Lady Redcliffe-Maud (Jean Hamilton); the late Mrs Rose L. Scott; Mrs Ursula Vaughan Williams; John Warrack and Miss Avril Wood.

In consulting various records and archives I received valuable assistance and I should like to acknowledge in particular that of R.J. Hampson, ALA, Area Librarian, Montgomery; Messrs Howard Son & Gooch; J. Johnson, University of Reading; Mrs J. Laurenson, University of Cape Town Librarian; Richard Osborne, Bradfield College; R.N.R. Peers, Curator of the Dorset County Museum (for making available half of the Hardy–Gardiner correspondence); Wayne Shirley, Library of Congress, Washington; Messrs Wood, Nash & Winter's; Alan Wykes, Hon. Sec. Savage Club; and Paul Yeats-Edwards, FLA, of Winchester College. My thanks are also due to the Army Records Centre, Ministry of Defence, Hayes, and the librarians of the Parry Room, Royal College of Music; the Vaughan Williams Memorial Library, Cecil Sharp House (especially for making available the Sharp–Gardiner correspondence); the Central Music Library, Westminster; and the Music Department of the Luton Central Library.

In connection with my research into Gardiner's friendships I am particularly indebted to the following for their willingness to make material available to me: concerning Heseltine, Dr Ian Copley and Fred Tomlinson; concerning Quilter, Brian Parkhurst; concerning O'Neill, Derek Hudson; concerning Delius, Dr Lionel Carley and Robert Threlfall, both of the Delius Trust, to which body I am especially grateful for granting permission to reproduce letters from its archive; concerning Bax, Lewis Foreman; concerning Holst, Imogen Holst; and concerning Grainger, Stewart Manville of the Grainger Library Society; Dr Kay Dreyfus of the Grainger Museum, Melbourne; Dr David Tall and Barry Peter Ould of the Percy Grainger Society; and John Bird, Grainger's biographer, who deserves a special vote of thanks for so generously putting his research at my disposal.

I would also like to record my thanks to John Kennedy Scott for sparing time to talk with me about his father; to John Eliot Gardiner and the Monteverdi Choir and Orchestra, David Wilson-Johnson, David Owen Norris, Leslie Howard and Peter Jacobs for enabling me to gain a deeper understanding of the music through their public and private performances of Gardiner's works; to David Wilson-Johnson again for kindly supplying copies of many of the manuscript vocal works; and to anyone whose assistance through oversight I have inadvertently omitted to acknowledge.

Finally, two special acknowledgements. I wish to express my gratitude to Lewis Foreman at whose instigation this book began, for his help, advice and encouragement throughout all its stages; and to the various members of the Gardiner family, especially the composer's great-nephew John Eliot Gardiner, for their kindness, trust and hospitality without which the present book would not have been possible.

The music examples are reproduced by courtesy of the following copyright holders: Chappell Music Ltd and Ascherberg, Hopwood & Crew Ltd for ex. 25; Curwen Edition (J. Curwen & Sons Ltd) for exx. 5 and 6 (both formerly Goodwin & Tabb); Forsyth Brothers for exx. 11, 12, 13, 15, 22, 23, 24, 29, 30, 31 and 33; the trustees of the Gardiner Estate for exx. 1, 2, 16, 17, 18, 20, 21, 26, 27 and 28; Novello & Co. Ltd for exx. 7, 8, 9 and 14; Schott & Co. Ltd for ex. 34; and Stainer & Bell Ltd and Galaxy Music Corporation for exx. 3 and 32 (both formerly Augener) and 19. Ex. 10 is © Copyright 1903 by Boosey & Co. Ltd, reprinted by permission of Boosey & Hawkes Music Publishers Ltd; and ex. 4 appears with acknowledgement to Breitkopf & Härtel Ltd.

All the photographs used in this book were found among the effects of Balfour Gardiner and are reproduced by courtesy of the trustees of the Gardiner Estate, with the exceptions of plate 13, which was kindly supplied by Imogen Holst of G. & I. Holst Ltd; plate 15, which appears by kind permission of Lionel Hill; plate 16, which appears with acknowledgement to the Percy Grainger Society; and plate 19, which was taken at the author's request with the consent of the Grainger Museum, Melbourne.

The sources of the literary quotations are credited in the text, but particular acknowledgement is due to the following for granting permission to quote from these works: The Bodley Head, for Warlock's *Frederick Delius*; Constable & Co. Ltd, for Bashford's *Lodgings for Twelve*; J.M. Dent & Sons Ltd, for Colin Scott-Sutherland's *Arnold Bax*; Harrap Ltd, for Eastaugh's *Havergal Brian: the Making of a Composer* and Foss's *Ralph Vaughan Williams*; The Holst Foundation and the University of Glasgow Publications Committee, for Short's *Gustav Holst: Letters to W.G. Whittaker*; Derek Hudson, for *Norman O'Neill: a Life of Music*; Longman Group Ltd, for Arnold Bax's *Farewell, My Youth*; and A.D. Peters & Co. Ltd, for Clifford Bax's *Inland Far*. Acknowledgement is also due to the editors of *The Daily Telegraph*, *The Musical Times*, *The Observer* and *The Times* for extensive quotations from their respective publications.

1 One of the 'Frankfurt Group'

1877–1901

Somewhere on a ridge of the North Dorset Downs a young oak marks the place where the ashes of one of British music's truest friends lie buried among the trees that he himself planted. Frederick Delius said of him, 'He is one of my oldest friends and one of the very few people I trust and admire implicitly.'[1] Arnold Bax wrote of his 'unfailing friendship and generosity',[2] and that fine choral trainer Charles Kennedy Scott spoke of him as 'an original splendid soul who did more good than he was aware of'.[3]

There is no plaque to identify this last resting place; its occupant is anonymous in death as he was self-effacing during his life-time, and the spot will be passed unnoticed by the casual walker through the woods. Reputations may rise and fall, but, when in the autumn of 1940 Gerald Finzi was visiting his fellow-composer Robin Milford at the latter's home near Newbury, he met for the first time someone who to him was almost a mythical figure. The genial but shy man staying with the Milfords, dressed in thick Norfolk tweeds, with the kindest pale blue eyes and a halo of white hair surrounding his beaming ruddy face, was Henry Balfour Gardiner. In those war-torn days stories of Gardiner's generosity and his early championing of British music clung to him like a legend. Here was a composer who for some personal reason had given up music and devoted his time instead to forestry work, a man who before the First World War had been at the very hub of English musical life and had been personally acquainted with most of its leading figures. Sadly, three of them – Gustav Holst, Frederick Delius and Norman O'Neill – had been dead for some six years, and a second world war was now sweeping away any remnants that the first had not already destroyed of an age to which he spiritually belonged.

In common with his close friend Frederick Delius, Balfour Gardiner was born into a family of merchants, though like Delius he was to take little part in the running of the business. His ancestral line can be traced back to the early seventeenth century, to the Merchant Venturers of Bristol. His grandfather Henry Gardiner, born there in 1809, worked in the woollen drapery business, a trade that developed into wholesale clothing with many connections in the West of England and South Wales. On its limited profits he lived in Bristol a very economical life

1

until, as luck would have it, the sudden flow of emigrants occasioned by the Australian gold rush of the 1850s brought unexpectedly a considerable increase in trade and with it a commensurate fortune. He retired in 1862, purchasing an estate at Caterham in Surrey, and he died in 1884 leaving assets totalling about £70,000. He was a quiet, unassuming man of great integrity with a reputation in his earlier days for strictness and severity, but with one commendable trait in later life that Balfour Gardiner was to inherit in great measure: benevolence.

Margaret Henderson, who became his wife, gave birth to six children of which Balfour's father, Henry John Gardiner, was the only boy. He was born in Bristol in 1843 and after receiving a somewhat limited education left school before the age of sixteen and went to Liverpool, where for two years he 'learned the trade' in a woollen warehouse. He entered his father's business just prior to Henry Gardiner's retirement. Some years of travel followed, after which he returned to Caterham and began gradually expanding his many business concerns. He established his own import-and-export merchant company, H.J. Gardiner & Co., and took much interest in various other financial undertakings, including some collieries. This led in turn to several positions of importance: he became a director and later chairman of Bradbury Greatorex (a wholesale warehousing firm now a subsidiary of Courtaulds), and he was for some years chairman of both the Blackwell Colliery Company and the Holborn Viaduct Land Company as well as being director of the Atlas Assurance Company, the Canadian Bank of Commerce and the Bolsover Colliery Company.

In 1870 he married Clara Elizabeth Honey, one of three daughters of an accountant. According to a delightful if apocryphal story,[4] Henry John could not decide which of the three attractive Miss Honeys he wished to marry. But playing croquet with them one day he chanced to notice as they bent low to make their strokes that the hems of their petticoats showed beneath their skirts and that, while two of these visible hems were frilly, Miss Clara's was plain. It was to her that he proposed. Their married life began in London near Hyde Park at 6 Orsett Terrace, where on 7 November 1877 Clara gave birth to their first child, Henry Balfour Gardiner. They then moved to Eltham in Kent and on 29 March 1879 their other child, Alan Henderson Gardiner, was born.

Tragically, a few days after giving birth to her second son, Clara died at the early age of twenty-seven. The two boys' maternal needs were attended to by a Miss Sophie Hopkins who came to keep house for their father, and when his sons were safely launched on their schooling Henry John Gardiner moved to 25 Tavistock Square, London. He also had the use of a house known as 'Moody's Down' in the heart of Hampshire at Sutton Scotney, Barton Stacey, where it became his custom to spend three days each week entertaining his shooting friends and other guests. In 1920 he had to give up this house when the landlord took possession, so for his country seat he looked elsewhere. After first renting a house in Newbury, in 1921 he took Hazel Cottage at Wonston in Hampshire until he finally acquired twenty acres locally on which he had Upton House built; it was completed in time for the Christmas of 1923.

In 1919 he added to his already impressive list of offices that of high sherriff of the County of London. Three years later, on the death of his partner, his own firm was liquidated, though certain business connections with Nyasaland tea plantations were retained in another form through the Cholo Land and Rubber Estate Company. Balfour in time became a director, under sufferance of duty if for no other reason, though he resigned soon after his father's death in 1940. Regarded by those in the business as the 'Grand Old Man'⁵ of the wholesale trade, outwardly Henry J. Gardiner had, like his father, that typically Victorian air of austerity which his imposing appearance enhanced and his manner on occasion could sustain. He was a stickler for punctuality, and, when dinner was once delayed because of the late arrival of relatives, he quietly informed them, 'You have wasted three minutes of my life.' Money wasted could be made again but time lost was lost for ever. For all his immense wealth, and without being extravagant with large sums, he was sometimes excessively 'penny-wise'. Once when giving a case of wine as a present to one of the family, he asked for the bottles to be returned in due course as there was money to be reclaimed on the 'empties'. Even when his sons were much older he was still held slightly in awe by them. Yet this apparent air of austerity is in part a tint that the perspective of time has placed on an era of rigid etiquette, something that the young Balfour inwardly reacted against, for he was always one to want his own way. As a consequence of Henry J.'s lack of easy intimacy in his dealings with his children, the father–son relationship was not as close as it might have been. Both love and respect were present, but they were restrained. How infuriated the young Balfour would be at his father's constant enquiry, 'How is my busy Bee today?' When Balfour was more independent the customary 'dinner on Sunday with father' had the ring of an ordeal about it and his visits were made partly out of a sense of obligation.

But there was a much warmer side to Henry J. Gardiner, a kindness, affection and consideration that like so many of his characteristics were to emerge in Balfour. He was certainly not lacking a sense of humour. When on one memorable occasion he had invited two friends to 'Moody's Down' for a week-end's shooting, he had the idea of taking each of them quietly aside beforehand, informing him that as the other was deaf he would have to speak twice as loud as normal to make himself heard. The outcome was worthy of P.G. Wodehouse. Henry John was a dutiful father and, although the loss of their mother was a severe blow to the children, with loving care he saw that they lacked nothing throughout their childhood – and indeed their later life. Financially he made it possible for them to indulge their own pursuits without the burdensome necessity of following a trade or profession. This helping hand was not wasted on Balfour, who became a skilful manipulator on the stock market and so in time was able to use his resources to the benefit of not only himself but, more importantly, others.

Although he had been christened Henry Balfour Gardiner, the 'Henry' was soon reduced to a mere initial which he invariably used when signing his name. To his friends he was simply Balfour, a name possibly derived from a distant relative, Colonel Henry Balfour (1767–1818) of the Bengal Artillery who had married into the Gardiner family. Both Balfour and Alan took full advantage of the free rein their father allowed them in their careers, and, although there were hopes that they might follow in the family business, Balfour chose music while Alan became an eminent Egyptologist. Alan's chief claim to fame in the layman's eyes was to be working at Luxor in 1922 at the time of the discovery of Tutankhamen's tomb. His work there mainly concerned the deciphering of inscriptions, and it was as a philologist that he made his greatest contribution to Egyptology. In 1949, at the age of seventy, Alan (by then Sir Alan) was one of those cited by the press as having outwitted the 'Pharaoh's Curse', supposedly responsible for the deaths of several archaeologists involved in the tomb's opening. He died in 1963.

Balfour Gardiner showed inclinations towards music at an early age. Although his father was not very musical, he did attempt the cello and occasionally held instrumental 'at homes' which were responsible for Balfour's musical awakening. It was listening to Corelli trios while only four that prompted the desire to learn the piano. This he was allowed to do as a special treat on his fifth birthday, for his father gave every assistance and encouragement to his sons' interests, and by the age of nine Balfour was composing small pieces for violin and piano. His schooling began at a day school in Eltham and he went on to private schools at Margate and Folkestone and later to Temple Grove, East Sheen (the setting of M.R. James's supernatural tale *A School Story*); from there he won a junior scholarship to Charterhouse which he entered in the winter term of 1891, his brother Alan joining him a year later. While at Eltham he had for several years studied the organ with a Mr T.C. Guyer, whom he affectionately remembered as a 'musician of pure and refined taste who developed my feeling for tone-colour'.[6] At Charterhouse, where he also won a senior scholarship, he came under the guidance of Mr A.G. Becker for the piano. Vaughan Williams, a Carthusian five years

1 Balfour Gardiner with his brother Alan (right), 6 August 1884

Gardiner's senior whom he missed by a year, spoke of Becker as being a very remarkable man and a fine teacher, regretting that he himself had not come directly under his influence.[7] Through Becker, Gardiner grew familiar with the classical piano repertoire and fostered an ambition to become a concert pianist. From his Charterhouse days comes his earliest surviving work – a setting for voice and piano of *The Banks of Calm Bendemeer* from Thomas Moore's *Lalla Rookh* (verses already set by Stanford in his grand opera *The Veiled Prophet of Khorassan* and published separately as *There's a Bower of Roses*).

From public school the next logical step for Gardiner to take would seem to be either Oxford or Cambridge. But instead of progressing straight to university, he chose first to continue his musical education abroad at a conservatory at Frankfurt-am-Main that enjoyed a considerable reputation. So, on leaving Charterhouse a little earlier than was the custom, at the end of the Cricket Quarter of 1894, he proceeded to Germany. There was nothing unusual about this decision because it was a generally held opinion at the time that musical education on the Continent was superior to that available at home, a belief underlined by the many famous names the German establishments could boast on their teaching staffs. There were a number of excellent training schools to be found abroad, outstanding ones being at Berlin, Cologne, Dresden, Frankfurt, Leipzig and Munich, most of them dating from around the middle of the century. If for English students the expense was often an obstacle, the appeal was still strong. Elgar had wanted to study at Leipzig but was prevented by insufficient funds. However, Delius went there in 1886 for an eighteen-month period with his father's financial backing. (One may speculate what might have happened had Elgar's father been a man of wealth and resource like Delius's and Gardiner's.) Many of the previous generation of British composers had furthered their studies abroad: Sullivan at Leipzig, Corder at Cologne, Stanford and Cowen at both Leipzig and Berlin, and Mackenzie at Sondershausen. Even the ebullient Dame Ethyl Smyth had taken Leipzig and Berlin in her stride (and won much operatic success abroad) before assailing the English musical scene. For them the choice of an English music college had been very limited. The senior institution at home was the Royal Academy of Music, founded in 1822 (whose successive principals of Macfarren, Mackenzie and McEwen once earned it the apt nickname of 'The MacAdemy'), and then came a long gap before the appearances of the Trinity College of Music in 1872, the Guildhall School of Music in 1880, and the Royal College of Music in 1882 which absorbed the earlier National Training School of Music set up in 1873.

Gardiner's choice of Frankfurt proved in several ways to be a happy one. He was fortunate in his professor of composition, he was to form

6

2   Balfour Gardiner at the time of beginning his studies at Frankfurt in 1894

lasting friendships amongst his fellow students, and his residence there engendered a deep love of Germany and the Continent. In later years he often looked back with much affection on his Frankfurt days. The Frankfurt Conservatory (Dr Hoch's Conservatoire as it was known and advertised in the English musical press) had been founded in the year of Gardiner's birth, 1877, and its building financed from the proceeds of a substantial legacy left by a well-known Frankfurt citizen after whom it was named. The first director was the Swiss composer Joachim Raff who held the post until his death in 1882. Raff's death in fact prefaced quite an upheaval. The Conservatory's staff could then be broadly grouped into two camps: the older conservative group (amongst whose number the name of Clara Schumann was prominent as head of the pianoforte department from 1878 until illness and increasing deafness forced her to resign in 1892) and the younger radicals who had mostly been pupils of either Liszt, von Bülow or Raff. Thus, in keeping with the schism then prevalent in nineteenth-century music, the Conservatory was evenly split between the proponents of Brahms and Schumann on the one hand and the Wagner–Liszt school on the other. The appointment of Dr Bernhard Scholz from Breslau as the new director gave fuel to the revolt within the Conservatory, for he was a signatory of the Brahms–Joachim manifesto denouncing the 'New Germans'. (In 1880, when Scholz was director of music at Breslau, it had been at his instigation that Brahms came to write his *Academic Festival Overture* in acknowledgement of the honorary degree conferred on him by the university.) Clara Schumann wrote in her diary on 21 January 1883: 'Herr v Mumm called on me and told me of the revolution in the School (one can call it nothing else). Three have given notice and three others have been given notice. There is a complete transformation – but it was needed. The lack of discipline was incredible.'[8]

The younger dissenting faction broke away to establish a new institute in Frankfurt which rather confusingly was called the Raff Conservatory, appointing Hans von Bülow (himself once a Liszt pupil) as honorary president. On taking up the directorship at the Hoch Conservatory, Scholz generally created a favourable impression and by the end of 1883 the internal troubles there had died down, so that Brahms could write to Clara Schumann: 'You never mention the school, and that is a good sign, because it shows that under Scholz things are getting better and more comfortable every day.'[9] By the following July Clara was able to write:

So far things are going well at the school and we have much to thank Scholz for. In many respects he makes a good Director, but he is very fidgety and seems always to be trying to make us stand out (as regards the other Conservatoires). At the smallest sign from the other side he gets excited, and then I always have to urge him to forge calmly ahead and take no notice of other people . . . But even if they really did do something good, that need not affect us. Frankfurt is big enough for two or three good institutions. I am much more concerned about the fact that there is so little real ability in the Raff Conservatoire . . .[10]

Seen through the eyes of Gardiner's fellow student Cyril Scott, Scholz was 'an imposing and awe-inspiring old gentleman with a very florid face and longish white hair, who walked with a slow shuffling gait and usually wore a black frock coat quite incongruous with the rest of his attire, which was of a bile-coloured texture without any pattern'.[11] Scholz was not the only member of the Frankfurt staff whose dress appeared somewhat peculiar to Scott (whose own flamboyant attire was anything but conventional) for the renowned professor of composition, Iwan Knorr, came in for some critical remarks as well:

He was of slender build, of sallow complexion, wore his iron grey hair *en brosse*, and had a short non-pointed and rather mangy-looking beard. His mode of dress was unaesthetically striking: he invariably wore elastic-sided boots with false buttons, and a cravat which looked as if two pieces of nondescript stuff had been glued on to a bit of cardboard . . Furthermore, browny-yellow trousers of a distinctly bilious shade, and far too full in the seat – which used to hang down in a very curious manner suggestive, if the simile be permitted, of the posterior of an elephant.[12]

Knorr was an outstanding personality on the Frankfurt staff, and the greatest influence on Gardiner. Although not actually born in Russia, he had spent a large part of his life there and his sympathies were similarly directed. He had been a close friend and biographer of Tchaikovsky and when the composer visited Frankfurt in 1889 Knorr's was one of the friendships he was pleased to renew. Knorr married a Russian, studied at Leipzig and later returned to Russia to teach before joining the Frankfurt staff in 1883 on the recommendation of no less a figure than Brahms. Knorr had sent him one of his compositions, asking for an opinion. The work, a set of orchestral variations on Ukranian folk-songs, much impressed Brahms and in 1877 Knorr joined the senior composer on a two-day walking tour.

Knorr had an enviable reputation as one of the finest teachers of composition. His strength, one that was highly appreciated by his pupils, was that his teaching was free from much of the rigidity common in a more academic approach. He fostered his pupils' individual talents instead of merely moulding them to an academic conformity. Placid, good-humoured and retiring by nature, he was not one to discourage originality providing it was in good taste. As he wrote himself: 'I have endeavoured to respect the individual and taken care not to impose my taste or my tendency on him.'[13] One of his precepts was that the rules of composition should first be learned so as to know how to break them later on. In this way his teaching ensured a firm foundation for the most forward-looking of his pupils, which included Oskar Fried, Hans

Pfitzner and Ernst Toch. Knorr's methods were not those of Scholz who also taught composition and was one of 'the old school'. There was some friction between the two men, each no doubt eyeing the other with a degree of disapproval. On Scholz's resignation in 1908 Knorr succeeded him as director, a post he held until his death in 1916.

The Hoch Conservatory generally lived up to its excellent name, offering a wide range of musical subjects at an annual fee of between 360 and 450 marks. Most of the instrumental tuition was given by members of the Frankfurt Opera orchestra and by each of the internationally acclaimed Frankfurt String Quartet whose leader, Hugo Heermann, was also in charge of the city's Museum concerts. Heermann remained at the Conservatory until 1904 when, according to Cyril Scott, having been indiscreet enough on more than one occasion to kiss his female pupils, he was asked to leave. The story goes that his wife protested to Scholz: 'Really, Herr Director, it is too absurd to make such a fuss about a mere kiss – in *our* circle, *everybody* kisses!' Unfortunately the girl in question had complained and such protestations were in vain. Whatever the truth of the story, Heermann went on to found a violin school of his own.[14]

Other prominent figures included the Frankfurt Quartet's cellist, Hugo Becker, acknowledged as one of the leading instrumentalists of his day, who spent many years at Frankfurt before moving in 1909 to the Hochschule at Berlin. In the piano department were Lazzaro Uzielli, James Kwast and Ernst Engesser. But of wider, lasting renown was the composer Engelbert Humperdinck who taught composition at the Conservatory from 1890 until 1896. While at Frankfurt he achieved fame on the strength of a single work, his opera *Hansel and Gretel* which he had written at his sister's request as a Christmas entertainment for her children. Knorr encouraged him to bring it before the public, which he did with great success at Weimar in 1893, and the opera has retained its popularity to this day. But as a teacher Humperdinck was much less successful. Originally engaged out of charity, he became known for his absent-mindedness and lack of punctuality. In 1900 he was appointed director of the Berlin Akademische Meisterschule.

Of the 250 or so students on roll at Frankfurt, over half were women, and during Gardiner's time there was a significant proportion of students from English-speaking countries, the greater number coming from Great Britain. Gardiner and his contemporaries were by no means the first British students at Frankfurt. Two British pianists famous in their day had studied there previously. Frederic Lamond had arrived in 1882 to study with Heermann and Schwarz, and with the shake-up that followed Raff's death he moved to the new conservatory of which Schwarz was the nominal director. Lamond was a protégé of Liszt and enjoyed the rare privilege of the master's presence at one of his London recitals.

Leonard Borwick studied at Frankfurt from 1883 until 1889 with Clara Schumann, who is said to have regarded him as her favourite English pupil, and she did much to further his career.

Gardiner's first Frankfurt term began on 1 September 1894, and thereafter his name was to be closely associated with four fellow English-speaking students. Known collectively as the 'Frankfurt Group' or even the 'Frankfurt Gang', they were Norman O'Neill, Roger Quilter, Cyril Scott, and the Australian Percy Grainger. With his good looks, his Irish charm and wit, O'Neill was very popular among the students. 'Norman came to call on me', Gardiner wrote of their first meeting, 'and made a great impression. He talked neither of cricket nor football; he was, like myself, intensely interested in music . . . and he had a charm of manner that he retained till the end of his life.'[15]

O'Neill came from a fairly well-to-do artistic family and his talents were soon to find an outlet in the theatre, where his chief contribution was the incidental music he composed for about fifty productions over a period of thirty years. While at Frankfurt, Norman met his future wife, Adine Ruckert, a pupil of Clara Schumann. They were married in July 1899 and remained among Balfour Gardiner's closest friends for life. Adine was a fine pianist and in years to come would often play Gardiner's pieces, especially his *Noel*, a slight jaunty work chiefly in 6/8 time concluding with a richly harmonised statement of 'Good King Wenceslas'. In 1934 he wrote complimenting her on a performance: 'I do not remember anybody since Frankfurt days whose playing I like so much . . . I have never heard a better rendering of *Noel*.'

Charm and wit were also the special characteristics of the gentle Roger Quilter. A fastidious composer and the most conservative of the Group, his elegant songs lie at the centre of his relatively small output. Whereas O'Neill found his musical niche in the theatre, Quilter was drawn to clothing fine poetry with music. In fact he spoke of liking poetry even more than music, and his preferences were for Shelley, Keats, Herrick and Shakespeare. Coming from an aristocratic line, Quilter was schooled at Eton and led a sheltered life that was not free from poor health. Like Gardiner he was to remain a bachelor. Apart from his songs, he is best remembered today by the music he wrote for the children's play *Where the Rainbow Ends* and his most frequently played orchestral work, *A Children's Overture*.

By sharp contrast the extrovert Cyril Scott and Percy Grainger were the Group's most original 'thinkers'. Scott had first visited Frankfurt in 1891 when only twelve for a stay of eighteen months to study the piano, and he returned in 1896 for further study, this time for composition with Knorr, having by then set his mind on becoming a composer. He clearly held his professors Knorr and Uzielli in sufficiently high esteem to

11

3 Norman O'Neill, the oldest member of the Frankfurt Group

4 Cyril Scott, adopting a typically flamboyant pose, in Berlin about 1901

dedicate to them an early set of *Six Pieces* for the piano 'in grateful remembrance of my student days'. Scott was an artist in every sense of the word, in his appearance, his manner and his talents, which were diverse and by no means restricted to music alone. He wrote much poetry, both original (with earlier overtones of Dowson) and translations of Stefan George (whom he knew well) and Baudelaire. Besides several published volumes of his verses, his other writings included the librettos to his four operas, several unpublished plays (which he wrote during the Second World War when for a while he lived in hotels without ready access to a piano), a study of humour, two books on music and philosophy, two autobiographies, and many books and pamphlets on his medicinal and occult interests. He once listed his recreations as therapeutical research, transcendental philosophy and mysticism. He countered criticisms of having dissipated his energies in too many spheres with the view that 'the more subjects one can, within limits, become interested in, the less time and inclination one has to be unhappy'.[16] But it is hard to escape the conclusion that he did spread his talents too widely and thinly to the detriment of his music.

Scott gained much ill-timed attention and acclaim before he had reached maturity as a composer, and furthermore, being a highly accomplished pianist, the success of many of his shorter piano pieces overshadowed his large-scale orchestral works and his substantial chamber music, in both of which fields he employed what were then considered rather daring innovations owing more than a little to Grainger. But it was Scott's occult interests that raised more than an eyebrow. In 1907 the music critic Robin Legge wrote to Delius that Scott 'is devoted now to "occultism" – & is seen everywhere with a black Yogi who is supposed to hold in his head all the secrets of the Universe. Scott is a whole-hogger in the matter.' Myrrha Bantock, daughter of the composer Granville Bantock, remembered Scott staying with them and how, when taking his afternoon sleep, he would pin a notice on his door: 'Do not disturb. I am in an astral slumber.'[17] After the deaths of his own and Grainger's mothers, Scott claimed to have made contact with them both through a medium. But stranger still to the uninitiated is the influence of the Master, a 'being' said to be of Kashmiri origin, well over 150 years old, that could speak English fluently and had been Pythagoras in one of his earlier reincarnations. Telepathic communication with him was made by means of a clairvoyant through whom, apparently at the Master's wish, the outline of one of Scott's philosophical books was 'dictated' to him. It seems that even Scott's marriage, from which there were two children, had come about at the suggestion of the Master, and when, at the age of 65, in the face of the almost total neglect of his larger works, Scott considered giving up composition altogether, it was at the Master's behest that he set to work on his opera *Maureen O'Mara*. Scott's works received rather more attention on the Continent than at home and, though he eventually outlived the rest of the Frankfurt Group, at his death he was an almost unknown figure.

At Frankfurt Cyril Scott had close musical bonds with the most individual of the Group, that lovable eccentric Percy Grainger whose life and directions were to be every bit as extraordinary as Scott's. A man of irrepressible energy, his music bubbles with sheer enjoyment though it is not without its deeper serious side, his moods of musical athleticism being matched by a deep and often harrowing emotionalism. If for nothing else his fame could rest on arguably the finest collection of British folk-songs on which he worked for many years. He was a tireless experimenter and in some spheres a true original. He arrived in Frankfurt from Australia in 1895 together with his mother who remained his constant companion and whose overbearing influence dominated him until her death. At Frankfurt the much younger Grainger found in Cyril Scott a sympathetic and guiding influence, recognising what he called Scott's 'amazing genius'[18] during their student days and how he 'out-soared all others in composition'.[19] Although Grainger later detected signs of his fellow-composer's 'creative laziness'[20] and was indeed to outshine him, he generously acknowledged his debt to Scott:

It seems to me as if I might never have been a modernist composer but for my contact with Cyril Scott. When he found me . . . I was writing in the style of Handel & seemed to know nothing of modern music. 'Aren't you interested in writing modern music?' he said to me. 'What do you mean by modern music?' I answered. He played me Grieg's Ballade & Tchaikovsky's Theme & Vars (both quite new to me). Then, his own modernist music was a fiery awakener of my own modernist powers. It is true that, as a boy of 11 or 12, in Australia, I had heard in my head my Free Music, made up of beatless lilts, gliding interval-less tones & non-harmonic voice-leadings. But this early tone-vision had no connection with the conservative composing I was doing in Frankfurt in the pre-Scott days . . . [21]

Even Knorr remembered Scott as 'brilliant, revolutionary',[22] and the conductor Basil Cameron (who had close associations with the Frankfurt Group) once stated in a BBC broadcast: 'There is no doubt that Cyril Scott's flamboyant originality in his music and his enthusiasm for experiment spurred Grainger on to carry into effect a whole train of innovations in musical composition that were already stirring in his mind.' The two acted in many ways as sounding-boards for each other's creativity.

The label 'Frankfurt Group' is little more than a term of convenience with which to denote this coterie of ex-patriate composers who, by studying abroad, stood apart in outlook and education from the mainstream of the conservative British musical establishment at the turn of the century. The label is slightly misleading since at no time were all the Group studying together at the Conservatory, partly because Gardiner chose to punctuate his spell in Germany with his university years in England after which he returned to Frankfurt for private study, and partly through the diversity of their ages which spanned seven years. By Christmas 1895 and the end of Gardiner's first Frankfurt term Grainger was 13, Scott 16, Quilter and Gardiner 18 (Quilter the elder by six days) and O'Neill 20. Neither Scott nor Quilter was resident during Gardiner's official period of study at the Conservatory, and when Scott returned in October 1896 Gardiner had already left to enter Oxford. Yet the nickname stuck and they generally remained close friends from their student days and, publicly and privately, enjoyed each other's company regularly up to the First World War, and thereafter with less frequency when their individual lives followed different paths. As Grainger hardly regarded O'Neill as being one of the Group, theirs was the only distinctly cool relationship amongst the fraternity.

Friendship was very much the Group's unifying element, for they scarcely formed a 'school of composers' to merit comparison with 'Les Six' or 'the mighty handful' of the Russian nationalist 'Five' led by Balakirev. They were united more by their outlook than by any similarity of style, though towards the end of his life Grainger tried hard to define other stronger, musical bonds between the Group:

As I think of the other ones (Scott, Quilter, Gardiner & myself) & seek to find a characteristic that marks our group off from other British composers it seems to me that an excessive emotionality (& particularly a tragic or sentimental or wistful or pathetic emotionality) is the hallmark of our group. When Cyril returned to F[rankfurt] in 1896 the books & pictorial art we got to know thru him were the plays of Maeterlinck (to which he wrote several overtures in those early days), the poems of Stefan George & Ernest Dowson, Walt Whitman, Aubrey Beardsley . . . [Many of Scott's early works] are informed with some agony which I would be inclined to attribute to German influence. All we 4 composers spoke German as fluently as English – tho not necessarily gramatically. I think it must be true that the exagerated tenor of Germanemotionality had some influence on us all 4. The influence, if any, lay in the willingness to take such emotional views of things. The feelings themselves were typically English in their wistfulness and patheticness. Perhaps it might be true to say we were all of us PRERAFAELITE composers . . . And what musical medium could provide the agonized emotionality needed? Certainly not the 'architectural' side of music & not the truly English qualities of grandeur, hopefulness & glory so thrilling in Elgar, Walton, Vaughan Williams & other British composers. I think the answer is 'the CHORD'. The chord has the heartrending power we musical prerafaelites needed. Based on Bach, Wagner, Skriabine, Grieg & Cesar Franck Cyril, Balfour & I became chord-masters indeed . . .[23]

Certainly 'the chord' was fundamental to Grainger's expressive language; of his own attitude towards composition he wrote: 'My efforts, even in those young days, were to wrench the listener's heart with my chords', adding that 'it is the contrast between the sweet & the harsh . . . that is heart-rending'.[24] Yet that very chord by which he set such store (defined by Sir Thomas Armstrong as a version of the chromatic chord on the major sixth of the scale with its ninth and *appoggiaturas*) was neither invented by the Group nor did it become their exclusive property, as a glance at the music of Delius will show.

If the Group had no musical distinguishing mark in common readily to set them apart from others, besides the geographical isolation of studying abroad, a degree of rebelliousness further marked them off. Sir Hubert Parry, who was director of the Royal College of Music, once received a letter from a friend speaking of Gardiner as a promising young composer, and in consequence Parry invited him to lunch, hoping that he would play him some of his music. But Parry's views Gardiner took to be poles apart from his own and so he declined the invitation, an action he regretted all his life when he found out the generous nature of Parry's true sympathies.[25] This rebellious spirit showed itself in other ways, the height of youthful irreverence being the Group's shared dislike of Beethoven. If rebels they were, and this became more apparent in the cases of Grainger and Scott whose music often seemed to cross the barriers of accepted musical convention, what the Group sought and cherished above all was their independence from such restraints, something which they achieved but at considerable artistic cost. One can only conclude that the Frankfurt Group ultimately failed to live up to the early promise and youthful aspirations of its members.

At Frankfurt Gardiner would sometimes take his mid-day meal with the Graingers at their pension. Rose Grainger expressed a special liking for Balfour of all Percy's composer friends. 'She said you would be the only one she would have cared to have been married to, had she been a young woman of your breed-link (generation)', Grainger wrote with typical frankness on 27 September 1941. Those of the Group in residence would occasionally gather in the city's pleasure gardens where they could eat, drink and converse to the strains of a small orchestra. Gardiner particularly enjoyed walking and cycling round the local countryside. A favourite haunt was a well-known beauty spot not far off, the village of Cronberg in the Taunus Mountains, some forty-five minutes' journey by rail, and many a delightful excursion was made there.

Gardiner still had serious intentions of becoming a concert pianist and he studied the piano, first briefly with Engesser and then with Uzielli who had been a pupil of Clara Schumann. At one of the student concerts Rose Grainger singled Balfour Gardiner out as the best of the pianists there and Percy called him 'a fine rich-toned player of Schumann'.[26] At a Conservatory concert on 4 December 1895 he played the first movement of Beethoven's Piano Concerto No. 1, but during that second year he had to abandon his hopes of becoming a concert pianist when over-practice resulted in partial paralysis of his hand muscles. So he decided instead to devote himself to composition. Fortunately, unlike Grainger, he got on extremely well with Iwan Knorr his composition professor, who at one time or another taught each of the Frankfurt Group and regarded Gardiner as the most understanding of all his pupils. Knorr suffered from liver trouble and consequently his place would sometimes be taken by the director. One such instance brought about a confrontation between Scholz and the opinionated and outspoken Gardiner who was then working on a composition he had shown to Knorr before his temporary absence. Knorr had not been happy with one passage for which he wrote in suggested alterations. When Scholz saw the work he picked out the very passage Knorr had rewritten, expressing his strong disapproval. 'But I like it very much!' retorted the independent Gardiner.[27] It was not long before he left the Conservatory and studied privately with Knorr instead.

17

With composition there came problems. To be met, as Gardiner was at Frankfurt, with a wealth of modern music he had never previously encountered was a bewildering experience. Outside the Conservatory there was a thriving musical life. Concerts were regularly given by the Museumgesellschaft and the opportunities for hearing modern music were frequent. It was to Frankfurt that the young Richard Strauss came in 1896 and 1899 to conduct the premières of his *Also sprach Zarathustra* and *Ein Heldenleben*. The city could also boast a splendid Municipal Opera House completed in 1880 with one of the largest and best-equipped stages in Germany. In 1882 Clara Schumann was writing to Brahms: 'A lot of Wagner is being given here – the *Rheingold* and the *Walküre*. One of these days I suppose I shall have to have it inflicted on me . . .'[28] For Gardiner at first the diet was almost too rich to be palatable. On the night of his arrival he heard *Die Walküre* for the first time. The music made little impression: he thought it incoherent and without any melody or attractive harmony that he could readily grasp. He had later to hear the prelude to *Tristan und Isolde* six times before he could make anything of it. That state of mind was not to last long. Ironically, over eight years later he recorded in his notebook: 'I have never in my life read anything so saliently inept as Dr Hubert Parry's article on Tonality in Grove's History of Music.' Against the statement that 'Tonality is the element of key, which in modern music is of the very greatest importance', he commented: 'Throws light on the doctor's ideas of "modernity"', and when Parry wrote that 'unless the tonality is made intelligible, a work which has no words becomes obscure', Gardiner added: 'Has the doctor read Tristan?'

If his love of Wagner started shakily, it was a very different matter with Tchaikovsky. On his first hearing, the Sixth Symphony made an immediate impact. Like Knorr, Gardiner came to regard Tchaikovsky as a model of clear orchestration. 'Old Tchai, he knew the way to do it', he would remark. Yet he was soon faced with a dilemma. His earlier musical training had been exclusively on classical lines. He was fond of experimenting with new chords but he now began to think in two different harmonic systems, one which gave him freedom to exercise his imagination, and the other in which he was restricted to the limits of accepted musical forms which he followed mechanically. He explained his predicament in an article in *The Musical Times* of August 1912:

One phase of my early attempts at composition consisted almost entirely of experiments in harmony, though at that time I was acquainted with nothing more modern than Schumann, excepting the *Tannhäuser* overture and the Horn Trio of Brahms. During my schooldays at Charterhouse these experiments were continued with increasingly strange results, to the neglect of other elements of music; and thus I entered the Conservatorium at Frankfurt with an exuberant harmonic imagination, but with very little resource in other respects. I soon found that a harmonic scheme in which tonic and dominant had no place was of small use in solving the simple formal problems that were put before me; and I was compelled accordingly to descend to a lower and, indeed, to a primitive plane of musical thought in order to cope with them. Thus I acquired a second style – formal, practical, and less imaginative – which co-existed along with my more intense, natural, original efforts; and it is on the basis of this second style that my musical development proceeded. Looking back on those bygone years, I cannot but feel that I paid a heavy price for the normal equipment of a composer in the loss of originality it entailed. Like all other students who undergo a conventional musical training instead of developing their style at every point on their own lines, I had to take the bad with the good; to learn to solve problems that would never have arisen if I had gone my own way; to utter things and acquire methods of utterance that were essentially alien to me: and I was thus left, as all apt students invariably are left, with a limited imagination, and burdened with a number of habits that had to be unlearned, and will still have to be unlearned till I come to my own again. While saying this, I wish to acknowledge to the full the efficient handling and sympathetic insight of my master, Professor Iwan Knorr, than whose teaching, on its own lines, I can conceive none better.

His quest for independence left him seriously doubting the wisdom of following a formal musical education, and he had some censorial comments to pass on the products of those colleges of music:

Those who defend the musical institutions that bring composition 'within reach of all' may say that I was losing myself in my own particular cul-de-sac, and might never have become a composer at all. Be it so. Let the strong overcome the difficulties they make for themselves: let the weaklings go to the wall. As things now are, all the weaklings are helped to compose: and compose they do, with lamentable results. I would have more danger, and no helping hand outstretched; and the man with the courage, skill and endurance to face the danger and overcome it will produce finer and truer music than the man who is shown the broad and easy path that leads but to conventionality.

After two years at Frankfurt, Gardiner resumed his more general education at home and entered New College, Oxford, on 17 October 1896. Many friends expressed doubts as to the advisability of taking such a step, Cyril Scott for one urging him to give up the idea and concentrate instead on composition. But Gardiner was never easily swayed by other opinions when his mind was made up, and while his stay in the city of Oxford resulted in a lasting love for the place, the move was otherwise hardly profitable. His views on the detrimental effect of his university education were quoted in the same *Musical Times* article:

As to the influence of Oxford on the musician, I should say that in my experience it was not stimulating. For it is the business of the artist as of the philosopher, to use his creative and selective faculties in defining his attitude towards his environment; and his character becomes firmer and fuller, and his expression of that character more complete, in proportion to the constancy and intensity with which he uses those faculties. His growth must be directed by impulse from within, not by imposition from without; and the imposition from without in the case of an Oxford education is such as to leave him lumbered with a mass of undigested and

19

unassimilable facts on the one hand, and stunted on the other by lack of nourishment that is congenial to him.

Quite why Gardiner chose to go up to Oxford and whether he was merely complying with his father's wishes remain somewhat a mystery. However, while at Oxford he thought it 'would be fun' to sit for a music examination. As he had expected, he failed. 'They asked me such silly questions,' he told his friends, 'that really I couldn't answer them.' One question had been on the greatness of Schumann as a composer. 'Well, I don't consider that Schumann *is* a great composer, and so I didn't answer the question,' he explained.[29] Here it seems he wasn't out of keeping with some contemporary opinions for, according to Richard Church in *The Voyage Home*, a professed fondness for Schumann's music could evoke strong reactions from other composers: from Bax – 'Dangerous! The wrong sort of romanticism', and from Bliss – 'The emotions of a schoolgirl!'[30]

One of the Oxford friendships that Gardiner valued was with Donald Tovey, a Nettleship scholar at Balliol College, who graduated in 1898. Tovey recognised Gardiner's skill in orchestration and Gardiner frequently called on him in his rooms. But otherwise he was restive as an undergraduate. In between terms he would usually return to Frankfurt and study privately with Knorr. In 1898 he gained a second-class degree in honour moderations and in 1900 took his final degree, scraping a fourth in *literae humaniores* and only just managing to satisfy the examiners. He was then free to go back to Germany. Yet, despite his strong dislike of the rigours he endured at Oxford, his affection for the city remained and in later years he was to make it a second home. Grainger could not understand this fondness and much later he wrote from America in a characteristic 'round-letter' to his friends:

Balfour Gardiner (one of the least yoke-able of Englishmen) has settled down to be, at least partly, an Oxford-liker. One would have thought that Balfour, being clever enough to lose his know-all-title (doctorate) by saying, 'But Schumann WASN'T a great composer!' would be yoke-shy enough to kick his mind-legs over the Oxford thought-traces; one would have thought that Balfour would have been at-rest-set (satisfied) with his earthy and salty over-souls (geniuses) Hardy, Barnes and Masefield and be glad to deaf-hear the lures of the robed pundits.

Late in the summer of 1900 Gardiner was once again back in Germany, studying privately with Knorr. In between his studies he continued to explore the district, either walking or cycling, and he regularly attended the opera and theatre at Frankfurt and Wiesbaden. Although all hopes of becoming a concert pianist had been earlier dashed, he had a piano installed in his rooms and kept up his practice. Composition occupied most of his time and his notebook details what may have been a typical day: Bach analysis at 9.30 a.m., piano practice at 11 a.m., composition at 5 p.m. and 9 p.m. Cyril Scott, who had by then left the Hoch Conservatory, was still occasionally to be found in Germany, and as a token of their friendship he inscribed to Gardiner printed copies of two early songs, *April Love* and *Ad domulam suam*, writing on the first, 'To Henry Balfour Gardiner as a small return for the sympathy without which one could never work – May 1900', and on the other, 'In remembrance of Frankfurt – Xmas 1900'. There were to be many mutual dedications among the Frankfurt Group and Scott was to choose his 'three oldest friends Percy Grainger, Roger Quilter and Balfour Gardiner' as the dedicatees of both his first autobiography, *My Years of Indiscretion* published in 1924, and his study of humour entitled *The Ghost of a Smile* which appeared in 1939.

By the end of 1900 Balfour Gardiner had more or less exhausted his studies at Frankfurt. The surviving works from that period include eight songs (of which two were later revised for publication) and *Four Studies* for piano. Other works contemplated and sketched at least in part include a work for piano and orchestra; a setting for choir, organ and orchestra of the *Dies Irae*; an early setting of the *Evening Hymn* (*Te lucis ante terminum*) quite different from the version published in 1908; an organ sonata (for he had kept up his organ studies at Frankfurt); and numerous other chamber and orchestral works no longer extant.

Early in January 1901 he went on from Frankfurt to a conservatory that no longer exists, at Sondershausen, about fifty miles west of Leipzig, where he studied conducting and had too the opportunity of his first orchestral performances. It was there, he recorded a year later, that he did 'the best work I have done in my life'. He still kept in touch with Knorr and would take the brief holiday at Cronberg in the Taunus Mountains. Easter found him at his father's Hampshire house, but he was soon back at Sondershausen working on, amongst other things, a symphony of which he had started the first movement the previous November. The Frankfurt Group, close correspondents, were always keen to hear of each other's progress and offer criticism. 'Dear old Scotty paid us a visit the other day bringing lovely things', Grainger wrote to Gardiner in July 1901:

Your lovely E♭ mel. is a fine invigorator of dull moments, it takes its place among the very lovely. I had a joke with Scott about it. He says he does not like it as well as most of your other things, but when I played it among other things, he started up with 'What is that lovely thing?' etc. So you see how much one may rely on a person's opinion. I am longing to hear more of yours. Just at your stage of development you are most confoundedly interesting, one never knows what will turn up next, there is no limit to possibilities.

Within a few weeks, on 13 August 1901, Gardiner heard from Scott:

So many thanks for your letter. Your remarks are quite right as they always are . . . After hearing Grainger's Cello Piece [*A Lot of Rot* for cello and piano, later renamed *Youthful Rapture* and also orchestrated] all my work seems insipid. The boy is a genius of the first water – possessor of a strength, an originality, pathos and beauty which baffles all description. And as to you, well I am very anxious to hear your new work – your idyllic phrase has been a source of great pleasure to me – and many others – May there be many more like it. Write to me whenever you can and describe your work a bit, even if it be only a post-card. I should love to see Knorr again. He always sets me straight.

Gardiner's moment of truth came in the summer at Sondershausen when he had the chance of having two orchestral works performed. The first of these was the symphony which he conducted himself. Built on a classical mould of four movements with an *andante* second movement followed by a scherzo and trio, there was much in the work to impress the listener. A critic from a Nordhausen paper referred to a string melody in the trio 'of unbelievable beauty, of which one could only wish that it didn't disappear so quickly'. A forceful finale brought the symphony to a rousing end. His *Heroic Overture*, played some days later, was equally praised, though neither work was performed again. Soon after the symphony's performance Gardiner reworked part of the first movement but nothing came of it. These prentice works soon gave way to others and a promising start had been made to his career as a composer. By the end of the summer he was home again, and on completion of his studies in Germany he returned, in Grainger's panegyric, 'a magnificent pianist, a resourceful conductor . . . a thoroughly practical music-maker . . . and . . . one of the most inspired composers of his generation'.[31]

2 'A Civilised Being . . .'

1902–1903

Home from Germany with his student days now behind him, Balfour Gardiner settled down with some difficulty to the disciplines of composition. Besides allocating a fair portion of the day to composition, he also set time aside for reading which he wisely regarded as necessary to his artistic development. A voracious reader, he read widely and critically, occasionally recording his observations. He showed particular interest in Nietzsche, Schopenhauer, Thomas Green (*Prolegomena to Ethics*) and Tolstoy (*What is Art?*), though he was not always in sympathy with the views they propounded.

In Nietzsche he found much to admire. *Genealogie der Moral* he thought the most interesting book he had read for a long time. From *Also sprach Zarathustra* he entered into his notebook an English translation of the 'Midnight Song' already set to music by Mahler and Delius (though at the time he was probably unaware of either setting). Turning to *Jenseits von Gut und Böse* he frankly confessed:

I do not understand all, but there is much with which I am heartily in sympathy. First of all he is on the side of my individualist and specialist tendencies. The colourless man who lives up to standards, and who has reached the perfection of type in the Average City Man, is a person I loathe and detest. So much so that 'die grosse Verachtung' has led me to hate even small talk. I can't stand it. That is, not unless the personality of the talker transforms everything & the personality is a great one. I cannot stand casual acquaintances – cousins, etc. and I shall make a general clearance of friends after these three months, when I am independent. (notebook entry, 3 February 1902)

However, a return visit to Oxford helped restore his bonhomie. 'Everybody charming', he wrote six days later. 'Contempt of City men and disposition to grumble completely knocked out of me.'

In the early months of 1902, when not at his father's London house in Tavistock Square, he stayed at his other house in the heart of Hampshire at Sutton Scotney which lies at the eastern extremity of Hardy's Wessex. Balfour Gardiner was well acquainted with Hardy's works and even copied out at the end of the year a short quotation from one of the early stories, *A Pair of Blue Eyes*, possibly detecting a relevance to himself beyond the mere fact that he himself had blue eyes: 'His constitution . . . was one which, rare in the springtime of civilisations, seems to grow abundant as a nation gets older, individuality fades and education

23

spreads: that is, his brain has extraordinary receptive powers, and no great creativeness.' Besides the novel's pertinent title he may have felt that the quotation's conclusion aptly mirrored his own condition with the compositional difficulties he was experiencing.

These were months of self-examination. Because of his father's generous provision the young Balfour was rid of any necessity of having to earn a living. But as a composer he had not resolved his earlier dilemma with any satisfaction. The core of the matter was what Cyril Scott referred to as Gardiner's 'mournful belittlement of everything he wrote . . . [a] hyper-self-criticism [which] was to be his undoing in the end'.[1] Gardiner was well aware of his own weaknesses. 'I am habitually afraid to think of – or rather to think out – things which I have begun (music, of course) for fear of spoiling it', he wrote in his notebook on 25 September. 'This is a lamentable lack of confidence; and unluckily it is not merely occasional, but an ingrained habit. It is only when I explore that I let myself go without looking before or after – without looking after – at any rate. This habit must be broken: it can easily become mere laziness.'

But it was not a habit from which he was able to free himself. Throughout his composing life he suffered continually from spells of depression when faced with problems to which he could find no ready solution. 'The moment I try to compose I get muddle-headed', he told his Frankfurt friends. 'I have plenty of ideas but I simply can't decide which are good enough to put down.'[2] He admired his fellow composer Frederic Austin's ability to see his way clearly to the solution to any problem that confronted him. And there was no lack of personal encouragement. The high hopes that Knorr held for him were echoed by his fellow students. In the middle of 1901 Scott had written to Gardiner: 'Percy wrote me such good news – namely that you had been doing such fine work – original and glorious, and such a change to what I heard. Well done! my dear friend – there is nobody more convinced of your genius than I was if it would only come out – and now it is doing so'. But at the end of that same year there came typical moments of despondency reflected by such entries in his notebook as 'Can do no music – In most pessimistic mood' and 'I can't do any music at all & am restless & wretched accordingly.'

Gardiner continued to feel disadvantaged by his education. He wrote some years later to Grainger, who had been exhorting him to better things:

My dearest Barbarian,
    You urge me to rape and indecent lengths, and I assure you I would if I could! But you must know that I am a Civilised Being and have been at Charterhouse and Oxford; and although I loathe and detest them with my whole soul, yet they have left their mark on me, and I write as I must . . . But, my dear Barbarian, I

cannot put it down to any real concern of yours about my music; for I hold it of no account, and I cannot imagine anybody else bothering about it. (26 September 1911)

He was still to some extent in search of a style. 'Shall I leave the idea of progress (according to alien standards) and try to develop personality – practically and *technically* too, building up (i) a harmonic system (ii) a melodic system (iii) a formal system, though (iii) must come last and only in the course of years?' he had written just before his twenty-fourth birthday. He was still torn between the directions in which his imagination wanted to lead him and the dictates of accepted musical form which he felt curbed his individuality. These 'alien standards' were constantly wagging a reproving finger. The Frankfurt Group's dislike of Beethoven did not exclude him from Gardiner's studies. Reading Wagner's *Ring* prompted the idea of extending the resource of instrumentation in both his orchestral and chamber music, and the mutual influences of the Group were strong. Nearly a year later on 12 September 1902 he wrote: 'Scott's style is not very rich in *dynamic*, Percy's is more so. Wagner certainly got a lot from Beethoven, who is perhaps the most powerful dynamitist [*sic*] that ever existed – but I find some of these effects unpleasant. In my own style I should try & introduce more dynamic effects.'

That February while at Sutton Scotney he was relieved to be in a 'most musical' frame of mind and worked hard at a string quintet. Chamber music occupied a large part of his early output. In moments of relaxation he enjoyed cycling round the neighbourhood and was pleasantly surprised to discover so much glorious countryside close at hand after the delights of the Taunus Mountains in Germany. But the first step towards the independence he so keenly sought was taking rooms in London at 5 Paper Buildings, The Temple. This brought him more in touch with the musical capital and his friends. Yet he was rarely at ease with London life of which he could be a cynical observer:

Everybody here in the City working at things that do not interest them, partly out of duty, partly as a means to pleasure. The game is not worth the candle. And above all things they sacrifice inner development to securing the means of enjoyment, outward agencies. And what are there? If you look into the faces of people, you see that they have all lost their lebenslust: they are all at heart grumblers, must be so – either that, or deadened. (notebook entry, 16 January 1902)

Even with his own freedom from such an existence there remained a grumbler within. When he had previously complained of finding it impossible to work in London for the noise of barrel-organs, his father had given him the run of his Hampshire house and had installed a piano. But his efforts were to little purpose as Balfour then complained that he couldn't work there either because of the sound of birds.[3] (He was not alone in suffering from such diversions, as Norman O'Neill also found it hard to compose in the country where he would be distracted by either a beautiful view or birds singing.[4])

If Gardiner could not abide casual acquaintances, his close friends were soon to experience the full measure of his generous hospitality and benevolence. He kept in constant touch with the Frankfurt Group who would often be present at the performances of each other's works. In January 1900 Gardiner, Quilter, Grainger and Knorr had journeyed to Darmstadt to hear the first performance of Cyril Scott's First Symphony. The work had a fairly hostile reception and midst cheers and hisses Gardiner is reported as overhearing a member of the audience comment: 'One ought to play that to the Boers then they'd run as far as the Equator!'[5] (The Boer War had entered its second year.) When in the winter of 1901-2 Hans Richter conducted Scott's *Heroic Suite* in Manchester and Liverpool, Gardiner went north to hear it. In May he similarly attended one of Norman O'Neill's concerts. Grainger, on the other hand, had decided against public performances of his own works. As a result of his mother's recent nervous breakdown he wanted to earn enough money as a concert pianist 'to secure for her a reasonable degree of comfort and security'. Although he was now combining the role of concert pianist with that of composer he feared that 'the radical nature' of some of his compositions would 'stir up animosities' and threaten his earning power as a pianist.[6] He had therefore for a while withheld his works from performance. But composition went on and one day, when the three were together at Sutton Scotney, Scott and Gardiner obliged Grainger, who was then working on his *Marching Song of Democracy*, by climbing a hillock a few hundred feet away and singing in fifths one of the work's themes so that Grainger could savour the effect of the sound ringing out from the trees,[7] a strange request that was nonetheless in keeping with the 'out-of-door' spirit of the work's original plan. On Gardiner's occasional days in London before he took rooms in The Temple, his chances were slender of spending an afternoon with Grainger, who was then living in the capital but usually to be found busily teaching for most of the day. But later on, when not so rigidly tied to a teaching and concert schedule, he became a frequent visitor at Gardiner's, sometimes arriving with the Danish cellist and fellow student at Frankfurt, Herman Sandby.

Another Australian acquaintance of Gardiner's in the early years of the century was Frederick Septimus Kelly. Known to his friends as 'Cleg' Kelly, he was one of a number of brilliant young musicians whose lives were to be ended so tragically by the First World War. George Butterworth, Ernest Farrar and W. Denis Browne were others to share a similar fate. Born in 1881, Kelly went to Eton and from there in 1899 to Balliol College, Oxford, with the Lewis Nettleship Scholarship. An outstanding sportsman, he rowed in both the Eton and Oxford eights, three times

5 F.S. Kelly, a brilliant musician and friend of Balfour Gardiner and
Rupert Brooke, killed in action in 1916

won the Diamond Sculls, and rowed for England in the 1908 Olympic Regatta. While at Oxford he exerted a strong influence on musical life there, becoming president of the University Musical Club and promoting the Sunday evening concerts at Balliol. After Oxford, as an adviser to the Classical Concert Society he was partly responsible for the inclusion of modern music in their London concerts. Gardiner had known Kelly from his last year at Oxford and had given the aspiring composer much valued advice, introducing him to Grainger whose freedom of harmony had much impressed Kelly. From Oxford Kelly progressed to Frankfurt and studied with Knorr from 1904 to 1908. An accomplished pianist, he went on an Australian concert tour in 1911 and on his return gave a series of London concerts either as soloist, accompanist or composer with musicians like George Henschel and Henry Wood. At the outbreak of war he enlisted in the Royal Naval Division, and at Blandford Camp in Dorset joined company with Rupert Brooke and the composer W. Denis Browne who had been a star pupil and fellow student of Brooke's at Rugby. In March 1915 they sailed for the Dardanelles, Kelly and Browne keeping up spirits by playing duets on a saloon piano. But *en route* for Gallipoli Brooke died from acute blood poisoning and was buried on the Greek island of Skyros, Kelly helping to heap lumps of white marble into a cairn over the poet's grave. A little over a month later Denis Browne was also to die, in trench fighting at Gallipoli, and on 13 November the following year, after being awarded the Distinguished Service Cross, Kelly was killed in action at Beaumont-Hamel in France. The *Elegy* for strings he wrote in memory of Brooke became his own elegy at a memorial concert conducted by Frank Bridge at the Wigmore Hall on 2 May 1919.

Circumstances prevented Kelly's friendship with Gardiner from being a long and uninterrupted one – a surviving portion of their correspondence and a few notebook entries are the only testimony of their friendship – but another musician, Frederic Austin, was more fortunate in becoming a close friend for life. Born in 1872, Austin was a man of diverse musical talents. As a fine baritone he was closely associated for several years with Beecham's operatic ventures, with the British National Opera Company of which in 1924 he became the artistic director, and with Rutland Boughton's Glastonbury festivals. He was also the soloist in the first English and subsequent early performances of Delius's *Sea Drift*. As a composer he scored a measure of success with several orchestral works, notably his *Spring Rhapsody* of which Gardiner was especially fond. But his finest achievement was the arrangement he made of John Gay's *The Beggar's Opera* which he followed up with the less successful sequel *Polly*. Ernest Irving has written of Austin that 'it was not until a look had been taken at the inside of his scores that one realised that here was a

6   A portrait of the versatile singer and composer Frederic Austin, inscribed:
'a token of valued friendship – Frederic Austin Jan: 07'

genius; not on the grand scale, perhaps, but one whose work, in its small way, was as exquisite as that of Mozart. Composers who reset *The Beggar's Opera* will find this out for themselves.'[8] When *The Beggar's Opera* was produced at the Lyric Theatre, Hammersmith in 1920 Austin's abilities as both singer and actor contributed much to its outstanding success, running for three and a half years with 1,463 consecutive performances. Austin had lived for a while in Cyril Scott's home town of Birkenhead and Gardiner quite probably came to know him through Scott, who found him there 'embedded in an academic rut' teaching at the Liverpool College of Music. After studying singing in London where he made his debut in 1902, he eventually gave up teaching in 1906, by which time he was launched on a successful career as a singer.

Early in the spring of 1902 Gardiner took a few days' holiday in North Wales. He was not a person to be stationary in one place for long; the 'wanderlust' was ever present and travelling seems to have been an essential ingredient in his way of life. In April he made two trips to Liverpool (possibly then making his acquaintance of Austin) and after returning from the first tried to settle down to composition but, in his own words, 'made myself utterly miserable in the attempt'. He was then working on a fantasia for horn, viola and piano but failed to complete it. Cyril Scott saw the sketches and told him how much he liked one of the themes. Gardiner's reply was characteristic: 'Aw, I hate the thing. I'll give it to you if you can make anything of it.'[9] This Scott willingly accepted and later wrote to him: 'Dear old boy, I have used up your glorious Steigerung in the finale of a Piano Sextet which I am writing.'[10] In 1911 Scott recast the work as a piano quintet which earned him a Carnegie Prize.

Between his journeys to Liverpool, Gardiner spent 24 April at the wedding of a New College contemporary, Humphrey Milford, later to be knighted and from 1913 to 1945 the head of Oxford University Press. His son Robin, born the following year, developed into a prolific composer, chiefly of vocal music, and studied with Holst, Vaughan Williams and R. O. Morris. He was also to receive much assistance in different ways from Gardiner. Later that year there was an event for the Gardiner family to celebrate as two days before Balfour's twenty-fifth birthday his sister-in-law Hedi gave birth in London to the first of her three children – Henry Rolf Gardiner. By the time Rolf reached his own twenty-fifth birthday a special relationship between him and his uncle was to form: in some ways he became the son and heir that Balfour never had.

In 1902 Grainger organised the first of many informal choral meetings to try out his own and other composers' choruses. They started at his Kensington rooms with a few amateurs swelling the 'Frankfurt' body of Quilter, Scott, Sandby, Grainger and Gardiner. Later meetings were held in the King's Road and on occasion were conducted by Vaughan Williams in Grainger's absence on tour. These were not the only opportunities for the fledgling composers to put their choral compositions to the test.

During those early London years Balfour Gardiner would sometimes be seen at certain social functions popular among the higher strata of society. These were musical gatherings held by wealthy and often influential persons whose large town houses lent themselves to these occasions. One such hostess was the tall, statuesque Mrs Lowrey whose residence in Cheyne Walk overlooked the Thames. She was a devoted admirer of Percy Grainger, attracted to him as much by his golden Apollonian looks as by his music, to which she gave much encouragement. On select evenings an *ad hoc* chorus would assemble at Mrs Lowrey's to perform some of Grainger's part-songs. The participants would often include Cyril Scott, Roger Quilter, Herman Sandby, Gervase Elwes, Frederic Austin, the painter and actor Ernest Thesiger, and another from Frankfurt student days, Baron Clemens von Franckenstein, known to his friends as Clé. After studying with Knorr, Clé had toured with an operatic company in America and then from 1902 until 1907 was engaged as conductor with the Moody-Manners Opera Company in England. He later took up appointments in Wiesbaden, Berlin,and Munich where he became Intendant at the Opera House. The composer of several operas and orchestral works (including a *Rhapsody* performed at a Royal Philharmonic Society concert in February 1926), he remained an especial friend of Gardiner and O'Neill.

Although by no means a social bird himself, Gardiner would occasionally sing at Mrs Lowrey's soirées, and Cyril Scott remembered the difficulties which some of the composers present had with part-singing, particularly Gardiner who exclaimed once at rehearsal in his Oxonian accent: 'The only way I can possibly sing my part is by closing my ears, so that I can't hear what you others are singing. As soon as I hear *you*, I inadvertently begin to sing *your* parts.'[11] And so the ensemble continued with Gardiner singing at the top of his voice with hands clasped firmly to his ears while the enthusiastic Grainger conducted with clenched fists. As well as providing much entertainment and fun, these meetings were a marvellous opportunity for trying out new works. It was at Mrs Lowrey's that Scott secured a performance of the Piano Sextet in which he had used up Gardiner's discarded theme.

Similar gatherings were organised during the winter of 1903–4 by Everard Feilding, brother-in-law to the celebrated tenor Gervase Elwes. Gervase and Lady Winefride Elwes had leased a house in Hertford Street with a large elegant drawing-room which once a fortnight was crowded with music-lovers of every sort, both amateur and professional. Everard Feilding felt that composers and performers were like races apart who

31

did not really know each other. So he devised what he called 'jamborees' to bring them together. The proceedings were very informal, some people coming in dinner-dress *en route* from parties, others in their day clothes, some sitting on chairs that flanked the walls, others on the floor in the absence of further seats. Everard set the ball rolling by mounting a chair, bell in hand, and he would cut short any formal ceremony by informing those present that, as there were too many to allow normal introductions to take place, once he had rung the bell they were to consider themselves introduced. That was sufficient on one occasion for a normally shy lady to approach Grainger straight away and greet him: 'I am so glad to be introduced. I have always wanted to meet you.'[12]

Grainger often encouraged a group to sing his part-songs, of which copies were circulated, and Elwes sang any new songs that came to hand, wherever possible with the composer at the piano. Roger Quilter (who had a special fondness for accompanying Elwes), Vaughan Williams, Scott and Gardiner all put in appearances. Also sometimes to be seen there was William Hurlstone, a composer of great promise who died from bronchial asthma in 1906 at the age of thirty. So too was Lady Dean Paul (born Irene Wieniawska and known professionally as Poldowski), the daughter of the famous Polish composer and violinist. She was herself a composer, her settings of Verlaine being much admired, and she became an acquaintance of Gardiner's.

These musical meetings ended when the lease of the house expired, though similar functions were continued by others, at Lady Bective's home in Eaton Place, and at the house in Cadogan Gardens of the financier William Rathbone (dedicatee of Grainger's *Handel in the Strand*). The composer–conductor Eugene Goossens, initially a violinist, remembered playing at many other such London parties and seeing there Cyril Scott, Roger Quilter and Percy Grainger. But Gardiner moved less easily in these circles and, possibly regarding the part-singing in which he might be called to participate as something that was distinctly not his métier anyway, drifted away from these social elevations. For him two places of his student days instead were to hold a continual attraction. He maintained links with Oxford through frequent visits there, and in February 1903 he made what was fast becoming a customary trip abroad, to Germany. On his return Scott chastised him for the non-musical distractions of Oxford; he urged him to abandon such interests that were doing little to further his career as a composer and instead settle down to a long period of composition with him at Helsby in Cheshire, where rooms with a piano could be had for twenty-two shillings a week with easy access to the countryside for moments of relaxation. 'Study as it were with me', he wrote to Gardiner on 20 April 1903, 'and at any rate we will get your technique in order. I will give you ideas how to go on when you get stuck to the best of my ability and even if your inspiration is not as happy as it might be you will find very soon on these lines it will pick up.'

Scott knew too well Gardiner's wayward despairing attitude towards composition and recognised his need for a spell of concentrated study. As a man of more than ample means Gardiner had never been faced with the struggles that men like Elgar and Holst had to contend with for their very existence. Indeed Holst, later a close friend who regarded Gardiner as a wonderful orchestrator, wondered about the composer Gardiner might have been if he had had to work for a living. Inherited wealth had robbed him of any necessity to write as if his livelihood depended on it. He could afford to set a work aside for a while for later reappraisal. This might have brought dividends had his self-critical nature not caused him to leave unfinished, withdraw or destroy many a work. He lacked the creative impetus and perseverance of another composer who became a close friend for life, Arnold Bax, whose similar financial independence had in no way curbed his productivity but who continued to compose throughout the greater part of his life in a late-romantic style contrary to the changing fashions of the times.

While it seems likely that Gardiner did go to Helsby, it is not clear whether he took up the invitation for the length of stay Scott had intended or indeed whether such a pooling of musical ideas took place. One may question whether Scott was the best person for the task anyway. Although he possessed much originality, his facility could often outstrip his invention and while he readily grasped new ideas, many products of his early maturity failed to gain the permanence that a steadier process and sounder judgement might have ensured. But fortunately for Gardiner the end of the year held the promise of a London performance which would bring his name before the public for the first time.

3 Hampshire folk-song collecting

1903-1906

The most encouraging news of 1903 was indeed of the first performance on 5 November of the String Quintet in C minor given by the Cathie Quartet – with an additional second viola – at a Broadwood concert in St James's Hall, London. The programme note by Robin Legge stated that the composer 'has already written a fairly large amount of chamber music, orchestral music and songs, of which the greater number are even now regarded as youthful indiscretions by their author'. Grainger had seen the quintet before its completion and was greatly impressed. 'Won't Scott dance when he hears it?' he wrote to Gardiner on 20 February 1902. 'For God's (and my) sake, *do* finish it quickly, I long to see it complete in its formal glory. I never looked for a great formal power in you, but must now own that I am eternally convinced.' And as if to emphasise his admiration, he added a plea: '*An especial favor* – If you have not decided to dedicate the Quintette to Scott would it be too much to ask you to concede that honor to me?'

The four-movement quintet, contemporary with Stanford's First Quintet composed and published that year for a similar combination of strings, created a favourable impression, the two inner movements being especially well received. *The Scotsman*, however, found an 'appalling amount of chromatic harmony at a very quick pace', and suggested that the orchestra would have been a more fitting medium than solo strings. The fact that this work, like so many others, no longer exists in its original form is indicative that Gardiner himself was not satisfied. The next year he made some attempts at reworking it but in the meantime he was more occupied by another chamber work, a string quartet, and the quintet had to wait many years for its final revision.

Over Christmas he and Cyril Scott made a prolonged visit to Paris, staying at a small hotel near the Louvre which had been recommended to Gardiner by Henry Biggar, the Canadian historian. Biggar was lodged in rooms above theirs and offered to show the two composers round the Parisian museums and galleries. He continually annoyed Gardiner by greeting him each time with the same remark: 'Well, going strong?'[1] Unfortunately Gardiner was far from going strong as he was suffering from a mixture of constipation, stomach-ache and general listlessness. He consequently restricted himself to a vegetarian diet (with the exception of fish) and consulted a French doctor who gave him a course of injections and some electric treatment to the stomach. He also prescribed a sweetened concoction of lemon and orange in equal portions. But this potion had little effect on Gardiner, and, while he nevertheless proved for Scott to be a delightful companion, he was musically 'down in the dumps'. At that time Scott dedicated to Gardiner his *Solitude* for piano which was published the following year.

Gardiner's spirits, often at their lowest during the winter months, were soon to revive as 1904 held the prospect of his first English orchestral performance. Furthermore on 3 June he was able to record triumphantly in his notebook: 'At last. Some formal ideas for a symphony.' The Sondershausen symphony had been relegated to that company of 'youthful indiscretions' and he now started afresh with new plans for a one-movement symphony. Even before commencing composition, the outline of the work was clear to him: it was to be in three parts. After an extended introduction, the first section would be basically fast with a slower distinct second subject. While loosely following sonata form, the second subject was to return before the first in the recapitulation, and this section would then conclude as it had begun. A slow idyllic interlude was to follow with a middle portion of contrasting faster music, and the whole work would end with an English dance.

7 'Some formal ideas for a symphony . . .' An early sketch for a beginning to Gardiner's Second Symphony, started in 1904, and revised and first performed in 1908

The English dance was a form much favoured by Gardiner and it was to recur in various guises throughout his output. It was in essence his expression of allegiance to the folk-song movement which provided the roots for so much British music of the pre-war era. It was also the name of his orchestral work which Henry Wood introduced at the Proms that year. Its origins may be traced back to Grainger, a debt acknowledged in the dedication, 'To Percy Grainger who first taught me "The English Dance"'. About 1900–2 Grainger had himself composed an *English Dance* which he dedicated to Cyril Scott. It was effectively his *Lebenstanz*, a 'tally of English energy' in which he had attempted to embody 'a peculiar spirit of athletic intensity and rollicking abandonment' that enthralled him in English life, and he cited such examples as 'furious football rushes . . . newspaper distributors swerving wildly . . . through London traffic on low bicycles, a profusion of express trains hurtling through the dark, factories clanging and blazing by night'.[2] He credited Gardiner with advice given about the scoring. Each of the Frankfurt Group, with the exception of Norman O'Neill, wrote an English dance by name. If Grainger's and Scott's (and to a lesser extent Gardiner's) may be taken to reflect some aspect of modern life, then Quilter's more countrified essays transport the listener back a couple of centuries. Whether or not Gardiner's *English Dance* had any pictorial idea for its basis, no programme was disclosed. Rosa Newmarch's descriptive note was dry and analytical:

In the dance a large orchestra is employed. The principal theme [example 1] is first given out by oboes and cor anglais over an organ-point in the cellos. It is then taken up by strings and treated in turn by almost every instrument in the orchestra. It appears also in inversion, and many counter-subjects of varying character are heard in combination with it. In this way the composer continues for sixteen pages of full score, which it is impossible to describe in fuller detail. At this point the time changes to 6/8, and a new theme [example 2] appears in the woodwind and harps, accompanied by pizzicato strings, the continuation of the theme being given to strings only. Next we have to notice an episode of two bars which assumes considerable importance, and a sequential passage for wind, first violins and violas of which also considerable use is made. With this material the composer concerns himself throughout the central portion of the work. Later the first theme returns again, being now heard in an augmented form in the trumpets, and also in its original shape in the horns in combination with one of the themes already mentioned. After a repetition of the four opening bars there is a short coda (*molto allegro*), the whole ending with continued reiteration of the second bar of the first theme.

Gardiner's *English Dance* was played on 21 October 1904 at the last night of the Proms. Its vigour appealed to the audience who at the end of a Prom season would have been in no mood for solemnity. But most critics were quick to point out the work's inherent weakness, a fault that was to bedevil Gardiner more than once: it suffered from insufficient

8   Balfour Gardiner in the early years of this century

Ex. 1

Ex. 2

variety chiefly due to a rhythmic monotony. With his fondness for a 6/8 measure it was only too easy a trap to fall into. Several critics remarked on the skilful orchestration but, as the *Musical Standard* critic suggested, the score needed 'overhauling'. Gardiner often returned to this work, even after he had had it lithographed, but twenty years later he had still not resolved the basic problem. 'I don't think the old English Dance will ever get done', he wrote to Grainger on 20 March 1926. 'I made the introduction fairly satisfactory, but could not find any means of relieving the terrible rhythmical monotony of the dance itself.' The work was not performed again after its première.

Balfour Gardiner's contacts within the musical world were meanwhile widening. He was by now well acquainted with Wood and Stanford, two influential figures. Towards the end of 1904 Vaughan Williams, five years his senior but not yet established as a composer of note, lunched with him for the first time, though theirs was never to be a close friendship. More importantly Gardiner had a valuable ally in Robin Legge, who for some years was the music critic of *The Daily Telegraph*. Legge was also the music editor for the publishing house of Forsyth Brothers and he later recalled with satisfaction his association in that capacity with members of the Frankfurt Group: 'I am proud . . . that it was my privilege . . . to print, I think, all the earliest compositions by Roger Quilter, Balfour Gardiner, Cyril Scott, Percy Grainger when he first used his curious phraseology . . . I still cling fondly to much of Cyril Scott's earlier piano music.'[3] (Grainger's 'curious phraseology' resulted from a desire to purge the English language of words with Latin and Greek derivations, so that instead of the conventional Italian terms that normally adorn musical scores he showed a marked preference for such expressions as 'louden lots' and 'soften bit by bit'. Grainger was to pursue this idea to almost ludicrous ends in the peculiar 'blue-eyed English' he adopted for his correspondence, and he was probably much encouraged in 1937 by Gardiner introducing him to the philological works of William Barnes who had similarly regretted the Latinising of English speech and had devised an 'alternative vocabulary' replacing, for example, 'accent' by 'word-strain', 'initial' by 'word-head', and 'dilemma' by 'two-horned rede-ship'.)

Robin Legge became an eloquent spokesman for that generation of composers, though he did not allow friendship to flavour his judgment, as his assessment of Cyril Scott's Second Symphony, in a letter to Roger Quilter on 31 August 1903, illustrates:

I don't agree that C.S.'s symph. *is* great . . . I am quite sure he will have to modify his idea of flow for flow's sake in instrumental music. That there is much that is astonishingly brilliantly good & beautiful of course I grant you, but the music does not seem to me to be abstract music – but to be, roughly speaking, a concourse of lovely, sweet & remarkably voluptuous – almost sensuous – sound. It is decadent rather than strong – exotic if you like, & magnificent, but 'great' is a very large expression. Every nuance *may* be & no doubt is influenced by Wagner – but C.S. adopts – half assimilates almost the actual texture of *Siegfried*, & there is a suspicion of mannerism in much of his harmony. After all, endless melody is a mannerism, an artificiality. Mind you, & believe me, I recognise as well as you all the great things C. S. says & I would not publish what I say here. I am sure C. S. himself, no fool, will see some of it himself as he grows in age & wisdom – *if* he can be kept from the petticoat influence. If not, then he'll be useless to the world & to himself, for he is not the strong man that Percy is though he is in a sense more purely musical. C. S. must develop his mental strength: he must live & live in the world, not in the fetid atmosphere of a crowd of mutual admirers & quasi courtiers – If he will, then he will by God's grace develop into the biggest – greatest – thing we have produced.

Legge's percipient and revealing remarks provide some pointers towards the path of eventual decline in Scott's standing as a composer. The symphony, played at the 1903 Proms, was one among several of Scott's works with which Gardiner helped in some small way, in this case by correcting at least the last two movements before they were sent to the copyist. Scott's declared intention in this and other works of this period had been 'to secure continuous flow, without a cadence from beginning to end of a movement'.[4] As the *Times* critic pointed out, Scott had set himself a very difficult task, not merely 'of avoiding the cadence, but of making the avoidance necessary'. Two other procedures in Scott's music which helped label him as a modernist were the avoidance of key signature and the use of irregular barring with its frequent change of time signature. This last device was one borrowed from Grainger who had already begun developing it so prominently in his *Hill-Songs* and the *Love Verses from 'The Song of Solomon'*. Gardiner made comparatively less use of irregular or alternating metres, although he was to exploit this procedure most effectively in one of his last songs, *Rybbesdale* (1920–2), where he breaks up the generally common-time pulse with occasional bars of 3/2, 7/4, 6/4, 5/4, 3/4 and 2/4 (example 3). But Gardiner's music was developing along more conventional lines without the daring experimentation in harmony and compositional techniques to be found in Grainger's and Scott's works. Stylistically his music falls more within the broad contours of the idioms of Bax and Delius.

Among the Frankfurt Group's early works to appear in the Forsyth catalogue under Legge's editorship were three piano works by Gardiner published in 1905: *Prelude* (*De Profundis*), *Humoresque* and *Mere*. The first two were dedicated to Evelyn Suart, a pianist to whom Gardiner had been introduced by Cyril Scott at a Broadwood concert (possibly in November 1903 when she had played three of Scott's pieces). Born in India in 1881, she had studied abroad with Raoul Pugno in Paris and Theodor Leschetizky in Vienna. She soon gained a reputation as an exponent of Debussy and Ravel, and she did much to help popularise Scott's and Gardiner's piano works.

The *Prelude* is the least distinguished of the three. Beginning with a plaintive chant above a soft tolling bass, it later dangerously nears monotony with the repeated phrases that build to a chordal climax. Evelyn Suart gave the first performance at a Bechstein Hall recital on 9

Ex. 3

May 1905. The other two pieces are technically more demanding and may well have been designed as show-pieces for their respective dedicatees. Both are in duple time, proceed at a rapid pace while requiring some intricate fingerwork, and are effectively written for the keyboard. *Humoresque* received its first performance in June 1904 but was later revised before publication and first heard in its final form in November the same year, Evelyn Suart being the soloist on both occasions. With its alternating left-hand chords of a fifth, *Humoresque* might initially suggest some kind of Grieg country dance. It illustrates Gardiner's occasional tendency to rely on little rhythmic figures to sustain the musical interest at the risk of overworking them, as the *English Dance* had already shown. Neither in *Humoresque* nor in the equally brilliant *Mere* is any relief afforded from the insistent rhythmic drive. *Mere*, dedicated to Grainger, was named after a village that took Gardiner's fancy when cycling through Wiltshire in 1902. Not that Gardiner set great store by titles, nor for that matter the acknowledgment of the composer of a work. As he expressed it to Grainger on 31 December 1943: 'I wish most music were anonymous, like ladies' hats or jewellery or even houses – it would have enormous advantages, cutting out all the silly talk about the composer & what he meant & whom he married & what his recreations are. It would be nice to see in a programme "No. 662 for piano & orchestra".' (Coincidentally, Mere was for twelve years the home of the Dorset poet William Barnes whose verses Gardiner later set.)

There were other first performances of note in 1905. In the Aeolian Hall, London, on 28 February the Cathie Quartet, who in 1903 had introduced his quintet, played the String Quartet in B♭ for the first time. This short one-movement work met with much praise. The *Times* critic referred to it as

a work that makes one wish Mr Gardiner's contemporaries would be as short, concise, and to the point as he. The work is so beautiful in its idea, atmosphere and workmanship that one would willingly have heard it again. The scoring, the warmth of colour and the invention alike are not only out of the common but on a very high plane and it is a small wonder that the composer and the players were called again at the close. (1 March 1905)

Before long the work was also taken up by other quartets. In his *Cyclopaedic Survey of Chamber Music* that amateur patron of chamber music, W. W. Cobbett, in 1929 praised Gardiner's quartet as 'one of the earliest examples of the renaissance of interest in chamber music shown by English composers in recent times'. Most of the development in this tautly constructed work stems from its sinuous lyrical opening theme (example 4), especially the rising figure in the first bar which is later whipped up into a *vivo* 6/8 coda.

Ex. 4

Within a few days of the quartet's first performance, Gardiner was represented in the third of the new Patron's Fund concerts, held at the Royal College of Music on 9 March. The programme consisted of new works by William Henry Bell, Benjamin Dale, Thomas Dunhill, G. Molyneux Palmer and Balfour Gardiner. Both Bell and Dale soon became firm friends of Gardiner who was now becoming increasingly involved with the rising generation of younger British composers. His new work at that concert, a four-movement *Suite in A major*, was the result of several years' gestation, known in its preliminary stages as a *Summer Suite*. According to *The Musical Times* he conducted it himself 'with alertness and verve' and it was generally considered the most mature and interesting work in the programme. *The Standard* wrote that 'it is so instinct with manly sentiment and vigour that it should speedily become well-known in our concert room. The last movement in particular is a splendid piece of exhilarating music that prompts the imagination and stirs the pulse of the listener.' *The Musical Times* also commented on the 'vivacious and manly themes . . . which are treated with a terseness, vigour and command of orchestral resource remarkable in a young composer'. There was a rare unanimity of opinion among the critics who similarly drew attention to the brilliant scoring and the inspiriting effect of the music. One or two detected a familiarity with the works of Wagner and Tchaikovsky, two life-long influences, but *The Daily News* fairly summed up the work's reception by concluding that 'the Suite is thematically interesting, in mastery of the orchestra it is mature, in invention ingenious and unflagging, and there is hardly a dull or laboured bar in it from beginning to end'. With such an enthusiastic welcome it is all the more surprising that the work has not survived for, although Gardiner conducted another performance on 29 April 1909 at Bournemouth where again, according to the *Musical News*, it 'left a most favourable impression', it has since disappeared without trace. In the mid-thirties, when he had given up all interest in music, Gardiner unfortunately burnt many of his manuscripts and one can only suppose that this *Suite* was one of those works which fed the flames.

In the early summer of 1905 there was a notable departure from Gardiner's normal musical activities as he was taken up with the current enthusiastic interest in folk-song collecting which played such an important part in the British Musical Renaissance. Collectors had been quick to realise that a precious heritage was in danger of being lost for ever and so, armed with notebook and pencil (and in some cases a phonograph), they searched out potential singers in fields, pubs and workhouses. Scouring the remotest corners of the counties, enthusiasts rescued hundreds of fine tunes that otherwise would have been gradually forgotten, and so helped to preserve a vanishing art. Composers too joined in the search, with George Butterworth, Vaughan Williams, Percy Grainger and later Ernest 'Jack' Moeran each making important contributions. A representative selection of these discoveries found their way into the numerous rhapsodies and other folk-inspired works that were current, like Butterworth's *The Banks of Green Willow* and Vaughan Williams's *Norfolk Rhapsodies*. As the composer C. W. Orr half-mockingly expressed it:

folk-tunes became all the rage; young composers diligently flattened their sevenths and modalised their tunes; parties of enthusiasts went back to the land, where they implored the rustics to warble songs their mothers taught them, which effusions were carefully noted down to be worked up into English Suites, English Rhapsodies, and English dance tunes. Nor was it surprising that with such a spirit of enthusiasm in the air new geniuses were discovered every month, and it became difficult to keep pace with the young men who were turning out masterpieces almost before they had finished cutting their musical teeth . . . It was, in fact, a healthy reaction against the foreign-musician worship that had gone on too long, but it overlooked the truth that you cannot create a ready-made renaissance by a form of folk-tune serum . . .[5]

Vaughan Williams had begun collecting in earnest in 1903 and the much younger Butterworth probably not until seven or so years later at Vaughan Williams's instigation. Grainger's enthusiasm had been fired by an illustrated lecture given in March 1905 in London by Lucy Broadwood, who was both a founder-member and the secretary of the Folk-Song Society and, like Cecil Sharp, a strong force behind such collecting. That April Grainger took down the now well-known Lincolnshire folk-song *Brigg Fair* which became the basis of Delius's extended orchestral rhapsody.

Balfour Gardiner became involved with the efforts of an amateur collector, George Barnet Gardiner. Neither a musician nor a relative, G. B. Gardiner was a linguist and a classics master at Edinburgh University and the compiler of several Latin primers. Once his interest in folk-song had been aroused, Lucy Broadwood suggested to him that Hampshire would be a promising field for research.[6] As a contemporary article stated, G. B. Gardiner 'had done a little collecting in the West of England, when Mr Balfour Gardiner, the composer, who lives at Sutton Scotney, offered to "note" songs for him if he came to Hampshire to reconnoitre and prospect'.[7] G. B. Gardiner's method of working was first to cover the area and collect any suitable texts and at a later date a musician would revisit specified locations to note down the tunes. To this end, in addition to Balfour Gardiner's assistance, he enlisted the aid of two other local musicians: Charles Gamblin, who was an organist from Winchester, and J. F. Guyer from Southampton. The three musicians worked independently, Balfour Gardiner being responsible for most of the songs gathered in 1905, and Gamblin and Guyer assisting G. B. Gardiner in subsequent years. Progress was slow at first for although they started in June their work was brought to a halt by the hay-making season with the harvest following soon after, and they found their singers either too busy or too tired to sing. Later, when their work was once more interrupted by the hay-making, they turned their attention to the workhouses where to their delight singers were readily available.[8] Many of them were in old age, one particular woman who sang for Balfour Gardiner being ninety.

Without the aid of the phonograph (which Grainger began using in 1906) there were problems in transcribing the folk-tunes. Describing such collecting in Sussex in his book *London Lavender*, E. V. Lucas wittily suggests that words are much harder to obtain than tunes 'because all the words are different, whereas the tune is the same all through' and as the older singers probably had few or no teeth it was sometimes difficult to know exactly what they were meant to be singing.[9] But as far as the tunes went this was not Balfour Gardiner's experience for he encountered other problems. He found that it was necessary to ask the singer to repeat the song until it had been accurately written down, and in these successive deliveries quite frequently there were variations on the original. Trying to take down *The Sweet Primeroses* he wrote: 'The above is as near as I could get to what J. C. *generally* sang: his variants were innumerable.' A degree of artistic licence permissible to the singer posed further problems for the collector as the rhythm and corresponding time signature were occasionally free and elusive. Regarding *Young Edwin in the Lowlands* he wrote: 'The singer generally started the first bars of this song in 6/8 time: but the crotchets soon got shorter & the quavers longer, till from the ninth bar onwards the time was unmistakably 4/4. The subsequent verses might begin with 6/8 or 4/4.' Nor was the text always above suspicion. With *Rap-a-tap-tap!* G. B. Gardiner noted 'the text is too broad to be sent in' and, fearing any impropriety, had substituted asterisks in the offending places.

The fruit of the 1905 collecting was gathered in the villages of Twyford, Hursley, Itchen Abbas, Old Alresford, Cheriton and Ropley. Further songs were collected at intervals in 1906 at Whitchurch, Andover and Easton. There remained a handful in May 1907 from the Kingsclere workhouse. In all, Balfour Gardiner notated nearly one hundred folksongs which were incorporated into G. B. Gardiner's collection of Hampshire folk-songs, now residing in Cecil Sharp House, London. A selection of sixteen from that collection formed Book III of *Folk-Songs of England* published in 1909 by Novello under Cecil Sharp's editorship. The piano accompaniments were by Gustav Holst and, while the introduction credits G. B. Gardiner's three assistants, *Sing Ivy* is probably the only one of the set to have been collected by Balfour Gardiner (although *Our Ship She Lies in Harbour* is a close variant of the one he took down). Holst was not an active collector himself; the heavy demands of his teaching and composition would have left him little time for such activities. But later, with folk-song very much in his bones, this tradition was an invaluable source on which he drew for many of his compositions. Of his numerous other folk-song settings, *The Seeds of Love* and *Swansea Town* are the only ones likely to have come as a result of Balfour Gardiner's collecting. Their close friendship was not to form for a few years yet, by which time Gardiner was no longer active in the folk-song field.

Balfour Gardiner himself made a few settings of Hampshire folksongs, though not solely of those he personally had collected, and in 1907 he showed four to Cecil Sharp, hoping that they might be included in the forthcoming edition of *Folk-Songs of England*. On 16 September he blithely wrote to Sharp:

I think you will have no objections to raise with regard to my treatment of modal tunes, which I have hitherto harmonized without the introduction of any note which does not appear in their scale (though sometimes, I believe, I have come near to a modulation to a major or minor key). As regards the 'modus lascivus' I cannot help allowing myself considerable license in the harmony. At the end of 'Old Swansea Town' (which I send) I believe I have not merely conformed to the spirit of the melody, but actually enhanced it by the employment of chromatics.

Gardiner's attitude to the treatment of folk-song was similar to Grieg's, whose aim had been to raise folk tunes 'to an artistic level through what may be called conventional harmonization', and also to Bartók who also coincidentally began collecting in 1905 and who wanted to 'bring back the spirit of folk-song and to harmonize the melodies in modern style'. Unfortunately Sharp was not in sympathy with the chromatic treatment of folk melody. He felt it was almost impossible to use 'modern chromatic harmonies without going astray'.[10] He sought a second opinion from Littleton of Novello who, while commenting that it seemed a pity to include any song harmonized in the 'modern manner',[11] ultimately left the decision to Sharp as editor. Sharp then suggested to Gardiner that he find another publisher willing to undertake a volume of his own settings.

Gardiner was naturally piqued at the rejection of his songs. 'I feel with regard to one or two songs for which I have an especial affection, that I should be sorry to see them harmonized & published by anybody but myself', he wrote to Sharp on 22 October. Accordingly next year he went ahead and had published his own version of *The Golden Vanity* for voice and piano, also orchestrating it. The tune was one collected by J. F. Guyer and quite different from that to be found in Lucy Broadwood and Fuller Maitland's *English County Songs*. The now seemingly innocent harmonies in the following extract (example 5) may well have appeared as musical solecisms to Sharp, whose conservative views on folk-song collecting and arranging were at about the same time being vigorously challenged by the refreshingly innovative and scrupulously accurate Percy Grainger, the latter even going so far as to express privately the opinion that 'Sharp's harmonic treatment of the tunes is revolting.'[12]

The Golden Vanity was dedicated to G. B. Gardiner who felt that his relationship with Balfour Gardiner had become somewhat frayed as a result of Sharp's attitude. While work was going ahead on the third volume of *Folk-Songs of England* he wrote to Sharp on 5 February 1908: 'I have had further correspondence of a delicate nature with Mr Balfour Gardiner, who justly claims and will certainly receive a few more songs and I have in consequence been compelled to ask Von Holst to suspend operations.' Five months later, on 31 July, he wrote again: 'Our relations with B. Gardiner are so strained that it may be as well to let sleeping dogs lie, that is, to omit his name altogether [from the volume]. I am sure he will be quite satisfied, if I give him "Swansea Town" and one or two other songs to harmonize in his own way.' But, despite these differences, the volume was duly completed with Balfour Gardiner's name included in the preface, though with a scant representation of the songs he had himself taken down. *The Golden Vanity* is his only surviving Hampshire folk-song setting. And on that sour note his involvement in folk-song collecting ended.

In October 1905 Gardiner was once more back in Germany renewing Frankfurt acquaintances, including his former teachers Knorr and Uzielli and the fellow-student Herbert Golden who had joined the Frankfurt staff on completion of his studies. Cyril Scott was also on the Continent and together they went up into the Taunus Mountains. Gardiner took the opportunity of going to the opera, but he also set time aside for composition, the major work in hand being the symphony he had begun in earnest the previous year, and he no doubt seized the chance of obtaining

Ex. 5

'Sir, what will you give me if I do her de-stroy?" It's I will give thee gold, and

I will give thee store,— And you shall have my daugh-ter when I re-turns on shore, If you

sink her in the Low-lands, Low - lands low, if you sink her in the Low - lands

low.

Knorr's advice. The following March he was abroad again, this time sight-seeing in Italy in the company of three Oxford friends and travelling through Florence, Perugia and Assisi. For a few days he linked up with Tovey and Kelly who were similarly delighting in the classical splendours of the land. Gardiner much enjoyed walking amongst such 'wonderful scenery' and visiting the Uffizi Gallery in Florence. Assisi he thought 'heroic'. As usual he took his music notebooks with him and would jot down ideas that came to him while in such fine spirits.

Because of his month's holiday in Italy he missed another performance of his String Quartet given by the Cathie Quartet on 29 March at a Broadwood concert in the Aeolian Hall. That year he was elected to the Savile Club. Both he and Roger Quilter became members at the same time and among those supporting Gardiner's candidature were Robin Legge, Everard Feilding, Gervase Elwes, Sir Charles Stanford, C. H. Lloyd (erstwhile Three Choirs Festival organist and conductor with many Oxford connections through which Gardiner may have come to know him) and Alfred Oppé, a friend from Oxford days. That May there was further folk-song collecting for G. B. Gardiner, and in June he was off to the Lincolnshire coast for a habitual holiday with Frederic Austin's family at Chapel St Leonards, where a Mrs Coote let bedrooms for 10 shillings a week.

Gardiner was represented at another Patron's Fund concert, held this time at Queen's Hall, on 3 July 1906 when he conducted the first performances of two orchestral songs, *When the Lad for Longing Sighs* and *The Recruit*, both settings of verses from A.E. Housman's *A Shropshire Lad*. When in 1896, after one publisher's rejection, Housman eventually had this slim volume printed – at his own expense – no-one could have then foreseen that this collection of sixty-three poems would be avidly seized upon by so many composers and further immortalised in their settings. The simple, direct utterance of the verses, their easy ballad-like metre, and their recurring universal themes of the brevity of life, the foreboding of youth's destiny in war, and the capricious fortunes of love, all enriched their appeal. Furthermore, their generally rustic atmosphere provided an added stimulus for composers with folk-song inclinations.

Housman's attitude to the union of music and his verses varied from indifference to an anxiety that his poems should not be tampered with in any way. 'My taste in music is rather vulgar', he is known to have declared.[13] But at least he did not withhold permission. On 18 August 1906 the poet wrote to his publisher, Grant Richards: 'Mr Balfour Gardiner may publish "The Recruit" with music if he wants to. I always give my consent to all composers, in the hope of becoming immortal somehow.'[14] Gardiner's Housman settings were among the very earliest in a long and distinguished line, with Arthur Somervell's fine *Shropshire Lad* cycle preceding them in 1904 and with other – in some cases better-known – cycles by Vaughan Williams, Butterworth, Gurney, Moeran and Orr yet to appear, besides numerous individual settings.

Gardiner's two songs met with much approval. *The Musical Times* commented that the composer had shown 'commendable avoidance of the conventional. *The Recruit* is a manly ditty with a swinging rhythm and, sung by Mr Frederic Austin, so pleased the audience that it had to be repeated.' The *RCM Magazine* noted that 'Mr Balfour Gardiner had the pleasure of scoring a popular success with the second song, *The Recruit*.' Indeed, such was the success that when a special Patron's Fund concert was held in 1911 to summarise the series' achievement to date, a programme was drawn up from the most successful items of earlier concerts and Frederic Austin sang again the two Housman songs. Only *The Recruit* was published, in a version for voice and piano. It made occasional appearances at the Proms (twice in the 1907 season) and elsewhere with singers like Austin, Albert Garcia and Frederick Ranalow, while the first song (and eventually both orchestral versions) disappeared.

The immediate appeal of *The Recruit* is readily appreciable. It is a stirring ballad in the grand manner, the emotion borne onwards – like Somervell's *The Street Sounds to the Soldier's Tread* – by a quick march pulse which in both songs is given an added impetus with a little repeated fanfare-like triplet figure. There are moments in the piano version where one regrets the absence of the orchestra for which the song was clearly conceived, as for example in the reflective middle section with its *tremolando* accompaniment and imitative bugle calls. Unfortunately the song's weakness, a serious failing, is its repetitive and over-emphatic ending which is curiously insensitive by comparison with what has gone before. Furthermore the bold twice-stated figure ten bars before the end bears too close a resemblance to Mendelssohn's *Wedding March* for the similarity, once noted, to be effaced from memory. There was one more Housman setting to come – *When I Was One-and-Twenty*, published in 1908. Here no such fault can be levelled against it. This splendid, sensitive setting bears comparison with the best of other better-known versions. The delicate, rippling accompaniment supplies a fragile foil for the 'sighs' and 'endless rue' of the two verses. It is one of Gardiner's finest songs (example 6).

Gardiner's notebooks or 'jotters' of this period give some indication of a more active involvement with British music on a wider scale through the Society of British Composers, which had been founded in 1905 principally to promote the publication of British works in the Avison Edition. Bax, Bell, Dale, Hurlstone, McEwen and Vaughan Williams were among those to benefit from the enterprise. Gardiner had his String

Ex. 6

Quartet published in the Avison Edition in 1907 and the song *Winter* in 1912. The part he played in the SBC's activities is not clear, but judging from his notebook entries he may have sat on a 'reading committee' and helped assess the merits of works submitted for publication. He was no more sparing in his appraisal of other composers' works than he was with his own. Of a Gavotte by Charles Hartog he commented 'musical invention of a low order', of a Wolstenholme sonata 'common stuff', and of a piano piece by James Lyon 'crudest musical thought – nothing to recommend it'. He probably did not maintain his connection with the Society for long, but it did at least quite likely bring about a lasting friendship, for one score that passed through his hands was a recitation

The Twa Corbies by Arnold Bax. In November 1906, together with Benjamin Dale, Bax made the first of many visits to Gardiner's recently acquired Kensington house. There were to be many occasions on which they enjoyed each other's company, either in the relaxation of Gardiner's home or on holiday abroad.

Gardiner's warm hospitality was always much appreciated by his many friends, especially at the new house he moved into during the summer of 1960 when he vacated his rooms in The Temple for the more spacious accommodation of 7 Pembroke Villas. This placed him almost opposite Norman and Adine O'Neill who lived at number four, and this road was to witness the comings-and-goings of many a composer. Much later that year came the first performance of one of the very few of Gardiner's enduring scores – the *Overture to a Comedy*. Its conductor at Queen's Hall on 28 November was Landon Ronald, who frequently played the work in subsequent years. This prompted Gardiner in 1922, on hearing of Ronald's knighthood, to write to him a congratulatory note adding, 'I suppose it's because you've played my Comedy Overture so often!' Ronald replied in a flash: 'Write me a symphony and they'll make me a peer!'[15] The work as it is heard nowadays differs from the original as it was revised five years later. A programme note outlined the changes: 'All the old material was kept and none added, so that the present version differs from the former only in the manner in which the themes are treated.' Gardiner was as disparaging of this work as of any of his. 'No good at all', he would dismiss it. 'I have always hated this work, and remember that I even looked upon some of it with contempt when I was writing it', he told Grainger in a letter on 21 December 1924. The test of time has at least proved him wrong in his assessment. It is a delightful, spirited work and expertly scored, though requiring a conductor's firm hand to restrain the brass and percussion from dominating the more boisterous moments. It is an excellent example of British light music at its best. The principal theme is a lively, bustling affair announced on *staccato* strings (example 7). After some vigorous discussion of this idea on full orchestra, an especially memorable (and eminently whistleable) second subject (example 8) is heard on the clarinets against a restless semiquaver pattern of *spiccato* first violins.

The scoring throughout is full of delightful touches, including one glittering passage in which two flutes take up the second subject over a back-

Ex. 7

Ex. 8

Clarinet

ground of triangle, glockenspiel, *pizzicato* strings and held notes on the horn. In later years the conductor Guy Warrack would often broadcast the *Overture to a Comedy* on the composer's birthday and many times he included it as an interlude between ballets at Sadler's Wells. It is this work, the more popular *Shepherd Fennel's Dance* of 1911 and the *Evening Hymn* that have kept the name of Balfour Gardiner before the public. But selfess as ever, his name is assured of further remembrance through his great friendship begun the next year, with Frederick Delius.

4 Delius, Beecham and Hardy

1907–1909

Balfour Gardiner's ability to form deep friendships once more became apparent in 1907 when he met Frederick Delius. Although born in Bradford, Delius was then little known in England as a composer. Since his privately financed St James's Hall concert in May 1899 not a note of his orchestral works had been heard in his native land, even though they had received much attention on the Continent. His father's business was in the wool trade, but he escaped the clutches of the family concern and after some years of travelling, including two years spent in America chiefly on a Florida orange plantation, he settled in France where he lived for the rest of his life. It was not until his Piano Concerto was played at the Proms in October 1907 and his *Appalachia* was given a month later that any real interest in his music was shown in England.

So in April of that year it was a still relatively unknown Delius who dined in musical company at Gardiner's house in Pembroke Villas. 'I dined with Balfour Gardiner last night and they played "Appalachia" through', he wrote on 16 April to his wife Jelka. 'A few musicians were there. All were tremendously taken with it.' As a result of their meeting Gardiner was soon invited to visit Delius in France at his beautiful home at Grez-sur-Loing, a small village some twenty-five miles south of Paris. Within a few days of dining with Gardiner, Delius wrote to his wife of meeting others of the Frankfurt Group. On 18 April he wrote: 'Cyril Scott I have also seen and he is really very nice', and three days later: 'I also met Percy Grainger, a most charming young man and more gifted than Scott and less affected, an Australian, you would like him immensely.' Two days previously Delius had also written to Quilter, expressing the hope that they would meet again.[1] Just as Balfour Gardiner was the focal point of a number of musical friendships, so he and many of his friends became fervent admirers of Delius. For many musicians, especially in later years, a visit to Grez was almost like a pilgrimage. All the Frankfurt Group with the exception of Cyril Scott were devoted to Delius and made journeys to Grez. Norman O'Neill's first visit came at the end of 1907, possibly in connection with the Musical League which was being mooted at that time. Gardiner went almost every year, except for the war period which brought a temporary halt to such visits.

From Lincolnshire, where he was staying in June, Gardiner was de-

9   Frederick Delius, a photograph possibly taken during one of his visits to
England during the First World War

lighted to accept Delius's invitation and he made the crossing to Grez in August. He found London life tiresome at times and not conducive to composition, and he needed little persuasion to leave behind the bustle of the city for the peace of Delius's riverside garden. 'London is dull and uninspiring, and I am waiting for the spring',[2] he once wrote to Delius, and on another occasion, 'We have had a wonderful autumn, nearly as fine as last year; but it is wasted on one in London.'[3] Little wonder then that he derived so much pleasure from his moments at Grez. He was a countryman at heart, even once declaring that he felt well only in the strawberry and raspberry season. 'It would be a sad reflection', commented Cyril Scott, 'to think that we might have had more enlivening works from this talented composer if only strawberries had fruited all the year round!'[4] Gardiner's visits to Grez were escapes, a means of ridding himself of the irksome worries that sometimes beset him. During his brief stays, which he eagerly anticipated, he would combine work with pleasure, at times cycling, at others attending to his own works or assisting the older composer by correcting proofs of his scores for publication. In this way for many years he performed an inestimable service.

Gardiner often dispensed freely of his time where his friends were concerned – of his time and of his money. His wealth found many worthy outlets and his generosity took many forms, even to the neglect of his own music which he regarded as being of secondary importance. There was proof-reading and the copying and checking of parts, the way in which he was soon to be assisting Delius. And there were smaller kindnesses. In his anecdotes Grainger remembered how in 1904 Gardiner had cycled with him round the small villages near Frome in Somerset and helped to rehearse the various sections of the Frome band scattered about the neighbourhood so that Grainger could try out a new work, *Sir Eglamore*. Gardiner's musical advice was keenly sought by his Frankfurt friends. From their student days they would listen with interest to each other's works and ideas while in the throes of composition, and here Gardiner's critical judgment was much valued. In April 1907 he was offering Quilter suggestions for improving a point of orchestration in a new suite. And there was help of a different nature. He wrote to Quilter on 24 April: 'I met Henry Wood at lunch today in the Savile. He said – of his own accord – that he wished you would write something for orchestra. I told him you had done so already, & that I had urged you to send him something. He said he wished you would . . .' Quilter's new suite, a three-movement *Serenade* dedicated to 'Prof. Iwan Knorr in gratitude and admiration', appeared in that year's Promenade concerts. Before long Balfour Gardiner's generosity was to blossom into musical patronage on a scale that would surprise even his close Frankfurt friends.

He was not fully to assume the mantle of patron for five years yet but later in 1907 he took on another unexpected – if less significant – role, by joining the music staff at Winchester College where Dr E. T. Sweeting was head of the music school. At the time of Sweeting's appointment in 1901, music was barely tolerated on the College curriculum, if not actively discouraged. But over the years he built up a firm tradition. Sweeting's previous teaching post had been for fifteen years at Rossall where a Thomas Beecham was among his pupils. As the music school at Winchester grew, so likewise the music staff numerically expanded. Harold Jervis-Read, two years younger than Gardiner, had joined in 1902 and Balfour Gardiner made only a fleeting and more-or-less unofficial appearance in September 1907, his stay being too short to warrant an entry in the College register. A single brief reference to him in the December issue of *The Wykehamist* concerns itself solely with a piano recital given in the music school by the dedicatee of the piano piece *Noel*, Arthur Newstead, who played amongst other things compositions by Jervis-Read and Gardiner. At the College Glee Club Christmas concert on 18 December, Gardiner and Jervis–Read were joint piano accompanists to Sweeting's conducting.

As Gardiner often stayed at his father's house at Sutton Scotney the proximity of Winchester was convenient. Yet it was customary for all the staff to live within a few minutes' walk of the College walls and so during the term-time he stayed at 56 Kingsgate Street. He probably only taught there for a term, sufficient time however to produce one of his most frequently performed works, the noble anthem *Te lucis ante terminum*, generally known as the *Evening Hymn*. Although he confessed to having done with religion after his first term at Charterhouse, this anthem had nevertheless been on his mind for many years and the opportunity for its performance in the College chapel must have spurred on its completion. It is the sole surviving product of his organ studies, with an important and impressive part for that instrument, adding strength to the full-voiced climaxes without any loss of clarity. The introductory ground-swell, underpinned by a sustained tonic pedal and briefly spiced with a short whole-tone run, builds up in an eleven-bar paragraph to the choir's powerful entry (example 9). The central hushed *a cappella* entreaties are framed by organ linking passages, and the choral opening returns in an impassioned statement that dies away with repeated amens. Gardiner dedicated the anthem to Sweeting.

Whatever his reasons for joining the Winchester staff had been, his reasons for leaving are similarly obscure. But when in 1909 he heard that Jervis-Read was resigning in order to devote more time to composition, Gardiner half expected to be invited to fill the vacancy. By then, however, Gardiner had other concerns and was unlikely to have accepted the post had he been offered it; the composer Adam Carse became Jervis-

Ex. 9

Read's successor. Yet that was not to be the end of Gardiner's teaching career as the lean war years were to call for his services elsewhere.

At the conclusion of his Winchester term he was off to Berlin, spending Christmas there with his brother Alan and his wife Hedi. The years that followed were to be increasingly busy ones, though the beginning of 1908 found his spirits at a low ebb. 'I am terribly depressed & am doing no work', he wrote to Delius on 19 February. 'If I don't begin soon, I think I shall take advantage of your hospitality & come to Grez.' Three days later came similarly despairing tones: 'The moments are frequent just now when I feel that I could write nothing in these surroundings.' Delius replied with a few words of comforting advice, and during April and May Gardiner consoled himself by travelling abroad to Florence and Venice, calling in at Grez on the homeward journey where he hoped that he would be able to assist Delius with the libretto of his new 'music-drama' *Fennimore and Gerda*, based on the Danish writer J. P. Jacobsen's novel *Niels Lyhne* with which Gardiner was already familiar. He was himself working on a setting of Francis Thompson's *A Corymbus for Autumn*, which sadly does not seem to have reached fruition. But more immediate work in hand was the revision of the symphony begun in 1904 which Henry Wood had requested for the 1908 Proms. The holiday restored Gardiner's spirits and he took to work more readily, yet he had reservations about the symphony. He wrote to Delius on 24 July:

I know by experience that I shall have no peace until it has been performed, criticised & forgotten. When all that has happened, I hope still to have three or four weeks of summer in which to start some new work. I cannot tell you how weary I am of my old music with its academic conventions & pretentiousness, & I am gradually coming to see what my new music must be like & am anxious to set to work on it. I have been very happy & peaceful this summer, & really feel as if I could write again with enthusiasm.

A new orchestral score, his *Fantasy*, was given its first performance at Queen's Hall on 13 June by Beecham and the New Symphony Orchestra. It met with a mixed reception: it had no avowed programme and the critics seemed somewhat at a loss without a peg to hang it on. Delius, whose *Appalachia* was in the same programme, received three accounts of the concert and of the *Fantasy*. Gardiner himself was pleased. 'Beecham . . . did my Fantasy well', he wrote the next day. 'It was a great event for me, & a great stimulus.' Nevertheless he withdrew the score for revision and it had to wait seven years before it was heard again. Beecham wrote a lukewarm report of the performance three days later: 'Gardiner's thing turned out alright – the scoring a bit queer in parts – imagine the effect of a flute, viola, and trumpet, with harp arpeggi for bass! That pretty sentimental tune in it of course pleased very much.'

Norman O'Neill was more congenial, though there was an ominous portent in what he had to relate on 22 June of Gardiner's changing attitudes: 'Balfour's piece everybody seems to have found very charming & he was quite warm about it himself. He is most amusing – he told me within a week that he was going to "give up music" & that *"now* he was going to work"!'

Prior to the concert Gardiner had been cycling round Oxfordshire in search of a house for the summer and the next day he was off to the small village of Little Barrington near Burford where he had rented a vicarage for two months. There he hoped to complete 'this frantic symphony'[5] in time for the Proms. He had wanted to join Delius on a holiday in Norway but the urgency of work forced him to forgo that pleasure. Fortunately it was a glorious summer that year and he felt 'another being'.[6] At the same time he had his eye on a house in the village which he considered buying and renovating, but the eventual house of his choice lay farther south, in Berkshire.

The symphony was completed in time for Henry Wood to conduct it at the Proms on 27 August. It was curiously announced as being in E flat when it was in fact in the key of D, though some tonal ambiguity in the introduction to the first movement was probably the cause of the confusion. The scoring called for a large orchestra including two harps and a battery of percussion. In its revised form it was now in three movements instead of the originally intended single movement, with the last two being played without a break. The *Observer* review on 30 August gives the clearest hint of the score which is now lost:

The work is in two divisions. After an introduction that avoids the suggestion of definite tonality, the first movement built on a short concise phrase cleverly and continually treated with glowing harmonic colour pursues a brisk, bright way leading naturally to a second subject, a broad well-drawn melody which is in sufficient contrast to vary the interest without changing the general mood. There is no episodal movement, no sidelight on either theme and no development in the ordinary sense of the word. The charm of the matter lies in the ever-varying harmonic treatment . . . The second part is not of so sustained an interest, the subdivision of the slow section into two distinct parts makes for patchiness. The first half is quite ordinary, for Mr Gardiner, but the last, a 6/8 movement in G minor, suggesting a folk-song if it is not one in actuality, seems to come logically into the general atmosphere induced by the first movement. With the aid of a very fine and effective rhythmic passage this merges into a brilliant finale which is not too long drawn-out. When the interest of thin thematic material is made dependent on harmonic colouring conciseness is a virtue and this Mr Gardiner's work decidedly possesses. Unquestionably it should be heard again.

With the *Daily Telegraph* critic remarking on a 'magnificent melody' near the end of the last movement and a 'lovely second subject' in the *andante*, the critics were clearly not in complete agreement over the merits of the symphony's thematic material. The *New Ages* critic wrote that 'such a row you never heard as the beginning of the last movement, but it is so decidedly cheerful and good-tempered that one forgets that it is not quite *à-la-mode*'. The Prom audience was less concerned with fashion and gave the symphony a rousing reception, calling its composer several times to the platform.

True to his word, no sooner had the symphony been performed than it was forgotten, and despite the *Observer* critic's plea it was not heard again and the score quite possibly later destroyed. The British Symphony had not quite arrived despite the efforts of Parry and Stanford whose canon then numbered four and six respectively, yet of those ten all but Stanford's latest symphony belonged to the last century. But one had only to wait until December, for concert halls would soon be resounding to the triumphant strains of Elgar's First Symphony, programmed three times in the next season's Proms and to achieve the unprecedented distinction of a hundred performances in just over a year of its existence.

Gardiner now had many other things on his mind to take his thoughts away from his symphony. On 7 October he went to the Sheffield Festival with Delius, who had come over from France to hear the first English performance of his *Sea Drift* in which the soloist was Frederic Austin (who a month earlier had sung Gardiner's *The Golden Vanity* at the Proms). Delius was in England again at the beginning of December for performances of *Sea Drift* conducted by Beecham at Hanley on the third and at Manchester on the following day when Gardiner was present. A week later Delius conducted the first performance of his *In a Summer Garden* at a Queen's Hall Philharmonic Society concert and stayed for part of the time at Pembroke Villas. That year Gardiner, with the aid of his father in his capacity as director of the Atlas Assurance Company, was trying to assist Delius in the disposal of his Florida orange plantation. But much of the time was spent attending as many rehearsals and concerts as possible given by Beecham who, in conducting *Paris* at Liverpool on 11 January that year, had begun his many years of loyal devotion to the music of Delius of which he became the incomparable interpreter. Having done little conducting himself, Gardiner felt that there were many benefits to be had by watching Beecham. In fact he went further. When Beecham's Symphony Orchestra made its first full public appearance at Queen's Hall on 22 February 1909 in a programme that included *Sea Drift* (with Austin once again the soloist) and Berlioz's *Te Deum*, playing the triangle and tambourine was none other than Balfour Gardiner while Benjamin Dale was at the organ. But his efforts were not a success, as he told Delius on 24 March: 'My scheme for playing the percussion instruments fell through, simply because I could not manage it; one has no idea how hard it is to play a triangle until one tries. I still may attempt the bass drum, if I get notice of rehearsals from Beecham. But that, of course, is a very doubtful prospect!'

Despite a seemingly harmonious beginning, it was hardly to be expected that Gardiner would get on well with Beecham, a man of totally different temperament. With his whirlwind pace, there were inevitably some eddies and disturbances left in Beecham's wake, and Gardiner was one such casualty. An underlying antipathy is evident even in their early encounters. When in 1907 Beecham was involved in the selection of a committee for the new Musical League, he wrote on 13 December to Delius: 'I am considering the question of the Committee. It is not an easy matter to find a number of responsible and energetic people among the younger men in Town. They are mostly of the mind and disposition of your host at 7 Pembroke Villas.' Their differences spanned many years but things first came to a head in 1909 when Gardiner was outraged at Beecham's failure to honour a debt of some £150. On 13 September he wrote to Delius:

Not a word from Beecham, & my solicitors seem to be as unsuccessful as myself, as far as getting an answer from him is concerned. Unless he pays by today, a writ will be served on him, & if that is disregarded, I suppose it will mean either a law-suit or putting bailiffs in his house & selling his goods! But making all the allowances possible, the least one can say is that he has behaved extremely badly. He knows his cheque was dishonoured a fortnight ago, & yet he does not write to me. It is abominable treatment & I have had enough of Beecham to last me the rest of my life.

On 23 October Norman O'Neill likewise acquainted Delius with the facts: 'I stayed with Balfour last week-end. He is going for Beecham with the arm of the law! I don't blame Balfour after the way he has been treated. It seems that our Tommy owes a good deal of money so I doubt if he'll pay – this won't prevent him living in state at the Langham!'

No doubt Delius, with divided loyalties, used some balm to placate the infuriated Gardiner, but that was not to be the end of the discord. Poor Delius, who had offered to cover the debt in question himself, could not have foreseen that unwittingly he was to be the cause of greater friction between Gardiner and Beecham at his own death. Beecham of course was quite unruffled by the whole affair and, despite the fact that he included *Shepherd Fennel's Dance* in his Symphony Orchestra's repertoire for their visit to Berlin in 1912 and twice performed the revised *Fantasy* in 1915, to Gardiner the name of Beecham remained anathema. Many years later Percy Grainger related to Gardiner Beecham's comment on his *Colonial Song*. 'My dear Grainger', Beecham had said, 'you have achieved the almost impossible. You have written the worst orchestral piece of modern times!' On hearing of this Gardiner (who in fact was not nearly so fond of the *Colonial Song* as he was of other Grainger works) rounded on Grainger in an angry voice and roared, 'Why didn't you fell him to the ground?'[7]

Towards the end of 1908, possibly following Delius's example,

Gardiner gave much thought to tackling a work in what was for him a new medium – opera. For the basis of his 'lyric drama' *A Village Romeo and Juliet*, first performed the previous year in Germany, Delius had taken a rural tale, and in a similar fashion for his subject-matter Gardiner looked to one of Thomas Hardy's *Wessex Tales*. The story he chose, *The Three Strangers*, is unusual among Hardy's output in having a happy ending. Three strangers in turn call one night at a lonely cottage on the Dorset coombs where a christening is being celebrated with dancing and ample refreshment. The host, Shepherd Fennel, has a frugal wife who intends to strike a balance between a sit-still party which invariably leads to excessive 'toping' and a dancing party which contrariwise results in ravenous appetites causing 'immense havoc in the buttery'. But she hasn't foreseen the musicians disregarding her instructions to keep the dances short, especially when one of the dancers is so enamoured of his partner that he bribes them with a crown to keep up the dance 'as long as they have muscle and wind'. The first stranger to knock at the door and be offered some ale and a fireside seat is, unbeknown to the others, an escaped criminal due to be hanged the next day for sheep-stealing. In a short while another stranger calls and receives similar hospitality. The two strangers fall into conversation with their hosts and the later arrival is asked his trade. In a song he explains that he is the hangman whose services are required the following day. During the hangman's song a third stranger – the criminal's brother – looks in at the door just as distant guns announce a prisoner's escape. Recognising his brother and his predicament, he flees for fear of giving him away. Assumed by the onlookers to be the criminal, he is immediately chased and the diversion he has unintentionally caused allows the first stranger to escape. When the truth is learned the hunt is resumed the next day for the true criminal, but the sympathetic countryfolk, while so busily exploring the countryside, are not quite so thorough when it comes 'to the private examination of their own lofts and outhouses'. And so the sheep-stealer escapes capture.

The Stranger's Song from this tale, on occasions also referred to as *The Hangman's Song*, had been Gardiner's first published work and was several times performed at the Proms with either Frederic Austin, William Higley or Albert Garcia as soloist. This splendidly stark setting is shot through with fine dramatic irony as the hangman with an almost workmanlike cheerfulness sings of his gruesome duties alongside his intended next victim (example 10).

Shortly after its publication Gardiner wrote from Paris on Boxing Day 1903 to Thomas Hardy:

I am having sent to you a copy of 'The Stranger's Song': I can hardly expect you to like it, but hope you will accept it nevertheless as a token of my sincere admiration, & also of my gratitude. Indeed, I feel a sense of personal indebtedness

Ex. 10

towards you, and am glad to have this opportunity of acknowledging it. Many of your novels (and I have read *all*) have not merely given me the temporary amusement which most readers derive from most novels, but have made on me a deep & lasting impression, such as I cannot describe but you perhaps will understand. It annoys me that I cannot give any better account of my appreciation of your work, but I know from experience the hopelessness of the attempt. I can only assure you of my sincerest sympathy . . . I live in Wessex myself, halfway between Winchester & Andover, & you have taught me to know the County & to love it.

Hardy replied from Max Gate on 21 January 1904:

I have only received 'The Stranger's Song' you have set to music. I think you have been highly successful in the composition, & you will probably win many singers of such a catching melody. If you had melodized one of the songs of a tender kind in my two vols of Poems you might perhaps have still better pleased drawing-room vocalists.

Gardiner did not take up Hardy's suggestion, finding a more sympathetic response in the poetry of Housman and Masefield. But the story remained in his mind. It had for some years existed in a one-act play version. J. M. Barrie had prompted its dramatisation, and as *The Three Wayfarers* it was performed in 1883 and well received. Not knowing of its existence, Gardiner wrote again to Hardy on 2 November 1908:

> I read in the 'Times' of today that a dramatized version of the 'Trumpet Major' is to be given in Dorchester, & that you are taking an active part in its production. This emboldens me to write to you about a scheme which I conceived in re-reading 'The Three Strangers' about a week ago. The hangman's song, & the tenseness of the situation while he is singing it, beside the dance to the accompaniment of 'serpent' & 'bass-viol', give admirable opportunities to the musician; & though I must admit, on reflection, that no dramatized version, with or without music, can be such a satisfactory presentation of the tale as the form you have chosen, the character of the plot & the opportunities it gives appeal to me so strongly that I have a great desire to make out of it a one-act opera.
>
> But there are great difficulties in the way: in the opera, much more than in ordinary play, the situations must explain themselves – one cannot rely on the audience to grasp the words when sung; & for that reason the statement of the convict's brother, when he is brought back to the cottage, & its confirmation by the gaolers would be ineffective, & the point of the story might be missed. But a far greater difficulty is the ending: for in any dramatized version of the story, as it at present stands, the final escape of the convict would remain doubtful. One might, indeed, be satisfied if the shepherd & his party refused to go out on a second search out of admiration of the man's bravery, & on hearing that he was condemned for nothing more than sheep-stealing, & the curtain might go down at the end of another dance. This would be effective enough musically; but I should not like to make the music an excuse for any inherent weakness in the plot.
>
> I am in great doubts about the matter, not being a play-wright myself; & if I am to carry out my scheme, I must seek assistance from somebody more competent than myself to dramatize the story. Above all things, I should like your help; but when I began this letter I did not intend to ask for that; but merely whether you would have any objection to having 'The Three Strangers' made a play for music. Some years ago I sent you a setting which I had made of the hangman's song: I should use the same music for that in the opera. In the matter of the dances, the costumes, & above all, in the matter of characteristic dialogue, your advice would be invaluable.
>
> Please let me know if my scheme meets with your approval: if so, I have no doubt that you will be so kind as to assist me with your advice: if not, I shall proceed no further with it.

In his reply on 29 November Hardy tried again to draw Gardiner's attention to other areas of his literary output:

> In reply to your enquiry I may inform you that there is already an acting version of 'The Three Strangers' in existence. It was played in London with considerable success several years ago. I believe I have a copy somewhere.

But why do you not choose a subject more worthy of music? – such as, for instance, an episode from The Dynasts, e.g. The Trafalgar episode in Part I – the Peninsular episode in Part II, or the Moscow or Waterloo episode in Part III. However, I do not know much about music.

But Gardiner was not to be diverted from his plan. The grander scale of those episodes from *The Dynasts* held little attraction for him. Grainger sensed the real reason for his preference for *The Three Strangers* when he wrote in 1951 after Gardiner's death:

I always feel that the irresistible appeal of Balfour Gardiner's music – behind all its flowing melody, heart-searching harmonies and surging orchestration – lay largely in what I would call the 'social justice' underlying his choice of subjects and texts. He felt so sharply the injustice meted out to countryfied heroic and athletic types in our Nordic civilisation – the country lad to be hung for stealing a sheep (*The Stranger's Song*), the parlous lives of sea-faring adventurers (*News from Whydah, An Old Song Re-sung*) and the like. This deep compassionate sympathy with the misfortunes of heroic types informs even his most lively and vigorous pieces with a singular poignance.[8]

Gardiner therefore wrote once more to Hardy, requesting a copy of the dramatised version, hoping that it might serve as libretto in its existing form. This he received in due course and on 6 January 1909 he wrote acknowledging its receipt:

I am extremely obliged to you for your kindness in sending to me the dramatized version of 'The Three Strangers'. It has been most skilfully done, & the difficulties which I mentioned to you in my first letter have been for the most part removed. I have had a copy made for my private use, & return you the M.S.

I should like to write the opera in any case: but it would be satisfactory to know, before starting it, that no objection would be raised to its production (if such a chance ever presented itself) on the part of your publishers or yourself. I wish I could have met you when you were in town: I was actually lunching at the Savile one day when you were there, & did not know of it till ten minutes after you had left the club. Perhaps if you are in town again you would be kind enough to arrange a meeting? If not, would you please let me know whether there are any considerations which would stand in the way of a possible production of the opera. I think it unlikely; but copyrights, etc. are troublesome matters, of which I know practically nothing.

Hardy replied promptly the next day:

No objection will be offered either by my publishers or myself to the production of 'The Three Strangers' as an opera.

I do not know if you are aware that the opera of 'Tess of the D'Urbevilles' has been produced with much success in Milan; & I may mention privately that it may probably be produced at Covent Garden, though it would be premature to speak of this. I only mention it now because it occurs to me that, if it were produced there, this might afford an opening for yours. But I know nothing of the musical world.

And with both contributors freely disclaiming certain areas of knowledge, this correspondence seems to have ended. It is not known if the

10   *The Three Strangers*. These sketches are virtually all that survive of
Gardiner's projected one-act opera based on the short story by
Thomas Hardy

two ever subsequently met. The opera *Tess* to which Hardy referred was by Frederic d'Erlanger and it was indeed given at Covent Garden, on 14 July 1909. Hardy attended both the rehearsals and the first night but the story had been Italianised to such an extent that he scarcely recognised it as his own novel.

Much to our loss, Gardiner's opera never reached the stage, nor was it completed. A few surviving sketches show that some work was done on it: existing pages dated 21 January 1911 in short score relate to the latter part of the story when the local constable, under pressure from the hangman, is organising a search party for the stranger who has fled. Balfour Gardiner has not been the only composer to consider operatic treatment of this tale. By some coincidence a one-act opera of the same name by a Julian Gardiner (no relation) was produced at the RCM in July 1936 and more recently a version by Elizabeth Maconchy was first produced in 1968. In 1913 Elgar had contemplated a Hardy opera and once again, just as he had in correspondence with Gardiner, Hardy mentioned *The Dynasts* as a possible subject. The war put an end to such ideas, yet, with that upheaval past, in 1927 it was Holst who penetrated as close as any into Hardy's world with his masterly short orchestral score *Egdon Heath*.

But that fortunately is not all that is left of Gardiner's project, for as a note in the full score of his most frequently played orchestral work states: 'At Christmas-time last year (1910) it occurred to the composer to call up from the past that merry dance which led to the depletion of Shepherdess Fennel's victuals.' This idea gave birth to the well-known *Shepherd Fennel's Dance*. It seems likely that the dance was intended as an interlude in the opera. A later sketch in 1911 is headed 'for operatic working of Shepherd Fennel's Dance', with the main motif rising sequentially every two bars. How much else of the opera was composed is not known, as any manuscripts would have fed the incinerator he used so drastically in later life.

5 '. . . a place of enchantment'
1909–1911

Music in England had long been under the shadow of the Continental Masters. In the first decade of the century the concert programmes were heavily dominated by such deities as Beethoven, Brahms, Mendelssohn and Wagner, and composers of Balfour Gardiner's generation were impatient for a fair representation of their own works in the orchestral repertoire. From 1907 Gardiner was loosely associated with the ill-fated Musical League, which at the outset had augured well for the future of British music but, after much activity and some mild initial success, eventually came to nothing.

The principal aims of the League were to hold an annual festival of new and unfamiliar works not necessarily of native origin (though there was a later proposal that 'foreign musicians should not occupy more than one and a half hours out of the estimated five hours of the two concerts'), and to encourage a fluid interchange of ideas among composers and musicians, professional and amateur alike. This, it was felt, would 'exercise a beneficial influence on the progress of music in this country'. It also sought to decentralise musical activity away from London towards the provinces, particularly the industrial centres of the Midlands and the North renowned for their strong choral tradition. In design it tried to emulate the Continental Tonkünstlerfest (at which in 1906 at Essen, Mahler's Sixth Symphony and Delius's *Sea Drift* were both first heard). But the result proved to be on a much inferior scale, owing in part to the lack of financial support from the English municipalities.

Early in 1908 a manifesto was drawn up, with Elgar nominated as president and Delius (who had been one of the prime movers behind the League) vice-president. But Elgar, then approaching the peak of his popularity, was not always free to attend committee meetings, and Delius, who had accepted the nomination partly on condition that some of Grainger's works were performed, lived abroad and could normally attend only those meetings that coincided with the performance of one of his works, for which he specially travelled to England. Living in France, he was probably more in touch than most with the Continental musicians who it was hoped would participate in the League's festivals. Mahler, Debussy, d'Indy and Max von Schillings all promised Delius to attend the festival and conduct their works, but these promises were not to be fulfilled.

68

Gardiner was a member of the League for the fee of one guinea and was in touch with its activities through Norman O'Neill, his close neighbour in Pembroke Villas. One or two of the early unofficial meetings had been held at Gardiner's house but he declined to hold any prominent office. In September Beecham and O'Neill met to discuss candidates for a London committee, and on the 21st Beecham sent the list of proposed members to Delius for general approval – with Gardiner's name at the bottom, and adding the wry comment that could hardly disguise his antipathy: 'the last – you see – is well amongst the females' (the names of Lucy Broadwood and the composers Liza Lehmann and Dora Bright were next to Gardiner's). Yet whatever their personal differences, Gardiner was in no doubt of Beecham's ability. When in 1909 the post of honorary secretary became vacant on the resignation of Copely Harding, there were suggestions of Gardiner filling the vacancy. But he wrote on 29 October to Delius:

I shall not undertake the secretarial work of the League. From what I hear, it seems that Beecham will become the moving spirit of the League & of the Society of British Composers, which I had always hoped for & thought possible. If it happens, Beecham can find a secretary for himself: if it does not happen, the prospects of the League are not good enough to make it worth my while to undertake their work.

Always the individualist, Gardiner was hardly cut out for committee work, even less secretarial work, and in the end it was O'Neill who took on the job of secretary.

Beecham did not, as it turned out, play a lasting role in the League. Together with Elgar, Delius, and the music educationist and editor of *The Musical Times*, W. G. McNaught, Beecham and Wood were elected on to a sub-committee which was to choose the music for the festival. For years there existed an estrangement between these two conductors, something stronger than mere professional rivalry, and, whatever the gulf was between them at the time, they do not seem to have both been present at any committee meeting. By the end of January 1910 Wood had seceded from the League, and in his biography of Delius Beecham only credits the League with one festival (which he misdates)[1] and presumably left at about the same time. The composer Granville Bantock had been another 'behind the scenes' figure at the League's inception, but it was left to people like McNaught to hold things together. There was understandably disarray among the ranks and Harry Evans, the festival conductor, was far from happy about the state of the League. On 6 September 1909 he wrote to McNaught:

We agree that the heads of the concern, Elgar, Bantock, etc., are doing *nothing*, & worse than all, are taking no interest in the thing . . . We must do all we can to avoid a fiasco in the matter of attendance. I am disappointed in Bantock over this business. I expect he has some new craze – a new kind of goose, or a new Chinese rag-shop.

There had even been some talk of disbanding the League the previous year, but despite the problems the much-hoped-for first festival eventually took place in Liverpool on 24 and 25 September 1909. Gardiner's String Quartet had the honour of opening the first (chamber) concert, with two orchestral concerts the next day. Adine O'Neill wrote to Delius on 3 October that the chamber concert had been 'a rather depressing affair as it was not well attended. There was an orchestral rehearsal the same evening, and Austin, Gardiner & Co all rushed to that from the concert.' A rule that had been felt necessary forbade the committee members to put forward their own works, though this was not strictly adhered to as four of Delius's *Danish Songs* with orchestra were performed. A bilious attack prevented their composer from attending in person. Gardiner had hoped that during his visit Delius might spend a few days with him at a cottage he had recently bought in Berkshire. He had also given the League some financial support, which he discussed with Delius on 21 September in a letter of commiseration:

I am very sorry to hear you are so poorly; & especially that you are prevented from coming to Liverpool & to my cottage . . . As regards the £100 for the League, Norman was here for the weekend, & we discussed how it had best be employed. It was decided that I should become a guarantor for £100, & renew my guarantee every year until the calls had reached that amount. If, however, I find an opportunity of using the money to better purpose, I shall do so. It might happen, for example, that a work was insufficiently rehearsed, & that if I was present I might arrange for another hour's rehearsal before the concert; but however the money is spent, I want to keep control over it myself, & see that it is not thrown away . . . You of course understand that my £100 is to be subscribed anonymously.

Under the terms of his guarantee, anonymity proved impracticable and his donation was minuted against his name at a meeting held on 12 November.

Many of Gardiner's friends had works performed at the festival: Bell, Scott, Austin, Bax and Grainger. Austin and Grainger also took part as soloists and Bax played the piano in a sextet by Holbrooke. Two suppers and a luncheon provided material nourishment for the League's members, and Gardiner was present on the morning of the second day for a general meeting held in the Liverpool Philharmonic Hall at which he seconded a vote of thanks to the chairman, Elgar. The musical content of that festival only illustrates the relative immaturity of emergent British music at the time, for few of the works played would fit comfortably into today's programmes. But it was a valuable testing-ground for the younger school such as Gardiner was himself before long to provide on a lavish scale.

The following years were difficult ones for the League, particularly as the death of the choral conductor James Whewall necessitated the cancellation of a projected festival for 1910 in Hanley. A rival organisation, the Incorporated Society of Musicians, caused such concern that when the second and final festival was given in conjunction with the ISM, Elgar resigned in protest at the union of the two bodies. The dissolution of the League occurred in January 1913, reasons being variously attributed to apathy on the part of many of the committee, a lack of vision amongst musicians, and little increase in membership. The last festival consisted of four concerts, two of chamber works and two choral and orchestral, given in Birmingham from 30 December until 3 January 1913. Gardiner played a prominent part in the final concert, conducting his own *Overture to a Comedy* as well as Bax's *Festival Overture* and Austin's *Three Songs of Unrest* with the composer as soloist. Other works in the programme were conducted by Edgar Bainton, Julius Harrison, Gustav Holst and H. A. Keyser. With the festival's conclusion the Musical League quietly passed into history.

The most significant event of 1909 for Balfour Gardiner was not a musical one but instead the purchase of a cottage in the secluded Berkshire village of Ashampstead. It was here in such comfortable surroundings that his closest friends were to experience the full warmth of his friendship and hospitality, and their memories of him would be unforgettably linked with this cottage. Here too he was to spend some of the happiest days of his life. He at once engaged an architect and a gardener – he also purchased a motor-car – and set about making extensive alterations to the building. The car he found a great convenience. He was now able to motor to Grez, and when Delius came over in September for his third and final conducting engagement, Gardiner drove over to Hereford to hear him conduct his *Dance Rhapsody* in the Shire Hall as part of the Three Choirs Festival. He had planned to drive the Austins to Liverpool for the first Musical League festival that month and invited Delius to accompany them. 'Austin & his wife will sleep here [at Ashampstead] on the Wednesday evening & travel up in my car the next day, starting early in the morning, if the weather is fine', he wrote on 13 September. 'I wish you could join us. My journeys to Hereford & back with the car were such a success that I shall adopt this mode of travelling whenever I can. Do come with us.' But Delius's bilious attack prevented him from joining the party.

The alterations to his cottage, which involved the addition of two rooms, took some time and by the following April Gardiner felt in need of a rest. An intended tour of the Pyrenees with Bell and Austin had fallen through as Bell had just been appointed director of a national pageant and Austin's professional engagements left him with little free time. 'Might I pay you a week's visit in ten days' or a fortnight's time?'

Gardiner asked Delius on 3 April. 'I am longing to get out of England, & have a thorough change: for so many alterations are being made at my cottage, and so many things there require attention, that it has been quite a worry to me. I want to get away & forget all about it, so that I may return fresh there & settle down to work.' He and Delius had intended to tour the Loire together, but Gardiner was by now detained by a commission from Bell. The prospect of a visit to Grez made him work harder, but he was as always most anxious that his presence in Delius's house should not prove an encumbrance:

You would of course not allow me to disturb your usual occupations in the slightest degree: I have a whole heap of books to read & shall be quite ready to do odd jobs in the garden; besides which I shall probably have to score the music to one of the Pageant episodes which I am writing for Bell.

And again twelve days later:

I shall bring my driver with me, and he & the car had better go to the hotel. If it is in the slightest degree inconvenient for you to have me in your house (owing to your servants) I will go to the hotel also . . . I am immensely looking forward to my visit; I have been worried to death about all sorts of things for the last 3 weeks, and I shall enjoy the peace of your garden, & the complete change, more than I have ever enjoyed it before.

And so he decided to give himself six days to finish the Pageant music before setting out by car for France.

The music that he had been asked to provide was for a spectacular Pageant of London to be staged at Crystal Palace in the coming Coronation year. Over four days it unfolded in twenty-eight episodes a pictorial history of London and the Commonwealth. Frederic Austin, Frank Bridge, Gustav Holst and Vaughan Williams were among those from whom music had also been commissioned, for an orchestra consisting of a much enlarged military band with string basses. Gardiner's contribution was for three episodes depicting the Plague of London, the Fire of London, and the Lord Mayor's Show. The spectacle attracted more attention than the music, though one reviewer commented that the Fire of London section contained 'some unusual effects of chromatic scales in complete chords which seem very daring for military band'.[2] Wagner was clearly the model for the march tune probably used in the Lord Mayor's Show episode and, according to the surviving sketches, intended 'to be developed symphonically for military band . . . like the *Huldigungsmarsch*'.

In January 1911 Gardiner went abroad to Italy and Germany. On 2 May he conducted the first performance of the revised *Overture to a Comedy* at Queen's Hall. This work was published two years later by Novello with a dedication to York Bowen, though little record of their friendship has survived. Later in May he attended the rehearsals for the Pageant of London which opened in June with Bell conducting. On 14 June Gardiner conducted his two Housman songs in a special Patron's Fund concert at Queen's Hall, and in July he spent three weeks in Finland, staying with his brother Alan's relations. But for much of the remaining time he either relaxed or entertained friends at his Ashampstead cottage once the conversions were completed.

While he kept the Pembroke Villas house as his London address, Ashampstead now became his real home. For the alterations to his new property he engaged Basil Sutton, a young architect of the Reading firm of Sutton & Webb. They became frequent companions over the years, either discussing architectural projects that later engrossed Gardiner, or enjoying walks in each other's company. In the alterations Gardiner was exacting to the minutest detail, and he gave the same detailed attention to the garden which abounded in lime and apple trees. One section he set aside as his bee-garden in which he kept up to a dozen hives. Bee-keeping became an absorbing passion which he tackled with typical thoroughness, equipping himself with the necessary veil and gloves. He was frequently stung but he cheerfully passed it off as being 'good for the rheumatism'. The bees were his preserve and his alone, and he took much joy in presenting friends with gifts of honey. 'I have a little honey for you', he would announce on calling, handing them a jar in each hand. Only after his departure would they discover that many more jars had been left on their kitchen table. At Ashampstead he also kept pigs for curing bacon as well as a sow for breeding. Looking after the pigs was usually delegated to other hands, though one story has it that he once broke off a holiday abroad and raced homewards across Europe to assist a sow in farrow.[3]

The longest serving of his employees was Elijah Cox, whom he took on in the autumn of 1910. Cox and his family were given a cottage adjacent to Gardiner's and, among other duties such as gardening, Cox became the chauffeur whose job it was to ferry the many visitors to and from the nearby Pangbourne railway station. Gardiner's employees always knew when he was in a 'composing mood'. Some mornings when they were working in the garden, he would come outside without a greeting and stroll about the lawn oblivious of their presence, beating out with one hand a tricky rhythm that was troubling him. Once the solution had presented itself, he would rush indoors up to his music-room and try it out on the piano. Soon he was out again, beaming genial 'good mornings' about him. Rhythm was fundamental to him, as Cox's son was to find out the hard way when Gardiner, who gave him some piano lessons, insisted on beating out the rhythm of the piece he was learning on his head.

11 Balfour Gardiner's cottage at Ashampstead in Berkshire
(with Gardiner just visible between the two trees in the foreground)

Apart from the visits of other composers, at times Gardiner held week-end parties, select in number and often including his friends and under-graduates from Oxford. During the warmer months tennis was usually the substance of these parties, for which Gardiner always dressed in im-maculately pressed white flannels. An occasional guest at such parties was the doctor and author Henry Bashford, who was later to pen an affectionate portrait of Balfour Gardiner in one of his books. Describing one visit he recalled how

glowing with enthusiasm [Balfour] arranged the sides; and thanks to the wrist power that he had developed during his executant training, he occasionally pro-duced, in an otherwise eccentric game, strokes that would have defeated anybody living. He greeted these with obvious satisfaction and was equally annoyed by the strokes that he missed, maintaining a running commentary, in both senses of the phrase, upon his idiocy, as he put it, and incompetence. But he never lost a point by not trying for it. He performed Herculean excursions after impossible balls . . . I forget when we finished, but I remember that [he] was totally exhausted – he had probably run at least a couple of miles more than the rest of us put together – and the candle-lit cottage, as we returned to it through the dusk, seemed more than ever a place of enchantment . . .[4]

Bashford married Basil Sutton's sister, and it was with Sutton that he first met Gardiner around 1912 at his cottage. Of that initial encounter he wrote:

And presently . . . I beheld a very large and extremely well-covered pedestrian advancing towards us. He was wearing a panama hat – or rather waving it – an old but admirably cut coat of dove-grey homespun, grey flannel trousers crisp from the press, and stoutly nailed autumn-brown shoes. For the rest, as he drew nearer, I saw that he had a broad pink face, flaxen hair, worn rather long, and slightly protuberant sea-blue eyes . . .[5]

In 1935 a collection of Bashford's personal reminiscences called *Lodgings for Twelve* was published, the twelve of the title being various characters of his acquaintance. One of these chapters, under the thin disguise of 'Bramber Guest', is devoted to Balfour Gardiner, a pseudonym no doubt adopted out of deference to Gardiner's preferred anonymity in public matters. Bashford's generally accurate and most informative account is the only lengthy portrayal of Gardiner to have hitherto appeared in print. Sensitive to such portraits, his subject complained that it made him appear like a 'cuddly pink teddy-bear', though inwardly he was neither dissatisfied nor really offended. Bashford, later knighted and during the Second World War physician to King George VI, remained on friendly terms with Gardiner and paid many visits to his home in Berkshire and, later, in Dorset.

Although the perfect host in every way, entertaining guests was an ordeal for Gardiner. So solicitous was he for his guests' comforts and needs that he became vexed in anticipation of their visits and required several days to recuperate after their departure. Despite the pleasure of their company, he rarely wished their stay to be a lengthy one and would even drop hints if he felt they had over-stayed their welcome. He was known to inform his guests not only of a suitable train by which they should arrive but also the one by which they should leave. Yet by the same token he would be conscious, when visiting friends, of possibly becoming a burden himself on his host and would similarly make his visits brief ones. And although generally friendly and amiable, he did not indulge the social conventions of paying and returning calls.

On 6 September 1911 Henry Wood gave the first performance of *Shepherd Fennel's Dance* at a Queen's Hall Prom. It was an instant success and immediately encored. Gardiner attended the rehearsal the day before and admitted in a letter written the same day to Grainger that he 'liked it very much'. Wood, to whom it was dedicated, played it again just over a fortnight later at one of his Sunday concerts, and it made another appearance at that year's Proms on 11 October. It quickly became Gardiner's most frequently performed orchestral work and for several years it turned up regularly at the Proms two or three times each season. While one cannot deny Wood's magnificent crusading work as a conductor, at the same time he did give the music public what they wanted – that of course in itself is no fault, but he had a habit of taking certain popular works under his wing and, frankly, over-playing them so that their success obscured other lesser-known but equally important (or even better) works by their composers. He did this with Delius's *Brigg Fair* and *Dance Rhapsody No. 1* as he also did with Bantock's *Pierrot of the Minute* and Holbrooke's much inferior *Variations on Three Blind Mice*. Gardiner's penalty of being plagued by the success of a single work is that he is widely known only as the composer of *Shepherd Fennel's Dance*, delightful though it certainly is.

This work combines to advantage many of the typical features of Gardiner's style. Its brevity, its lively pulse and the expert and colourful orchestration all commend it to the listener. Just as characteristic is the way in which the dance (yet another form of that 'English dance') is built around an insistent rhythmic figure (example 11, from the piano

version), in this case very similar to the one which propels Svendsen's *Carnival in Paris*. It catches perfectly – almost in visual terms – the gaiety, the vigour, the exhilaration, in a word the 'earthiness', of the rustic dance. Notwithstanding the piece's short duration (under six minutes), a masterstroke is the non-reappearance of the lovely pastoral interlude intended to depict 'the simplicity and bonhomie of the shepherd and his wife' with its accompanying chromatically descending line (example 12, becoming twelve bars later example 13). Its return is almost hinted at just before the boisterous close, and the listener longs for it to come again. A masterstroke of restraint. Curiously enough, after he had put the work in the hands of the publishers, Gardiner wrote to Grainger on 26 September 1911: 'I begin to see now how I could have amplified it and made it more effective by more insistence. It is too late now: I am tired of it for one thing, & then publishers are wanting to issue it at once in every possible & impossible form, & I think it wise to consent.' It is difficult to imagine the dance being made more insistent

12   Balfour Gardiner entertaining Arnold Bax (seated right) and
fellow composer and pianist Frank Hutchens (left), who taught at the
Royal Academy of Music from 1908 until 1914 when he was appointed
professor at the State Conservatory, Sydney

Ex. 12

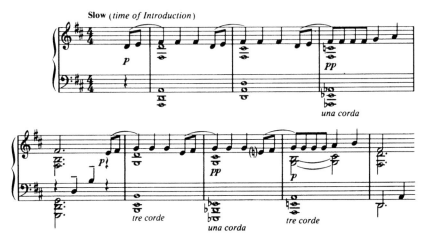

Ex. 13

without labouring it. However, the work was also published as a piano solo and in an arrangement for military band by F. Winterbottom.

Also in that season's Proms was *The Recruit*, sung on 7 October by Frederick Ranalow. Four days before Christmas Gardiner conducted his *Overture to a Comedy* at Bournemouth. The concerts there, a launching pad for many a British work, were in the very capable hands of Dan Godfrey who has written that 'no one could ever mistake the music of Balfour Gardiner for anything but the work of an Englishman. Both in his choral and orchestral examples there is the right cadence, and my only regret is that he does not make more frequent contribution.'[6] If Gardiner's works were 'all too few'[7] then, there was good reason, for he was preoccupied with a scheme that was eventually to earn him the undying gratitude of his fellow composers and was to place his name prominently before the musical public. He planned to promote and himself finance a series of concerts with the specific aim of bringing recognition to the many British composers who up till now had received rather scant attention. Into the production of these concerts, known as *The Balfour Gardiner Choral and Orchestral Concerts*, he threw himself wholeheartedly.

6 'Oriana will sing for me . . .'

1912–1913

'Who wants the English composer?' With this challenge Vaughan Williams launched his outspoken article of 1912 in which he expressed many truths about the existing state of music in England. He continued:

Nobody wants the young English composer; he is unappreciated at home and unknown abroad. And, indeed, the composer who is not wanted in England can hardly desire to be known abroad, for although his appeal should be in the long run universal, art, like charity, should begin at home. If it is to be of any value it must grow out of the very life of himself, the community in which he lives, the nation to which he belongs . . . The English composer is not and for many generations will not be anything like so good as the great Masters, nor can he do such wonderful things as Strauss and Debussy. But is he for this reason of no value to the community? Is it not possible that he has something to say to his own countrymen that no one of any other age and any other country can say?[1]

That article voiced the feelings of young British composers whose frustrations the Gardiner concerts were to do much to alleviate. Indeed, the staging of these concerts was timely. Then as ever, art without charity faced a shaky existence. In that pre-war era with no broadcasting, no Arts Council, and without any government subsidies, the young composer's chances of obtaining a hearing were very few indeed. The 'official' body, the Philharmonic Society, founded in 1813 for the encouragement of orchestral and instrumental music and granted its Royal charter in November 1912, held only about seven concerts each year. So the openings there were few beside the normal concert diet. There were some hopeful signs in the prevailing musical climate, for this was a time of expansion, with the births of three new London orchestras to stand in healthy rivalry alongside Henry Wood's well-established Queen's Hall Orchestra: the London Symphony Orchestra in 1904, the New Symphony Orchestra in 1905, and Beecham's Symphony Orchestra in 1909. But it may also be regarded as the last important period of private musical patronage, with many organisations, and in some cases individuals, relying on certain wealthy businessmen for their support, a function nowadays largely taken over by industrial sponsorship. At the turn of the century three such philanthropists readily come to mind, all men of German descent to each of whom Elgar, for one, was indebted for his support: Frank Schuster, Alfred Rodewald (whose benefactions are especially associated with Liverpool), and Sir Edgar Speyer (who financed the Queen's Hall Orchestra).

One patron to whom many composers owed a special debt of gratitude was Sir Ernest Palmer, who in 1903 initiated the Patron's Fund at the Royal College of Music specifically for the encouragement of young British musicians. For this purpose he donated £20,000 in 1903, followed by a further £7,000 three years later. Gardiner was one of many to receive performances in the Patron's Fund concerts which were made up entirely of new works without any financial necessity of including standard classics to draw an audience. These concerts (which after the First World War became public rehearsals instead of formal concerts) were in some ways the model for the type of programme Gardiner was to put on, and in 1906 he acknowledged his indebtedness by dedicating *The Recruit* to Sir Ernest Palmer. The Patron's Fund also gave other forms of assistance to young musicians: it enabled students of poorer means to continue their studies either at the Royal College or abroad, it purchased opera tickets for young singers to attend performances at Covent Garden, and it helped towards the expenses of the preparation of parts or the publication of select works. In 1906, for example, Holst received such a grant towards the publication of his choral ballad *King Estmere*.

Leading conductors of the day with international standing like Richter and Nikisch, while not ignoring the existence of British music (especially Richter with his championing of Elgar), tended to show more their native sympathies in their programmes. So one looked elsewhere to figures like Dan Godfrey in Bournemouth, Granville Bantock in the Midlands, and Henry Wood and Thomas Beecham in London and the provinces (the last two names seeming to acknowledge Nikisch's pre-eminence by modelling their appearance on him, particularly in the cut of the beard). They were held in great respect for their continual advocacy of British music. There were, as has already been seen, some efforts to boost British music on a grander scale by the formation of the Society of British Composers and the Musical League. But it still fell to individuals to take up the torch in the various series of concerts they promoted in which British music occupied a prominent place.

Some of these consisted of chamber music, songs and solo instrumental items. Such were the Broadwood Concerts, an annual series of about twelve fortnightly programmes given in St James's Hall in connection with John Broadwood & Sons, the piano manufacturers. These began in November 1902 and by 1905 all the Frankfurt Group had been represented, sometimes appearing as performer as well. Gardiner's quintet was played in the first concert of the second series, and his quartet in the fourth series. Though by 1907 the programmes had become less ambitious in scope, these concerts nevertheless provided a welcome platform for young executants as well as composers. Through them Frederic Austin, Gervase Elwes and Percy Grainger secured useful engagements in the early stages of their careers.

Two other important series of that period, chiefly of chamber works, were organised by composers: Josef Holbrooke and Thomas Dunhill. Holbrooke's music, rarely performed nowadays, thrived on its composer's own idiosyncratic promotion and on the support of men like Beecham before the First World War, after which it fell into a steady decline. As well as being a vigorous promoter of his own works, Holbrooke was an ardent campaigner for British music in general through his chamber concerts begun in 1902. And if some names like Waldo Warner, Algernon Ashton and Edith Swepstone mean little today as one looks through his programmes, this is not to deny the generous support he gave to native music. Gardiner's quartet appeared in one of the 1913 concerts. Holbrooke's campaigning was not restricted to the concert hall for he was, as Cyril Scott wrote of him, 'a forceful fighter with the pen, albeit not for himself alone,'[2] carrying on his polemics in the press and his programme notes alike. For many years Holbrooke was fortunate enough to enjoy the backing of a wealthy patron, Thomas Evelyn Scott-Ellis, 8th Baron Howard de Walden, whose interests lay chiefly in the stage. He was the librettist of Holbrooke's operatic trilogy *The Children of Annwn*, a sort of post-Wagnerian 'ringlet' steeped in Cymric mythology, and he gave much financial assistance to the Arts, becoming president of the British Music Society set up after the First World War and donating £5,000 to its foundation fund in 1920. But, by then in the post-war climate, patronage on that scale was becoming considerably rarer.

The other promoter of chamber concerts, Thomas Dunhill, was, like Holbrooke, a contemporary of Gardiner's and is today chiefly remembered as a teacher as well as the composer of chamber music and operettas. But in 1907 he started a notable series of chamber concerts whose special function was to revive works by young British composers that had been performed once and then forgotten. There were probably many deserving works for which a second performance must have proved just as hard to obtain as the first, and in that respect these concerts supplied a splendid service.

For nine years Dunhill served as assistant music-teacher at Eton College on a distinguished music staff headed by C. H. Lloyd. The other assistants included Colin Taylor (a guiding influence on the young Philip Heseltine who studied at Eton for a short while) and a musician who made a significant contribution to British music in those pre-war years, Edward Mason. Born in 1878 and a student at the Royal College, Mason first came into the public eye as the cellist of the Grimson Quartet, whose other members were Frank Bridge, Ernest Tomlinson, and its leader

Jessie Grimson who became Mason's wife. (The quartet played Dunhill's horn quintet in the first of the Broadwood series.) In June 1906 Mason conducted the New Symphony Orchestra (of which he was soon to be a director) in its first Queen's Hall concert, with his wife as soloist in Bruch's First Violin Concerto. The following year he formed a choir bearing his name, initially numbering about one hundred voices, with the object of producing new works by young British composers. From 1908 until 1914 he staged an enterprising series of choral and orchestral concerts which came closer in magnitude and importance to Gardiner's than any other of that period. For seven years an annual concert was given, usually in March or April, and in all over thirty British composers were represented, with Holst being particularly well served. Gardiner's choral ballad *News from Whydah* was played in the 1913 concert. Like Gardiner in his concerts, Mason engaged the New Symphony Orchestra of which he was otherwise its principal cellist and in that capacity may well have played in Gardiner's series. (He certainly played in Gardiner's only Philharmonic Society concert in 1913.) Mason's choir was not restricted to his own concerts; Holbrooke and Beecham made use of it, Holbrooke in some concerts mainly devoted to his own works, and Beecham in his 1911 Queen's Hall all-Delius concert. The importance of both Mason's and Dunhill's concerts was recognised by grants from the Palmer Patron's Fund. But in March 1915 Mason went to France as second lieutenant in the Northamptonshire Regiment, and on 9 May he was killed in action near Fromelles, bringing to a sudden end a most promising career.

The last of these important concerts organised by individuals before the First World War were those mounted by Francis Bevis Ellis, also of the de Walden family. His three concerts in March 1914, one chamber and two orchestral programmes, which came after Gardiner's, brought forward some important works, with the first performance of the original version of Vaughan Williams's *A London Symphony* and the first London performance of Delius's revised *In a Summer Garden* being of outstanding interest. Bax was well represented in these concerts in which the conducting was shared by Ellis and Geoffrey Toye. But war was not far away and Ellis was soon to enlist in the Northumberland Fusiliers. In September 1916 he, like Edward Mason, was killed in action.

In spite of much individual effort, British music before the war still lacked a corporate identity, even perhaps in the public's estimation an air of respectability. It needed the kind of stimulus that the Musical League had failed to give – a festival that would display the range and wealth of music coming from those younger composers struggling for recognition. And this was just the creative spur that Gardiner was able to supply. It was characteristic of him always to put his friends' music before his own, and the series of eight choral and orchestral concerts which he organised, financed, and in part conducted in 1912 and 1913, is arguably his finest achievement. Each concert, almost without exception, was devoted to the works of British composers. Here Gardiner was unselfishly sparing in the presentation of his own works, concerning himself instead with the careful selection of his friends' compositions that would show them in the best light. To this end he was involved in considerable work in the preparation of scores, many of which were unpublished.

Grainger wrote that 'it was difficult to get Gardiner to explain the exact purpose of his concerts, but there was never any doubt in my mind that the impulse behind them was deeply patriotic. And when I said to him, "Aren't your concerts like a kind of flag?" he answered, "Yes, I suppose that is as near as we will get to it".'[3] In 1943 Arnold Bax described the concerts as through 'the princely generosity and selfless enthusiasm of Balfour Gardiner . . . the most ambitious plan for the encouragement and dissemination of native work that had ever been devised'.[4] He went further to add that while Vaughan Williams and Grainger 'owed him a debt of gratitude impossible to repay . . . he had saved Holst from neglect and a weighty sense of personal failure'[5] and had fairly launched Bax himself on his orchestral career. Not without good cause did Grainger call Gardiner the 'good angel of British composers'.[6] With his financial resources, his conducting ability and considerable artistic judgment, he was ideally qualified for the role of patron.

The outstanding success of the concerts was due in part to a generous provision of rehearsal time, a shortage of which plagued English orchestral life for many years, and also to the care taken in the selection of programmes (which are listed in full in Appendix B). These were a refreshing blend of the new and the old, with a variety of forces and textures from full choir and orchestra down to smaller unaccompanied choral groups, from the most recent orchestral scores to Tudor madrigals. An early problem that arose during the planning stages was one of finding a choir capable of tackling unfamiliar works. But fortunately in 1911 Norman O'Neill introduced Balfour Gardiner to Charles Kennedy Scott, conductor of the Oriana Madrigal Society. This choir had begun informally with Kennedy Scott, Thomas Beecham and a few others meeting occasionally at each other's house to sing madrigals, with Beecham singing bass and surprising the others by the quantity of music he was able to memorise. By 1904 these casual meetings had developed into a society whose declared intentions were to 'press the claims of our Elizabethan school' and 'to devote itself solely to the singing of English madrigals'. The first concert took place in the Portman Rooms on 4 July

1905, with Beecham still singing bass, though other commitments were soon to draw him elsewhere. Kennedy Scott, a year older than Gardiner, had studied abroad at the Brussels Conservatory and as a choral trainer his ideals were perfection, ever intent on raising the standards of his choir. Indeed, at an Oriana concert in June 1922 he felt compelled to turn impatiently to the audience and apologise for the choir's poor singing on that occasion. Norman O'Neill had been associated with the Oriana Madrigal Society as early as 1907 when at the fourth concert he and his wife Adine played Norman's *Variations and Fugue on an Irish Air* for two pianos, the first work by a living composer to be performed at an Oriana concert. After securing the choir's services for his own concerts, Gardiner became an honorary member in 1912 and was soon closely involved in the Society's activities. Following his intervention the Oriana programmes began to show an increasing slant towards modern British choral music, though Tudor music always maintained a firm place in the repertoire. Before long the Oriana concerts were being acclaimed for both the catholicity of the programmes and the high standard attained.

On 3 May 1911 Gardiner wrote to Grainger of his meeting with Kennedy Scott:

Kennedy Scott has been here this evening, & after talking with him, I realise that there are likely to be great difficulties in the way of getting an adequate chorus, if one gets it up oneself: & if one engages one already formed, of eliminating the conductor. Now Kennedy Scott is quite ready to be eliminated, as far as modern works are concerned, & apart from that negative merit, is extremely helpful and willing, and an entirely satisfactory person to deal with. I know of nobody who could aid us as he can.

So the Oriana choir, then sixty in strength, was engaged and Gardiner was able to write in his notebook: 'Oriana will sing for me & I will give £26 to them & tickets to their subscribers.' Kennedy Scott's singers appeared prominently in two of the Gardiner concerts, one each in 1912 and 1913, chiefly singing madrigals and ayres. When larger forces were needed Gardiner turned to Arthur Fagge's London Choral Society. To Grainger, whose choral works formed an important feature of the series, he wrote from Ashampstead on 12 July: 'Fagge came here the other day & I received the most favourable impression of him. I think there can be no doubt that your things will be well done.'

The New Symphony Orchestra was engaged and Queen's Hall provisionally booked. Gardiner originally intended having five concerts in 1912, one of them devoted to music for military band and chorus with some of his own Pageant music, Wagner's *Huldigungsmarsch* and works by Grainger being played. But this did not materialise, and many dates had to be changed to accommodate both Grainger's concert and Frederic

Austin's operatic engagements. Towards the end of May 1911 the dates were finalised for four concerts to be held at fortnightly intervals, starting in the coming March.

Right up to and during the series Gardiner's diary was full of appointments to meet and often dine the many musicians connected with his programmes. Sometimes they would be guests at Pembroke Villas or at Ashampstead, and frequently they were dined at Pagani's, the fashionable restaurant in Great Portland Street close to Queen's Hall. Kennedy Scott had many happy memories of those busy days and paid a warm tribute to the Gardiner series:

Norman O'Neill had introduced me to Balfour as being of possible service to him with the Oriana Madrigal Society. It was through these concerts that I (and many others far more deserving) gained a footing which we had never had before. Almost without one's being aware of it, a great ferment of musical activity had been taking place in our midst – great in quality as well as extent. We discovered, almost suddenly, that we had produced a veritable 'school' of composers, though its elements were so diverse and individual: a school already cemented by very close personal friendships (destined to be further extended) which had arisen largely through the instrumentality of Balfour Gardiner himself. Balfour's concerts were probably the most important series of concerts that we have ever had, not excepting those of the Delius Festival in 1929. They consolidated English music as never before or since . . . Short lived though they were . . . they were sufficient to demonstrate a new note in our native art; an indubitably English approach free from Continental fetters, by which perfectly sincere emotions could be expressed in an original way; a liberation not only of formal processes but, what was of far more importance, of the imagination itself.[7]

Kennedy Scott wrote too of the excitement and comradeship of the preparations:

Balfour Gardiner was their natural leader: not perhaps the most outstanding musician amongst them, though he was a considerable composer, but by reason of his taste and judgement, his enthusiasm, his financial resources, and utterly unselfish personal character. Everyone loved Balfour as a dear friend, who not only helped us all with unsurpassed largesse, but steered music into channels that literally inaugurated a new era of artistic freedom. If anyone deserved the title of Maecenas it was Balfour. He . . . had a small house in London, just off Edwardes Square, Kensington, opposite to that of his friends Norman and Adine O'Neill. Here we would meet: Gustav Holst, Delius, Percy Grainger, Frederic Austin, Roger Quilter, Benjamin Dale, Cyril Scott, Norman O'Neill, Arnold Bax, and occasionally others – though it was strange that Vaughan Williams was never of the number . . . Many were the delightful evenings spent at Balfour's house when, with Balfour as a perfect host, the general project was aired, and works were submitted for approval. It was at these meetings that Arnold Bax was so invaluable. None of us had his powers of sight-reading. He could play anything that was put before him at the piano, from a big orchestral score to a two-stave arrangement so that it was possible not only to select what was required with greater assurance but to have a pretty good idea of what was wanted in performance.[8]

Prior to the start of the series Arnold Bax and his wife Elsita were among those occasional guests at Ashampstead, for new works by Bax opened the first two concerts. These were just two of the many scores which Gardiner was busily preparing for performance, as hurried entries in his notebook indicate. Bax was asked to send three hundred copies of the chorus parts of *Enchanted Summer* (which began the series) to the Memorial Hall at Farringdon where Fagge was training his choir, while Gardiner was occupied with the orchestral parts. 'All the bass parts of Enchanted Summer have to have tempo marks inserted after (40) . . . Look through Solo and Ist violin parts of Enchanted Summer. 2nd violin part done' are typical of the reminders he jotted down. Work was simultaneously in progress on Bax's *Festival Overture* which was dedicated to Gardiner. 'Get back score of Festival Overture & let 2nd copyist go on with Ist violin part of E.S.', he noted. And while he was also going through several of Grainger's scores, rather more attention was having to be given to Cyril Scott's for reasons his comments to Grainger make clear. 'I looked at Cyril's Scherzo going home in the train last night. Even that – every note of it will have to be rescored', Gardiner wrote on 3 May 1911. Next to come under his scrutiny was Scott's ballad for baritone and orchestra, *Helen of Kirkconnel*, about which he wrote to Grainger three days later: 'Austin is staying with me; & we have been rescoring Cyril's "Helen". I have never come across a work with such possibilities of instrumentation. Needless to say Cyril has missed them all.' (These were not the only occasions on which Gardiner was critical of Scott's writing for orchestra, as when in November 1914 Beecham conducted the *Two Passacaglias on Irish Themes* he commented that 'the scoring was far from flawless'.[9])

In addition to the Memorial Hall in Farringdon, rehearsals were held in both the small and large Queen's Hall, though the small hall was barely sufficient to accommodate the larger forces with any comfort and clarity of sound, the chorus sometimes having to stand throughout the rehearsal. Where possible, composers directed their own works. Otherwise it generally fell to Gardiner to conduct. 'The sight of Gardiner conducting rehearsals', Grainger wrote, 'with half an eye on the orchestra and the other half on the composer of the work in hand – with every nerve strained to realise the most minute intention of the latter – was an object lesson in the art of winning artistic (as distinct from mere professional) victories.'[10] Ever since a harrowing experience from his student days Bax had stuck firmly to his rule of never conducting, so his works were among those left to Gardiner to bring off.

Three days before the opening concert Grainger, full of boyish enthusiasm, wrote to Gardiner, thanking him for his generous patronage and suggesting at the same time that the new and relatively little-known works to be performed would reach a wider audience if free tickets were distributed:

As for yourself, I feel we know more really about you from seeing you these days in public activity than from years of mere personal friendship frousting. Curious how the cold problems of public activity call forth a man's inner warmth where the glow of friendly meetings chiefly entice his stubborn aloofness. Good job too, I loathe small pattings-on-the-back & joint bolstering-up clubs of small friends. This expensive public game is far glossier. Chorus & band & all of us love you at your public work, & all will get to love you who see you at it: – & 'God is love'!

You are really giving us chaps *lovely chances* apart from musical honey-moon days; not the chances a rich man gives poorer, but the chances that only a thoroly pure sweet noble abstract lofty healthy animal can give others of his own ilk. For the joy & good of all this is the human panorama it unrolls. If I didn't feel your human support behind me, encoraged [*sic*] by yr absolute fairness, made momentarily happy (& therefore fit, & artistically digestive) by yr friendship alongside one, & bold by the sure knowledge that yr gentlemanliness will give you the corage [*sic*] to *force* things thro (where need be) for us chaps, I wouldn't be able to learn deeply from these experiences, & would merely feel bodily sea-sick & wash my inner hands of the whole bloody show. For I am aristocratic enough to 'will have my (human) dues' first, & refuse to profit artistically in wrong human company.

As I said to mum (who has never had so happy a week in her life, she says) last summer, about this scheme: 'With old Balfour it won't matter how rottenly the things go, it'll be a human feast all the same.' The accident that the things all go toppingly *is* an accident, as far as I'm concerned.

Now, on the other hand, as to yr being a bloody fool: I hear you don't propose giving away lots of free tickets. Let me begin by saying that I *personally* don't care *in the least* whether you give away none or 12 thousand. But I ask you to lend me an ear re a point (concert managing & giving) in which my judgements have been successful in several countries, just as I (very thankfully by the way) profit by yr advice in a province (orchestration) in which I'll never know as much as you can afford to forget.

You are giving these concerts precisely because other conductors & societies don't, & works ditto. The public, therefore, don't know these works, nor such schemes, & can't be expected to feel any interest in them in advance, since advertising conveys no tempting portrait of the actual dish, in such cases. Your (& consequently our) only hope is that a stray listless outsiderish & thro-free-tickets-*enveigled* public will go away & caution its friends to turn up to the following concerts of this series, & to *next year's series*, if there's to be one. Those *not* the friends of the free-ticketby-enveigled public for Wednesday must be influenced by the *enthusiasm* of the press, which enthusiasm can *only* be born of the influence of the enveigled public upon the press. The press, like all the rest of us, lack corage, in erste linie. It takes corage to write coldly of works warmly welcomed by a large audience, just as it takes corage to write warmly of works performed before practically no audience (& therefore seemingly coldly received): Let us, for God's sake, appeal to the Ist cowardice. If you can, get Smith shake his feathers up a bit & send out *so many* free tickets *now at once* that any or some of the last minute *paying audience* are *turned away*. You will make lifelong enthusiastic adherents of those turned away paying people *for life*. This is not a joke, or Graingerism, this is *really life as she lives*.

Be a gentleman, & look the tyranny of commercial life in the face & realise that you can only stoop to conquer, & that you might as well try & do 'Enchanted Summer' with an amateur band (why not?) as give the works you are so nobly bringing forward *their fair chance* without *sowing* London with free tickets . . . *Don't* listen to what Smith (E. L. R.) [E. L. Robinson, Concert Management of Wigmore Street, London] says: 'His is to do & die.' *Wire Smith if you agree.*

Gardiner did give away free tickets – if perhaps not to the public at large on the lavish scale Grainger suggested, at least to his friends and those connected with his concerts. A recent addition to his circle of close friends (and well represented in the series) was Gustav von Holst, to whom he gave twenty tickets for each concert.

As for the critics' response, there was no doubting either the artistic success or the achievement of the series. After the opening night on 13 March the *Daily Telegraph* critic wrote: 'The concert was superb in its exposition of a vitality that one happens upon so rarely nowadays, and it is eminently satisfactory to note that a large and very warm-hearted audience was present.' There was evidently some truth in Grainger's assertion of the audience's influence on the critics, for by the third concert the same critic was commenting: 'In every respect it was successful, and in the place of the usual bored audience people seemed for once happy on hearing British music: moreover, nearly all of them waited to the very end of the concert' (19 April 1912). Robin Legge (who was probably the author of the above notices) was almost ecstatic in his praise. On 27 April in his *Saturday Telegraph* column he confessed:

Frankly, I have never seen any such enthusiasm or such good spirits in connection with music of British origin as at these concerts of Mr Balfour Gardiner . . . The performances are better than those of almost every other series, because a sufficient number of rehearsals is allowed to the various composers. And, equally, the works chosen have been works characteristic of their composers and (either because of this or in spite of this, whichever you please) they have proved in every case well worth hearing . . . Since Arthur Nikisch conducted Tchaikovsky's Fifth Symphony for the first time in England I have never witnessed such enthusiasm in a London concert-room as greeted Mr Balfour Gardiner after the performance of *News from Whydah* or Mr Percy Grainger after his conducting of various compositions, or Dr Vaughan Williams after his *Norfolk Rhapsodies*. Why this enthusiasm? . . . There is no reason to doubt, it seems to me, that it was called up by the fact that at last a British public had heard the kind of British music that it had long sought, music that was not half folk-song and half German or French workmanship . . . I have no hesitation whatever in saying that, in my opinion, they are the finest English concerts I have ever experienced.

The *Times* critic was also generous with praise, and at the conclusion of the first series he neatly summed up the fresh ground it had broken:

There have been plenty of concerts given in the interest of the British composer in the past, and there always are plenty in the interest of the general public, but few, if any, have given such hopeful signs of reconciling the two, which too often seemed opposed to one another. (2 May)

When even at an early stage the success of these concerts became apparent, many – critics included – expressed the hope during the first

89

series that they would be continued the following year and were consequently delighted when such an announcement was made at the fourth concert on 1 May. That evening the *Daily Telegraph* critic wrote: 'They have not been equalled in the past generation, either for the ability exhibited or for the genuine and spontaneous enthusiasm they have called forth.' So in 1913 the series was duly continued at Queen's Hall, this time on Tuesday evenings instead of Wednesdays. Again they proved a great success, bringing forth a eulogy from the *Daily Telegraph* critic at the completion of the seventh concert that might well have set in motion a practical response, if not exactly on the lines suggested: 'If ever a statue is erected to Mr Balfour Gardiner it will surely be set up by a representative body of British composers in grateful recognition of what he has done in their cause' (5 March).

Individual performances in the 1912 series had come in for special commendation, with critics remarking on the high standard of both choral singing and orchestral playing. Grainger was singled out as 'not only a choral conductor of sheer genius but also a choral composer in a line by himself'.[11] His choral works were found to be rhythmically irresistible and in many cases encores were demanded and given. But when Gardiner's own works met with similar acclaim he would not allow a repeat. He felt that the instant popularity of both his and Grainger's works was detracting from the full appreciation of the longer works by others. So he suggested to Grainger that in the next series their own works should be placed at the beginning and end of the programmes where they would not make as much effect. Grainger, with his oddly prejudiced racial attitudes, would have nothing of it. 'Do what you like with your own works, dear Balfour', he replied, 'but for my part I am the only Australian represented, and I won't be a party to having my Australian music handicapped in that way.' Gardiner threw up his arms in a characteristic gesture of despair. 'How tiresome!' was his only comment.[12]

The 1912 series was curious for the inclusion of three non-British works. In the second concert Tchaikovsky's B♭ minor Piano Concerto was almost certainly chosen as a vehicle for Grainger the soloist. It was a war-horse with which he was already closely associated. (The *Times* critic wrote that 'his touch . . . was so clear and hard that it made some passages in the first movement sound as if they were picked out with little hammers'.[13]) Gardiner's special fondness for Tchaikovsky would anyway mean that he would have had no objection to the work's inclusion. In the same concert Borodin's *Polovtsian Dances* (performed without chorus) was a stranger choice, though the work's vigour and directness would have found favour with Gardiner – it was in essence another form of the dance he took so much to heart. Elgar conducting his Second Symphony, then not yet a year old, somewhat redressed the balance. In the third concert one can suspect Grainger of suggesting Grieg's *Psalms*. For the last year of the Norwegian composer's life Grainger had been an intimate friend, he was to make his own English translation of the *Psalms* (though the one used on this occasion was by Beatrice Bulman), and as an encore in the second concert he followed the Tchaikovsky concerto with one of Grieg's folk-song arrangements for the piano.

When it came to the second series in 1913 there was some doubt whether certain works would be ready in time, in particular Dale's *Christmas Hymn* and Grainger's *Sir Eglamore*. 'I shall never consent to do second-rate works', Gardiner had written to Grainger on 29 July 1912. Indeed the success of the whole ambitious scheme depended on that very factor, and he was most keen on *Sir Eglamore* being included and Grainger busily revised his 1904 version in time for the seventh concert. There was some doubt about the inclusion of another Grainger work as Kipling had proved unwilling to allow his verses to be set in *At Twilight*. So Gardiner suggested that Grainger should write his own words, which he did, with lines that closely parallel the introductory verse to Kipling's *The Rhyme of the Three Sealers*. But when the work was completed it was ultimately sacrificed to make way for Holst's *The Cloud Messenger*.

Only three of Gardiner's own works featured in the whole series. The popular *Shepherd Fennel's Dance* was given three times, and his part-song *The Stage Coach* to words by the Dorset poet William Barnes was introduced by the Oriana choir. But of greater importance was the first performance of his short choral ballad *News from Whydah* conducted by Gardiner himself at the opening concert. Completed the previous October, this grim but stirring setting of verses by John Masefield followed in the popular ballad tradition well cultivated by Stanford in such works as *The Revenge* and *Phaudrig Crohoore* and explored by many others including Cyril Scott, Bell and Holst. *News from Whydah*, dedicated to Arnold Bax, tells of a 'dark Senhora' asking a 'tarry buccaneer' news of her pirate lover whom she is soon to marry in Sligo. 'Yes, I saw your fancy man', comes the tart reply, 'hanging from a tree, dangling in a running noose . . . and won't you marry me?' The choice of text illustrates Grainger's perceptive observation of how Gardiner's sympathies often seemed to lie with the misfortunes of the under-dog, a feeling evidently shared by Masefield in 'A Consecration' which prefaces his *Salt-Water Ballads*:

> Not the ruler for me, but the ranker, the tramp of the road,
> The slave with the sack on his shoulders pricked on with the goad,
> The man with too weighty a burden, too weary a load.
> . . . Of these shall my songs be fashioned, my tales be told.[14]

91

What Grainger called Gardiner's 'social justice' pervades several of his works and, musically, with no other poet does he seem to have identified more closely. Altogether he set six Masefield poems, and after completing *News from Whydah* was contemplating another, *St Mary's Bells* (which John Ireland set seven years later). *News from Whydah* was his only work for chorus and orchestra to achieve any real success with choral societies. He said of it himself in 1919 that it was 'by far the best, most effective & most popular work I have written'.[15] Yet had he not asked Holst to prepare a version with reduced orchestration, the large orchestra specified by the composer might well have weighed against the work's performance by smaller choral societies. As Imogen Holst has written, 'Balfour Gardiner was one of the most generous of Holst's patrons. He was always finding tactful opportunities to help struggling composers, which must have been the reason that he asked Holst to orchestrate this version of *News from Whydah*.'[16]

Although vividly scored and undeniably effective in performance, the success of *News from Whydah* was not so much because of any superior craftmanship, for it has the odd weakness and mannerism absent in the two later and finer choral works, *April* and *Philomela*, but more for reason of its immediate appeal and directness. Again brevity is on its side. Another practical consideration towards the work's wider performance was its publication the same year. There is the briefest possible of introductions – one strong *fortissimo* held chord – and without further preliminaries the choir enters (example 14) with a characteristic dotted rhythm familiar in type from the *Gavotte* of the *Five Pieces* for piano published the previous year (example 15) and also from *Shepherd Fennel's Dance* (example 11, p. 76)

Being essentially a strophic setting, the opening idea serves for each of the six verses and, apart from some elaboration in the fourth, variety is otherwise obtained through augmentation and richer scoring and harmonisation. While in places the writing seems almost bombastic in the theme's grandiose inflation, at the end Gardiner subtly eschews mere show with the choir's dying cry, a *diminuendo* both anguished and final. While this work has merited what popularity has come its way, one can nonetheless regret that similar attention has not also been directed towards the other more deserving choral works.

Both the 1912 and 1913 series brought forward some large scores that taxed the available orchestral resources. In addition to a sarrusophone, Delius's *Dance Rhapsody* called for what was then one of the most unreliable of instruments, the heckelphone or bass oboe which had caused minor havoc at the work's first performance.[17] Holst had specified a double bass trombone rather than a tuba for *The Cloud Messenger*, while euphonium and tuba were needed for both Grainger's *Father and*

Ex. 14

Ex. 15

Daughter (in addition to a large band of mandolin and guitar players with sixty of them accommodated in the front row of the stalls) and his *English Dance*, a particularly demanding score.[18] Bells were required for Vaughan Williams's *Fantasia on Christmas Carols* and Austin's Symphony, and it seems that Gardiner and the two composers went off in vain searching for bells as Vaughan Williams's work was the only instance of the critics remarking on a score's requirements not being fully met.

Delius's *Lebenstanz* (*Life's Dance*) was yet another large score programmed, and here Gardiner's conducting came in for special praise. 'The performance of the NSO was magnificent, and the greatest possible credit goes to the "young British" conductor, who here showed an ability as conductor far in advance of anything he had previously exhibited', wrote the *Daily Telegraph* critic on 26 February 1913. In the final concert Evelyn Suart performed Delius's Piano Concerto and for one nineteen-year-old Royal College student this was a magical awakening to the music of Delius. That young student was E.J. Moeran, and as his friend and fellow composer Philip Heseltine wrote eleven years later:

This was one of the admirable series given by Balfour Gardiner – concerts that will be long remembered in the annals of British music, though they were insufficiently appreciated at the time they were given – and the programme contained the Delius Piano Concerto which accomplished for Moeran the same sort of miracle which Tristan and certain works of Grieg had effected for Delius in the eighties, and revealed a new world of sound to his imagination.[19]

Moeran's own account of his introduction to contemporary British music is also worth quoting for the additional light it throws on the impact of the Gardiner concerts, particularly on receptive minds of tender years:

In the years immediately preceding the First World War, there took place in London some remarkable choral and orchestral concerts at which the programmes consisted largely of British music. They were held due to the generosity and enterprise of H. Balfour Gardiner and many first performances of the works of such composers as Holst, Vaughan Williams, Arnold Bax and Percy Grainger, names at that time quite unfamiliar to the general public, were given at this time.

Having just left school, I had come to London as a student at the Royal College of Music; apart from a certain amount of Stanford and Elgar, I knew nothing of the renaissance that had been taking place in music in this country. So one winter's evening, when I had been to St Paul's Cathedral intending to hear Bach's Passion music and failed to obtain a seat there, feeling in the mood for any music rather than none at all, I went to the Queen's Hall where there was a Balfour Gardiner concert, prepared to be bored stiff. But, on the contrary, I was so filled with enthusiasm, and so much moved by some of the music I heard that night, that from then on I made a point of missing no more of these concerts.

Among other works I heard was a Rhapsody of Vaughan Williams, based on songs recently collected in Norfolk by this composer. It was my first experience of a serious orchestral composition actually based on English folk-song, and it caused a profound effect on my outlook as a young student of musical composition. This, and other works which I encountered at these concerts, seemed to me to express the very spirit of the English countryside as I then knew it. My home at this time was in Norfolk, where my father was vicar of a country parish, so I determined to lose no time in rescuing from oblivion any further folk-songs that remained undiscovered . . .[20]

For Moeran these concerts had been seminal. His own melodic line became governed by the contours and inflections of folk-song, and in the inter-war years he was a visitor to Delius's home at Grez, his love of Delius culminating in the beautiful *Nocturne* for baritone, chorus and orchestra written in his memory. Moeran became a casual acquaintance of Gardiner's, their encounters being probably on most occasions in the company of their mutual friend, Arnold Bax, whom Moeran knew better.

If one discounts for a moment the Oriana choir's contribution of Elizabethan and Tudor madrigals and the like, nearly half the works in the Gardiner series were receiving their first performance either in London or anywhere. Some works represented their composers' second thoughts, as in the case of Cyril Scott who had been dissatisfied with his Second Symphony after Wood had introduced it at the 1903 Proms and subsequently reworked three of its four movements as symphonic dances, of which his *English Dance* was one. A handful were already reasonably seasoned scores, even if some of those have since fallen into obscurity. Austin's *Spring Rhapsody* had first been given at the 1907 Proms and was later taken up by Beecham. Harty's *With the Wild Geese* of 1910 had proved successful under its composer's baton, and McEwen's border ballad *Grey Galloway*, first performed at a 1909 Philharmonic Society concert, became one of his best-known works. It also briefly received the attention of Beecham.

McEwen was brother-in-law to W. H. Bell, who at the time of Gardiner's concerts had left England to become principal of the South African College of Music at Cape Town. In Bell's absence the first performance of his choral border ballad *The Baron of Brackley* was entrusted to Arthur Fagge, while his other work, *The Shepherd*, was conducted by Gardiner. *The Shepherd*, based on a poem by Herbert Trench, was first played in its original version with soprano soloist at the famous Beecham concert[21] on 20 January 1908 when Holbrooke's symphony with choral finale, *Apollo and the Seaman* (likewise based on Trench verses), was also receiving its first performance. The retrospective interest in this concert is not so much in its musical content as in its novel and experimental presentation of the Holbrooke work. At the poet's suggestion the inspirational verses of the symphony were, with the aid of a magic lantern, projected across a darkened Queen's Hall onto a screen that concealed Beecham and his orchestra. Gardiner had attended that celebrated concert and his reactions were illuminatingly described by Rose Grainger two days later in a letter to Roger Quilter:

On Monday I went . . . to hear 'Apollo' – & to see 'Apollo' – & – my dear – it was awful – real Pish Tosh. No wonder I was in bed next day. The house was full of fashionables & they applauded much – Bell's 'Shepherd' was quite enjoyable – Gardiner & O'Neill were there – & before the music began, the former said to me 'Bell's stuff is dull & decent, Holbrooke's dull & indecent.' However he quite enjoyed it & so did I. He introduced me to Bell, who seemed to be a nice young- ster – But really, people can stand a lot after hearing and witnessing the effect of Holbrooke's music – with all the applause, he failed to come forward, however – I am afraid he goes in for sensation.

For later performances, generally conducted by the composer, Bell revised *The Shepherd* and deleted the soloist's part.

While the representation of composers in Gardiner's concerts was on a broad spectrum and included the establishment figure-heads Stanford and Parry (the latter conducting his latest – and last – symphony), inevi- tably there were omissions. 'Indecent' or not, Holbrooke's music was absent and the composer and conductor Julius Harrison (who had studied with Bantock in Birmingham) had apparently been unsuccessful in getting one of his own works accepted for the concerts. News of his exclusion reached the ears of Havergal Brian, who wrote with obvious disgust to Bantock in December 1912:

[Harrison] told me of being invited to lunch by Balfour Gardiner at which were O'Neill, Bax and another: all their time was spent in railing and cursing at every- body and everything. Gardiner pretended to be interested in Harrison and said he would produce some of his works. He asked for scores and Harrison sent some. Julius told Gardiner that his Variations [on *Down among the Dead Men*] were to be done at the Proms and G promised to make a special effort to hear them. Harrison saw him afterwards and Gardiner replied – in the Oxford manner – that 'I just managed to get in for the finale.' He has recently sent Julius word that he has no room for his works in his programmes!!![22]

As well as his sensitivity to differences in social background, the infre- quent performance of Brian's own compositions had probably incited his partisan sympathy. By chance, within a fortnight of Brian writing, the three were to be linked, on paper at least, at the last concert of the Musical League Festival in Birmingham when Harrison conducted his *Variations* as well as Brian's comedy overture *Dr Merryheart* and Gardiner conducted his *Overture to a Comedy*.

On a lighter note, Bax's tone-poem *Christmas Eve on the Mountains* received its first performance in the seventh concert, Gardiner conduct- ing. In his entertaining autobiography *Farewell, My Youth* Bax describes what purport to be his feelings while listening to the work's première. But poetic licence permits him to veer from the truth, and in a whimsical sketch entitled 'Philharmonic'[23] he transposes the performance to one at a Philharmonic Society concert with a different programme. Furthermore, next to Bax is none other than the conductor of the true first performance – Balfour Gardiner, with his 'round blue eyes peering shortsightedly through their glasses' as the two men find their seats in Queen's Hall. But such lapses may be forgiven as Bax's attention seems constantly drawn to a black-haired 'elfin child' in the audience peering at him 'round the very manifest bosom of a director's lady'. One may suppose that RAM student at whom he steals glances to be Harriet Cohen, for she claims in *A Bundle of Time*[24] that Bax once told her that he had attempted in his own autobiography to describe his feelings on first setting eyes on her.

After the Gardiner concerts there were supper parties at Pagani's. But if everything appeared superficially to be running smoothly, behind the scenes towards the end of the series matters were far from comfortable. Four days before the advertised date of the final concert Gardiner wrote to the young Heseltine: 'My concert, I fear, will not take place. I had a row with the orchestra, and cancelled their engagements.' In *Farewell, My Youth* Bax put his finger on the cause of the trouble:

Gardiner, testy, choleric, and accustomed to have his own way, had little experience as a conductor, and in the course of an unwise preliminary address to the orchestra told them so, very politely begging them 'to bear with him' and allow for any mistakes he might make. Now orchestral players in those far-off pre-BBC days were for the most part 'toughs', very much more unregimented than the docile ranks of Broadcasting House, and the NSO, indifferent or positively hostile to nearly all this new music, and taking advantage of their conductor's alternating diffidence and uncontrolled outbursts of irritation, behaved at times like a herd of sulky schoolboys. Matters were not improved when late at one afternoon rehearsal a lady in the chorus rose on her stalwart hind legs and, in a voice shaking with temper, charged the players with scamping their job. 'We in the choir have put our hearts into our work', she shouted, 'and we think it is up to you at least to take some interest and not let us down!'

One morning during the second series Balfour was to meet me after rehearsal for lunch at Pagani's. He kept me waiting – an ominous sign – for usually he was as punctual as the sun, and when he did turn up his face was red as a turkey's crop and his blue eyes were ablaze. 'I am sorry, Arnold', he burst out, puffing slightly, 'that you will not hear "In the Faery Hills" to-night, but the concert is off!' He made a furious gesture with both arms. 'Those people are simply intolerable! I have told the manager that I'll pay in full, but I'll have no more to do with them. Never again! Never!'[25]

Modern British music was hardly new territory for the New Symphony Orchestra for, besides the Gardiner series, they had already played much under Edward Mason and Beecham. But the control of the orchestra had by now passed to Landon Ronald whose programmes were by comparison more orthodox, and a surfeit of new scores may well have aggravated any irritation they harboured. However, matters were fortunately settled, possibly through the intervention of Norman O'Neill, and the final concert took place a week later than originally announced with extra rehearsals in the meantime. Robin Legge was able to announce in his column: 'It is with great pleasure that one hears that all difficulties in connection with the rehearsals for Mr Balfour Gardiner's final concert have now been satisfactorily overcome, and that in consequence the concert will take place in Queen's Hall on Tuesday evening next – not to-night, as originally planned.' Gardiner wrote back to Heseltine, offering him tickets for the concert and inviting him to the supper party after-wards. But the Deliuses, who were staying a while in England, had already planned their return journey to Grez for 14 March and so missed hearing the Piano Concerto. The postponement may well have been the reason for Bantock not conducting his *Fifine at the Fair* as earlier an-nounced. Gardiner conducted the whole concert instead and the *Morning Post* reported that 'the performance [of *Fifine*] directed by Mr Balfour Gardiner was of marked excellence; sensitive and forcible in turn'.

From this occasion arose the only general criticism of the series – that the concerts had been a little over-long, a curious remark when one con-siders the enormous festival programmes that were typical of that period, though the unfamiliar nature of most of the works was quite likely responsible for an awareness of length. Despite their success, the concerts never quite succeeded in filling the hall, a fact that would hardly have gone unnoticed by Gardiner who was deeply disappointed that in spite of much acclaim the public's response had not been greater. There were renewed hopes for a continuation of the series but his immediate reaction had been 'Never again!' He despaired easily. There was an ele-ment of the spoiled child in his make-up, and his upbringing had not equipped him with the ability to ride a storm of troubles and difficulties with the equanimity of a more experienced musician. His natural reac-tion was to avoid such situations: experiences of that kind left a wound of bitter resentment which would deter him from trying again. In time he did nevertheless consider promoting further concerts. But by then there were troubles on a wider front: a world war intervened.

7 'Full of unexpected harmonies . . .'

1912–1914

As well as blowing much welcome fresh air into English concert life, almost overnight the Gardiner series established several reputations among the emergent composers of the younger generation. On 18 April 1912, the day after the third concert, the New Symphony Orchestra appeared again at Queen's Hall, this time with the London Choral Society and their conductor Arthur Fagge in a programme that conveniently provided second hearings of *News from Whydah* and Bax's *Festival Overture*, both works having received their first performance a few weeks earlier under Gardiner's direction.

But it was Grainger's career that had received the greatest boost, a debt he readily acknowledged. On 13 and 19 May there were busy rehearsals for the first all-Grainger concert, to be held on the 21st at the Aeolian Hall. Many friends were among the performers: Austin, Elwes, Quilter, Grainger's mother Rose, and of course Percy Grainger himself. An unusual feature of the programme was Grainger's predilection for guitars, something that had contributed to the outstanding success of his *Father and Daughter* at the first of the Gardiner concerts, and had even encouraged Gardiner to express a desire to have a few lessons on that instrument. Grainger rarely wrote for a standard orchestra, and the nucleus of strings on this occasion was the Langley-Mukle Quartet in which Eugene Goossens was second fiddle. Apart from assisting in the preparation of the scores and parts, Gardiner's contribution to the concert was to conduct the final item, *Scotch Strathspey and Reel*, which in common with several other works was vociferously encored. The guitarists under Gardiner's baton were Roger Quilter, Rose and Percy Grainger (the latter alternating in the programme between guitar, piano and conducting). The hall was crowded to the doors, and the members of the audience were not the only ones bowled over with enthusiasm, for two days later Gardiner wrote to Grainger:

I am still intoxicated with your music & my head reels with morris tunes & strathspeys & clog dances & all sorts of other exhilarating rhythms. I have not had a similar experience for years, except after my own Oriana concert, which had the same freshness as yours . . . Since you want to dedicate a work especially to me, may it be the Strathspey, for I have been more intimately associated with it than with any other work of yours, and I like it very much.

99

On 18 June at Westminster Hall Kennedy Scott conducted the Oriana Madrigal Society, of which Gardiner was now an honorary member, in the two Barnes part-songs, with Adine O'Neill as soloist in the first half of the programme. Then on 23 July Gardiner conducted his *Overture to a Comedy* at Queen's Hall in another Patron's Fund concert attended by King George V and Queen Mary, at which works by Holst, York Bowen and Vaughan Williams were also played. In August Gardiner took a short holiday in Cornwall where he was delighted by the natural good nature and friendliness he found in the Cornish people. Ever the country-man at heart, he was generally happy when passing the time of day with ordinary country folk. The stiffer social conventions and formality of town society life found him much less at ease.

At the 1912 Proms Henry Wood twice played *Shepherd Fennel's Dance*, its popularity by then being assured. Wood was also in charge of the Birmingham Triennial Festival that year and he had put Delius's *Sea Drift* down for performance on 3 October with Thorpe Bates as soloist. Delius had been invited to conduct the work himself but he declined the offer, most likely because his three conducting engagements in this country had proved uniformly unsuccessful. However, he came over from France to attend the performance and stayed at the Queen's Hotel in Birmingham. It was an important festival (to be in fact the last in a series spanning 144 years) with eight concerts spread over four days and, like most big provincial ones, solidly constructed of choral works, including the two mainstays of the English choral tradition, *Elijah* and *Messiah*, as well as the *St Matthew Passion* and the Requiems of Brahms and Verdi. Elgar conducted the first performance of *The Music Makers* and closed the festival with *The Apostles*. Sibelius made his fourth visit to England (in his forty-five remaining years he was to come again only once, in 1921) and conducted his most recent symphony, the fourth, staying with his friend and champion Granville Bantock. Being placed as it was amidst such conservative programming, the Sibelius symphony must have fallen on a good number of puzzled ears in the Birmingham Town Hall. Delius attended the final rehearsal and is reported to have drawled, with cool admiration, 'Damn it, this is not conventional music.'[1] Another listener was far more open in his appraisement, calling it a work of great beauty, absolutely original and genuine Nature music.[2] That admirer was the eighteen-year-old Philip Heseltine, who was also a fervent devotee of Delius, whom he had first met during the interval of Beecham's 1911 all-Delius Queen's Hall concert. One of the first fruits of his enthusiasm for the music of Delius had been an arrangement he made for two pianos of *Brigg Fair*. At Delius's suggestion he had made a similar transcription of *In a Summer Garden* and as they were staying at the same hotel for the Birmingham Festival they were able to play it through together the day before the *Sea Drift* concert. Delius expressed his satisfaction with the two arrangements and many more were to follow.

Philip Heseltine, who became better known under his composer's pseudonym of Peter Warlock, was an enigmatic figure in British music; a critic, an early biographer of Delius, an acknowledged authority on Elizabethan and Jacobean music, and a song-writer *par excellence*, ultimately to take his own life. At the time of the Birmingham Festival he already knew of Balfour Gardiner, who was due to arrive at Birmingham in time for the performance of *Sea Drift*, and he had been thrilled some months earlier to read the prospectus for the 1912 Gardiner concerts. He was then studying in Cologne and he had written on 9 February 1912 to Colin Taylor, his music teacher at Eton: 'I would give anything to be at the concert on March 13th – Bax, Delius and Grainger etc. but I fear it will not be possible for me.' Gardiner's arrival at Birmingham gave him the opportunity of making his acquaintance, and on 9 October he wrote an account of their meeting to Colin Taylor:

On Thursday evening Balfour Gardiner turned up in his motor car to hear 'Sea Drift', and I had a long conversation with him after the concert: he is an extremely nice person – very cheerful and 'hearty'. He wants me to make a piano score of Delius's orchestral work 'Life's Dance' for him: he is going to perform it at his concerts next year. I have done about a quarter of it, but my progress with it is far from rapid, as it is frightfully complex: I am not surprised that B.G. wants a piano version, if he has to read such a score!

In thanking Heseltine for completing the arrangement, Gardiner wrote on 21 October that year: 'You yourself will realise how much it will facilitate the study of the score, & especially the apprehension of the big lines of it: indeed, an arrangement such as you have made is almost indispensable to a conductor producing the work for the first time.' In return he offered Heseltine tickets for his next series of concerts. That it was all worthwhile is clearly shown by one critic writing of the resulting performance that 'this Mr Balfour Gardiner conducted, from memory, with a more complete success than he has ever achieved before'.[3]

From the Birmingham Festival Gardiner drove Delius to Ashampstead and both very nearly came to an untimely end, as Delius later informed Heseltine in a postcard from Grez: 'We motored to Oxford & looked over the cottage. We nearly got killed in the motor car. The steering broke – luckily we were in a village & going slow – otherwise my career would have ended abruptly.'[4] Gardiner was well-known for his fast driving, not that he necessarily enjoyed speed for speed's sake. But the previous June he had been convicted of 'driving at a speed dangerous to the public' on the Huntingdonshire roads and fined £5 with £9 13s 7d costs. For the passenger Gardiner was often a terrifying driver as he had

101

the unnerving habit of carrying on long conversations with his head turned over his shoulder so that his attention was not always on the road. Sometimes this would even cause his companion to insist on taking over the wheel. And if a young relative were riding with him he would not be beyond a little playful tomfoolery. 'Shall I show you how a Frenchman drives?' he would suddenly enquire, and squeezing the horn's large rubber bulb he would swerve wildly from one side of the road to the other, hooting and swerving with childish delight until the sight of an approaching car restored sanity.[5] Gardiner certainly enjoyed motoring, for in later years there were occasions when he would be seen driving while Cox his chauffeur sat alongside. Like Heseltine and Moeran, Gardiner was also a motor-cycle enthusiast and often used one during his Ashampstead years.

News from Whydah now began to show signs of popularity and on 29 October it was first heard at Leeds, conducted by Herbert Fricker. In November *Shepherd Fennel's Dance* had its first Bournemouth performance. That same month Gardiner went with Arnold Bax to Ireland for a short holiday. Bax had deep affinities with Ireland, his spiritual home, and on the trip he felt some concern for his companion's well-being, writing to a friend of his 'anxiety and responsibility' for Gardiner, and adding that 'our friend presents a somewhat massive English bulk for the faery arrows of Gaelic romance to pierce. However he is very pleased so far.'[6]

Towards the end of the year, with his increasingly active interest in the Oriana Madrigal Society, Gardiner was invited to become vice-president, with Elgar its president. The early weeks of 1913 brought several noteworthy performances of his works: on 3 January he conducted his *Overture to a Comedy* at the Musical League concert in Birmingham; on 27 February at Queen's Hall the enterprising Edward Mason gave *News from Whydah* together with works by Delius, Grainger, Holst and others; on the 28th the String Quartet was played by the Saunders Quartet at a Holbrooke concert in the Aeolian Hall; on 1 March Henry Wood once more paraded his favourite work of Gardiner's and the following day in the Albert Hall Landon Ronald produced his – the *Overture to a Comedy*. Meanwhile the second series of Gardiner concerts was well under way.

When on 18 March after a week's delay the final concert brought the two series to an end, Balfour Gardiner shook off all the problems and worries of their production by taking a first holiday in Spain and the Balearic Islands in the company of Arnold Bax, his brother Clifford, and Gustav Holst. Despite what was to be a life-long friendship, this was the only holiday he took with Holst who, having to earn his living by his music and teaching, was unable to share his companion's life of relative ease. When the party assembled at Victoria Station on 27 March it was the first time that Clifford Bax and Holst had met. Clifford, an author and playwright, has since claimed that it was on this holiday he introduced Gustav to astrology, much to Balfour's disapproval,[7] thus sowing the seeds of *The Planets*. Holst was still feeling rather bitter at what he felt to have been the failure of *The Cloud Messenger*. The last of his 'Sanskrit' works, he had revised it for its first performance in Gardiner's concerts, and although some reviews spoke kindly of it (the *Daily Telegraph* critic thought it the most interesting novelty of its concert) he had not been satisfied. The failure was not due to insufficient rehearsal for there had been ample, thanks to Gardiner's generosity. Indeed, the *Morning Post* critic, who considered that there was 'no questioning the ability, not to say genius, revealed in the music' which showed 'immense imagination', found the performance 'admirable' with the choral and orchestral forces giving the composer 'support of uncommon efficiency'. But Holst was unmoved and to make matters worse he considered it his best work so far. 'The whole thing has been a blow to me. I'm "fed up" with music, especially my own,' he had written to a friend,[8] in a mood of dejection that mirrored Gardiner's occasional spells of despondency, which is probably why Balfour invited Gustav to go with them to Spain.

Clifford Bax has fortunately left a vivid account of their holiday in his autobiographical 'book of thoughts and impressions', *Inland Far*, which appeared in 1925,[9] an account that gains much strength from the fact that it is based on notes made at the time and does not merely rely on embellished memories from across the years. Gardiner was not altogether pleased with the result, feeling that the picture it drew of him was not entirely accurate and that he was being made a fool of. Clifford should have realised that travelling in the company of three composers would lead to the inevitable: before leaving Dover they had touched on orchestration, on arrival at Calais they were discussing the emotional value of the trombone (Holst's instrument in his early days when touring with the Carl Rosa Company and the Scottish Orchestra), and half-way across France 'their rapiers were making merry play and the sparks began to fly. With irreproachable courtesy they demonstrated misjudgment of orchestration by quoting from each other's works.' Approaching Gerona 'they were brandishing the most tremendous generalisations' until an armistice was called. One evening in Gerona they came across a blind Spanish peasant lustily singing a ballad to a reiterated tune. Perhaps with the finale of *Beni Mora* in mind, Gardiner muttered: 'I wonder what's happened to Gustav – he'd love this.' 'He does', came the voice from behind.

All responsibility for planning the itinerary and booking tickets they happily left to Gardiner for whom Bradshaw was almost a bible. With his organisational mind that left nothing to chance he was well suited for the task. He had already acquired a modicum of Spanish and in time was sufficiently conversant with the language to be able to read some Spanish novels and short stories. From Gerona they progressed to Barcelona where, with some hesitation, the party witnessed a bull-fight since Clifford and Balfour were eager to judge for themselves that contentious sport. Gardiner then suggested that they spend a night in the spectacular nearby monastery of Montserrat. For the final ascent to the monastery there was a choice between mountain railway and going on foot. Holst characteristically elected to walk while the others chose the less arduous approach. The following dry they returned to Barcelona and took a steamer for Majorca, spending about ten days at Palma. There the evening discussions would usually be concluded in Gardiner's room in the company of a pleasurable local liqueur, and with his individual views Balfour would often be turned to for some outspoken comment.

From Palma the party went by train to Soller where the railway was a sufficient novelty for the villagers to assemble at the station to greet the train's arrival. At Soller the four were not parted from the excellent liqueur that had proved such a fine catalyst for conversation as Gardiner had thoughtfully packed several bottles. Engagements at home brought the holiday to an end with Clifford having to leave first. By 21 April they were all back in England, their friendships firmly cemented. For Gardiner at least, the holiday had sparked off a lasting affection for Spain.

During the summer months Gardiner closed up 7 Pembroke Villas and divided his time between Oxford and Ashampstead. He considered one or two excursions, along the Kennet and Avon Canal or exploring the valley of the Teme. Norman O'Neill was one of his visitors in June. Then on 28 July he put the finishing touches to a new orchestral score, *A Berkshire Idyll*. He generally scored for a large orchestra and this was no exception, yet the treatment here is particularly sensitive and the mood more impressionistic so that this work occupies a special position in his output, standing well apart from his leanings towards the 'English dance'.

Heseltine was willing to tackle further piano transcriptions and two days after completing the work Gardiner wrote inviting him to Ashampstead, adding:

The only score I have at present of which I should like to have a piano duet version is a new work of my own called 'A Berkshire Idyll': it is short & the MS is clear: but it is in places full of unexpected harmonies & would not be too elementary for you to tackle. You must not let me thrust the work upon you: but if, as you say, you really like doing things of this sort – a strange taste, to my thinking – there it is, & I should be delighted to have your transcription.

But this was only a passing whim, as by 28 August he had a change of mind:

My suggestion about the Berkshire Idyll was made while I was still full of enthusiasm for it, shortly after it was written. At the present moment it seems as bad as it then seemed good, for only yesterday it was subjected to the most adverse criticism at the hands of one whose opinion I value very highly:[10] & I have no heart to consider it as a finished work & allow you to waste your labour on it. But thank you very much indeed for offering to do so.

The fervour and excitement felt during composition were often dissipated under a later colder analytical light, and his fondness for a work would fluctuate according to his mood. Though he was later to reappraise the *Idyll* more favourably, it remained unperformed during his life. In time it may well be judged as his finest surviving purely orchestral work. Like Frank Bridge's *Summer* (1914-15) and Bax's *Summer Music* (1917-20), this delicate evocative nature-poem conjures up for the listener halcyon summer days of cloudless skies. In both time and place it is close to Bax's 'hot windless June mid-day in some woodland place of Southern England'. One may imagine the Berkshire Downs bathed in a shimmering heat-haze (divided *tremolando* strings at the opening), everything drowsed in stillness as time hangs heavily in a sultry afternoon. The flute arabesques may inevitably recall Debussy's *Prélude à l'après-midi d'un faune*, and at moments *Nuages* from the *Three Nocturnes* may be brought to mind. In its mellow feeling and similar harmonic language there is even some affinity of mood with the closing pages of Schreker's Chamber Symphony of 1916. Yet these are passing resemblances and *A Berkshire Idyll* remains for all that a very personal statement. For the rest, the work is suffused in warmth with a glowing, passionate intensity – yet never hurried. A sleepy laziness steals through the score. It is the song of a tone-poet at one with his surroundings.

The principal subject (see figure *x* in example 17) is announced at the beginning by solo violin over *tremolando* divided strings with a touch of glockenspiel and celesta, to be answered immediately on flute and bassoon by a scalar phrase (example 16) that descends almost chromatically through five notes before returning to its starting point. At the *andante non troppo* section, this second idea becomes much elaborated, chiefly on the strings, while the initial figure is freely treated in a series of arpeggiated arabesques on woodwind. At bar 53 a broad line emerges for divided violas and cellos (example 17), comprised in close succession of

Ex. 16

105

Ex. 17

the opening subject (figure *x*, now based on C sharp instead of F sharp), a related pattern (figure *y*) that is rhythmically similar to example 16 in inversion, and the same pattern much transformed into a dignified rising-and-falling phrase (figure *z*) which again encompasses only five degrees of the scale. These eight bars of thematic evolution provide the argument for the greater part of the work; the second full statement, on clarinets in thirds and then solo violin, is an especially magical moment that seems to distil the very essence of a summer's heat. After a climax of considerable intensity, the coda introduces a radiant theme on muted strings (example 18) that is expanded with much warmth of feeling, but the last word is given to figure *x* on five solo strings before the full contingent resolve onto a chord of B major, mediant uppermost.

Ex. 18

In October Heseltine went up to Christ Church, Oxford, though he was to regard his time there as if in a 'pool of hopeless depression and stagnation',[11] and within a year he had abandoned his course. Yet with Ashampstead about twenty-two miles away he was able at least to keep in touch with Gardiner who frequently visited the city. That same month he was invited to Ashampstead for lunch, and in November they had tea together at Christ Church. Heseltine also made the acquaintance of another of the Frankfurt Group, writing to a friend on 20 November: 'Last Sunday I met Roger Quilter, and heard him play over several of his exquisite lyrical songs; on Monday Balfour Gardiner came to tea with me and brought me the proof sheets of a new orchestral and choral work of Delius, "The Song of the High Hills".'

Gardiner asked him to make a piano arrangement of the Delius work and not only did Heseltine gladly take on the task but he also checked the score and parts. He even intended making a vocal score but this was probably never done. Delius was delighted with Heseltine's willingness to accept such work and wrote to him on 18 January 1914 with some advice about the piano reduction that Gardiner had asked for:

All the corrections you sent me of 'Song of the High Hills' were right – It is wonderful how one oversees mistakes – you seem to have an eagle eye. You are doing me a great service by correcting the score & parts of this work. I will send you more parts as soon as I receive them. Your arrangement of the Song of the H.H. is wonderfully good in parts. You seem tho' to have hesitated between putting everything in & eliminating. For Gardiner I would put everything in & then afterwards make a playable 2 hand arrangement – I do not know much about piano arrangements but they must be playable & give a good idea of the work . . .

Heseltine completed his arrangement for solo piano early in 1914. Grainger was later to make another arrangement, this time for two pianos, in 1923.

Three days after his meeting with Heseltine, Gardiner was once more in the public eye. On 20 November he made his only appearance at the Royal Philharmonic Society as conductor with a programme that was clearly of his own choosing. It kept to the same formula as his own concerts by mixing orchestral with unaccompanied choral works, and he was again assisted by Kennedy Scott and the Oriana choir. Nearly all the works in the programme had in fact been heard in his 1912-13 series: Bax's *In the Faery Hills* (dedicated to Gardiner), Austin's Symphony, *In the Street of the Ouled Naïls* from Holst's *Beni Mora* (conducted by the composer), and Vaughan Williams's *Third Norfolk Rhapsody*. All, save the Holst work, were conducted by Gardiner, while Kennedy Scott conducted his choir in ayres and madrigals similar to those in the third 1912 concert with the addition of part-songs by Stanford, Parry and Gardiner (his two Barnes settings).

Quite apart from its unusual format, this concert had a special significance, for it was the first time in the 101 years of the Philharmonic Society's existence that a programme had been devoted exclusively to British music. Obviously regarding the occasion as a bold departure from tradition, *The Times* announced that 'Mr Balfour Gardiner at the head of an army of British composers stormed the defences of the Royal Philharmonic Society . . . and occupied the position of the Queen's Hall through the whole evening.' Unfortunately flesh and spirit of the Society's members were both weak and unwilling since, as they were 'not fond of new experiences', there were many empty seats. The harshest critical tones came from the *Musical News*, whose critic wrote of the Austin Symphony that 'so very unpleasant and tiresome a meandering was it that not a few newspapers came out from the pockets of those present, and they settled themselves to something of more interest than the Austinian strains'. (That critic's opinion of the symphony differed significantly from the view expressed in the same journal at its first performance earlier that year.) There was also a discordant note at the conclusion of the review:

It is rumoured that this unfortunate experiment was pressed on the directors by the conductor of the evening, Mr Balfour Gardiner; if so, the direction needs strengthening. The comments one heard in passing through the passage and corridors of the Queen's Hall were evidence that this truncated attempt at a presentation of natural music was a mistake.

One is reminded of Beecham's comment on the reception of a lengthy all-British programme he conducted during the Great War: 'Well, I think we have successfully paved the way this afternoon for another quarter of a century of German music!' Gardiner as yet had no official connection with the RPS, not being elected member until January 1914. Much later he was to become closely involved in the Society's affairs, though without actually taking office, unlike Norman O'Neill who became a director in May 1915 and co-treasurer the year after. But the 'experiment' as such was not repeated. Indeed, any all-British RPS programme was to be a rare occurrence, there being only four in the Society's next hundred concerts.

Fortunately not all organisations fought shy of presenting concerts solely of native music, and almost a fortnight after the Philharmonic affair, on 3 December, Arthur Fagge gave further proof of the excellent work he and his choir were doing in the cause of British music. In a bold programme that made few – if any – concessions to popular taste, the London Choral Society introduced new works by Speer, Barnett, Jervis-Read, Grainger and Gardiner. Grainger's new work was *At Twilight* which had necessarily been dropped from the 1912–13 Gardiner concerts, and his choral folk-song setting *Brigg Fair* was also sung. Gardiner himself conducted both *News from Whydah* and his new work *April*, a setting for chorus and orchestra of words by Edward Carpenter.

Like Thompson's *A Corymbus for Autumn* which sang of the 'Gipsy of Seasons' (Gardiner's setting sadly being either unfinished or destroyed), Carpenter's *April* verses are an impassioned celebration of those moments in the year during which Gardiner felt creatively at his peak. This was the 'month of the Sun-god's kisses, Earth's sweet passion. . . of breathless moments, hotter and hotter growing', and musically Gardiner responded with equal rapture. He started work on his setting of *April* in June 1911 and the score curiously bears three dates of completion of which the earlier two, 17 May 1912 and 20 May 1913, appropriately enough suggest that much of its composition was done either during or close to the month of the text's inspiration. The final date added to the score, 16 September 1913, may refer either to some later corrections or to his making a duplicate full-score, the existing copy (the original manuscript at present being missing). Although only of about nine minutes' duration (none of his surviving works lasts much more than fifteen minutes), *April* calls for a large orchestra with triple woodwind. The scoring is exemplary and Gardiner seems to have been in no doubt as to the tonal balance he wanted to achieve, adding a note to the MS full score that while the celesta is 'desirable but not absolutely necessary . . . the second harp is not ad libitum and its omission would result in a considerable diminution of the effect intended by the composer'.

The work opens with a string of florid arabesques on woodwind and harp, imitative as elsewhere of bird-call. There is a teasing ambiguity of tonality at the beginning, with a persistent A natural throughout the first eight bars and the principal theme attempting to establish itself in D before the choir enters to plant it firmly and unexpectedly in the home key of E flat (example 19). Even then the tonality occasionally pulls

Ex. 19

towards B flat, with an excursion into G flat for the introduction of a new, contrasting theme. The choir's initial statement contains two important elements: an arched phrase to the words 'O April month' and an upward-thrusting quaver triplet figure that gives an added impetus to the music, matching what Deryck Cooke has called 'the dithyrambic ecstasy of the words'.[12] The development of the thematic material is masterly, in that respect far superior to *News from Whydah*. Cooke found an echo of Wagner at the words 'Clouds and daemonic thunder' and this may also be felt in the *molto stringendo* orchestral passage which follows, most noticeably in the movement of the basses and the whipping up of excitement on the strings.

Less easy to pin-point but all the same making its presence felt is the underlying influence of Delius, more in the refinement of textures and the heady, Dionysiac freedom in the music's forward thrust than in mere harmonic procedures, a number of which had become common currency among the late Romantics. The rising triplet figure already mentioned is a typical Delian fingerprint, and in *April* Gardiner seems to be moving closer in style to the Delius of *An Arabesque* and the latter half of the *Requiem* dating from 1914. Yet what distinguishes this exultant and yearning score, with its close identification with the spirit of the text, is its clarity and freshness. To quote Cooke again, 'there is much here to delight those who can look back across the years, and feel affection for the peaceful landscape of an England which has vanished from our midst'. The score bears a dedication to Arthur Fagge.

Of the other new works in Fagge's programme that had included *April*, there was one in which Gardiner may well have taken a special interest: *Dream-Tryst* by his former colleague on the Winchester staff, Jervis-Read, who had achieved a few Prom performances since devoting more of his time to composition. His choice of text was a poem by Francis Thompson that Gardiner had himself already twice set. Gardiner's versions, dating from 1902 and 1909 respectively, were both for baritone and orchestra but otherwise quite different from each other. Jervis-Read's setting, for chorus and orchestra, was first published in 1913 and after further revision republished in 1922. (He later composed a setting of Thompson's most famous poem, *The Hound of Heaven*.) Whether Gardiner withheld his own *Dream-Tryst* from performance in deference to his friend's (in a somewhat similar fashion to Elgar's dealing with Cyril Rootham over their settings of Laurence Binyon's *For the Fallen*) one cannot be sure, but in those immediate pre-war years there would surely have been an opportunity for the performance of at least one of his versions. Considering how ruthlessly he dealt with his own scores in the thirties, the fact that both manuscripts were preserved would suggest that he was not dissatisfied with either, though neither seems to have been performed in his lifetime.

The 1909 version calls for the slightly larger orchestra and the textures there are rather more elaborate in evoking the mystical atmosphere of the poem's death-hour at dawn. In terms of actual number of bars, the later setting is just the longer, 144 compared with 139, though Gardiner's metrical response to the text was not the same in each case, the earlier setting being more trochaic while the 1909 version has longer uneven bar-lengths with frequent changes of time-signature, as a comparison of the baritone soloist's entry in each work illustrates (examples 20 and 21: 1902 and 1909 versions respectively. In the 1902 version Gardiner altered the original 'mingled' to 'mingling', perhaps in consideration of the vowel sound for the tied notes across bars 6 and 7).

In those last remaining months of peace there was little hint of the on-

Ex. 20

Ex. 21

coming clouds, no foreboding of the upheaval that war was to bring. At
a Royal Philharmonic Society concert on 20 January 1914 (the day after
Gardiner's election as member) Mengelberg gave the first English performances of Delius's two pieces for small orchestra, *On Hearing the
First Cuckoo in Spring* and *Summer Night on the River*. The pair, first
performed the previous October by Nikisch at Leipzig, were dedicated to
Gardiner, who was justly proud of the honour. Sir Thomas Armstrong, a
close friend of Gardiner's in later years, remembered walking one day
with him along the Woodstock Road in Oxford when a boy passed by
whistling the tune of *The First Cuckoo*. Gardiner turned to the boy and
said to him: 'Perhaps you don't realise that that is *my* piece – it was
dedicated to me.'[13]

April was heard again at the Oriana Madrigal Society's most ambitious concert so far, on 10 March at Queen's Hall, when works with
orchestra were included in their programme for the first time. Mendelssohn's *A Midsummer Night's Dream* overture opened the concert,
followed by Delius's *Sea Drift* with Thorpe Bates, *April*, the first performance of Holst's *Hymn to Dionysus* which was dedicated to Gardiner,
W.G. Whittaker's *North Country Folk-Tunes*, and Grainger's *We Have
Fed Our Seas for a Thousand Years*. A late addition to the programme
was the second London performance of *On Hearing the First Cuckoo in
Spring*. Holst and Whittaker conducted their own works, while the

111

remainder were entrusted to Kennedy Scott. Gardiner himself attended more to the promotional side of the concert. The previous May the Society had announced a guarantee fund entitling annual subscribers to two reserved seats for all Oriana concerts in return for each five pounds promised. Arnold Bax's father and Balfour Gardiner were the chief guarantors for £50, with F.S. Kelly and Roger Quilter each promising £10. For this concert it seems likely that Gardiner continued his earlier practice of distributing free tickets, purchasing two hundred at five shillings each which he then circulated to friends and acquaintances, some going to his father, Delius, Holst, Whittaker, Thorpe Bates, Grainger, Mrs Edward Mason and Dale. A well-attended if heavily subsidised hall was clearly preferable to a meagre paying audience. Gardiner similarly saw to the distribution of tickets to the honorary members, the mailing of circulars, and the placing of advertisements in the press. The scores and parts he checked at Ashampstead. Delius was unable to be present, as was Heseltine, who two days later heard from Gardiner: 'We had a glorious concert on Tuesday – the press, as usual, did not think much of it.' Not without cause, Gardiner had by now a growing antipathy to the press and the public with their tepid attitude towards British music, a feeling that was to intensify yet further.

During the early months of 1914 Gardiner was in touch with Bevis Ellis who in March mounted his own brief series: two concerts of modern orchestral music in between which was sandwiched a programme of chamber music. These followed to a lesser degree the example Gardiner had set. While the orchestral concerts contained works by Balakirev, Dvořák, Franck, Ravel and Richard Strauss, some important British works were also played. Bax's *Festival Overture* opened this short series and, together with most of the works, it was conducted by Geoffrey Toye who became a fairly regular acquaintance of Gardiner's.

At the same time Gardiner was also seeing much of Heseltine, who in February with a friend drove from Oxford to Ashampstead in a Humberette borrowed for the occasion. Four days later he and Gardiner went to a Henry Wood Queen's Hall concert at which Delius's *Dance Rhapsody* was played ('disgracefully badly' Heseltine wrote to a friend[14]) as well as the first English performance of Stravinsky's *Fireworks*. Near the end of the month he again visited Ashampstead and in mid-March they both attended a RPS concert, at which Gardiner introduced Heseltine to Ernest Newman who gave the young aspiring critic some advice. Heseltine also had serious inclinations towards becoming a composer. Indeed at intervals during the past three years he had been composing songs. On a visit to Ashampstead on 16 May he asked Gardiner's opinion of these songs. Four days later Heseltine wrote to a friend an account of the visit:

. . . I actually pushbiked 30 miles in the sweltering heat to see Gardiner! He was in a very genial mood, and was also most encouraging about the songs – this pleased me greatly, being unexpected, since his views on song-writing and mine are widely divergent! He and Delius and I are all going to Wales together in July – either on mo'-bikes or push-bikes.

Gardiner suggested to Heseltine that if his intentions of becoming a composer were serious he ought to study for a while with Holst, of whom he wrote on 8 October that 'it would be impossible to find anyone better'.[15] That came to nothing, but until 1925 Heseltine occasionally either showed Gardiner or sent him printed copies of his compositions in exchange for frank advice and criticism. The difference in their attitudes towards song-writing became more apparent in 1918 when he sent Gardiner two unaccompanied carols, *Kanow Kernow 1 & 11*. The comments he received prompted him to write on 19 July to Colin Taylor:

Do tell me if you like the second Cornish carol; I should be very greatly interested in your view of it. It seems to me a very simple and unpuzzling composition, but I sent it to Balfour Gardiner and he seemed to think it was a kind of essay in the style of the 16th or 17th century. I was flabbergasted: Is there anything 16th or 17th centuryish about it: and first of all what is 16th centuryishness in music?

Gardiner's opinions never lacked candour and with all honesty he had openly admitted to Heseltine that, while he wanted to offer some useful comment on the carols, he felt less fitted than most musicians to pass judgment. 'This sort of music . . . makes the same impression on me as a lot of 16th Century stuff that is declared, without a dissentient voice, to be excellent', is what he had actually written on 6 July. He had detected a hardness in the settings but at the same time added that they would be a joy to hear sung well. Gardiner and Heseltine's tastes did not run parallel courses anyway, for although they shared a deep respect for Delius's music, Gardiner was far less enthusiastic about van Dieren's work which exerted a powerful influence on Heseltine from 1916, the year in which he met the Dutch composer for the first time. On 12 August 1918 Gardiner wrote to Heseltine: 'On my first two attempts to read van Dieren's Symphony [the *Chinese Symphony* for five solo voices, chorus and orchestra] I suffered acute mental distress.' He was struck by its freedom, resource, and beauty of outline in the polyphonic parts, but was critical of much of the orchestration. 'He uses combinations that I cannot imagine I shall ever bring myself to tolerate', he complained.

In 1914 Heseltine was engaged on further work for Delius, making a translation into English of *Eine Arabeske*, a setting for baritone, chorus and orchestra of a German version (by Jelka Delius) of a poem by the Danish poet and novelist Jens Peter Jacobsen, whose writings inspired among other things Delius's opera *Fennimore and Gerda* and Schoenberg's *Gurrelieder*. When Delius had seen the result he wrote to

Heseltine on 24 April: 'In your translation of Arabesk there are still 4 or 5 places which will not do – they seemed too awkward & too much like a translation – I sent it to Gardiner. He & Bax may be able to help us.' Heseltine stayed with Gardiner on 23 June for two days and Delius, who had crossed from France and spent a few days at the O'Neills', joined them the next day and stayed for a week. The proposed cycling tour, now intended to centre on Gloucestershire and the Wye Valley, seems never to have materialised. However, Heseltine was able to relate to a friend on 2 July: 'I repaired to Gardiner's delightful cottage in Berkshire where we were joined by Delius and two other [unidentified] musicians, all of whom contributed liberally to the gaiety of things.' Delius, Gardiner and Heseltine were all present on 8 July for Beecham's all-Delius concert at the Royal Academy of Music when, besides other works, *In a Summer Garden* and the two pieces for small orchestra were played. A few days later Delius was back in Grez and any plans the three may have had for the rest of the year received a rude shock when war was declared on 4 August.

One such plan to be terminated abruptly by war was for a third series of the Gardiner choral and orchestral concerts. Towards the end of May an announcement had appeared in an Oriana programme stating that three concerts 'devoted mainly to Modern Music' were to be given on 18 November and the two successive Wednesdays. A specially augmented Oriana choir was to sing at the last concert. Works by Austin, Grainger, Whittaker, and even César Franck were under consideration (the latter possibly being suggested as a result of Bevis Ellis having conducted his own orchestration of Franck's *Pièce héroïque* at one of his concerts that March). Other more definite proposals were Bax's *Fatherland* (for tenor, chorus and orchestra) and his symphony *Spring Fire* (which had been put down for that year's Norwich Festival, also to be cancelled because of the war), Delius's *The Song of the High Hills* (of which Heseltine had made a piano reduction for Gardiner), Holst's *Hecuba's Lament*, Albeniz's *Catalan Rhapsody* (evidence of Gardiner's love for Spain and Spanish music), and most interestingly his own choral and orchestral *Philomela* which was not to be completed until 1923, though but for the war's intervention it could possibly have been ready in time for the proposed concert. Sadly the third series never took place, nor were they to be resumed after the war. One may instead speculate whether in the absence of a world war they might have become an annual event for the continual promotion of British music.

8 'The wasted years . . .'

1914–1919

Balfour Gardiner was thirty-six when Europe erupted into war. His upbringing, his attitudes, his way of life had attuned him to an era that was never to be recaptured. Even though he was not in the front line of active service, for him the experience of war and military life was traumatic. The disruption it brought into his creative life and more importantly the change it ultimately wrought in the English musical climate were crucial factors in his post-war development.

He had not, like many, been blind to the possible outbreak of hostilities. But he was nonetheless torn by his love for Germany. He had too an admiration for the systematic approach he recognised in the German way of thinking. One day when discussing the publicising of British music with Arnold Bax he remarked: 'Well, I am convinced that advertisement is the secret, my dear Arnold. We've all been too scrupulous, too much afraid of soiling our hands. But we must stiffen up about this business of British music – become harder, and I believe that advertisement should be studied as an exact science.' And he went on to mention an American psychologist's book he had just read on the subject. 'He goes most systematically into the whole matter. It might have been written by a German . . . After all it's the old Deutschers that have the method. Oh yes, they understand all that kind of thing . . . !'[1] The subject was to arise again in the course of one of those evening discussions on the Spanish holiday with the Baxes and Holst. When the argument had reached a particularly nebulous stage Gardiner declared: 'The fact is that nobody can talk sense about abstract ideas because nobody has satisfactorily defined our first terms. We are like these so-called statesmen of Europe, – simply guessing, making shots in the dark. The Germans are the only people who have begun to make abstract thought scientific . . . If there's another war between France and Germany you will see what their system has produced . . . People in England have no conception of what the Germans have done.'[2] He related how he had studied a railway map of the Franco-German border and discovered that Germany appeared to have built its railways right up to the border in such a way as to facilitate any invasion of France. He spoke too of the potential threat of the Zeppelin as a bomber (a danger a contemporary magazine had highlighted). He certainly regarded Germany as a considerable force to be reckoned with.

All speculation and scepticism were soon brushed aside by the reality of August 1914. During the succeeding months many of Gardiner's acquaintances enlisted, some like Edward Mason, F.S. Kelly and Bevis Ellis to join the ranks of 'The Lost Generation' of musicians. Of his close friends, Delius was living in France and Grainger had left for America where he was to spend the greater part of the remainder of his life. Others like Bax, Holst, O'Neill and Cyril Scott were found unsuited for active service during the course of the war and were exempted for varying reasons. But as the expected early end to the war kept its distance and the prospect of conscription became more serious, Gardiner found himself in a most unsettled condition and hoped for means of exemption in his case too when the blow fell.

A refreshing contrast to the gloom of the hour was offered by a new work, *In Maytime*, given on 3 October 1914 at the Proms by Henry Wood. To some extent a reworking of his *English Dance*, this was a short vigorous dance celebrating the revels of a Maying festival, and inviting comparison with the ever-popular *Shepherd Fennel's Dance* which received two Prom performances that year. As with several works no longer extant, the only clues to the work's shape are to be gleaned from programme notes and reviews. Rosa Newmarch's descriptive note gives the clearest picture:

Of the three main themes on which the work is built, two are taken from an old English Dance, a much earlier work – the first example of Mr Balfour Gardiner's music ever played at the Promenade Concerts. The scoring is for full orchestra, including bass clarinet, double bassoon, and a variety of percussion instruments (with pianoforte). The opening theme is simple and pastoral in character, and the instrumentation is appropriate. It forms the basis of a fairly long Introduction (Andante 2/4). A dance-theme follows (Allegro 6/8) which develops into a jovial, light-hearted section. As in *Shepherd Fennel's Dance* the movement becomes boisterous at times; for Mr Balfour Gardiner's country-folk are not Watteau figures, but able-bodied and vigorous English lads and lassies. Eventually some allusions to the subject of the Introduction recall a more tranquil mood. Another section will be noticed which begins with a double-bassoon solo in A flat, and ends with a pause before the change to A major. Towards the end the first theme is heard in augmentation against the second subject. The pastoral mood of the Introduction returns in Molto Moderato (F major) when the quiet beauty of the spring morning is remembered with a touch of regret. But the last moments of a holiday are not spent in repining, and the work concludes with an outburst of high spirits in an energetic Molto Vivace.

Despite its charm and inventiveness, its vigour and strong concluding climax, Gardiner did not regard it as a great success and lacked the patience to rework it further. Although both work and composer were warmly received, it was not given again and a Manchester performance announced for 9 January 1915 did not take place.

Another first performance of the early war years was of the revised

Fantasy for orchestra, given (like the original version in 1908) by Beecham, at a Royal Philharmonic Society concert on 15 November 1915. The revision chiefly concerned the addition of a new middle section. The composer's own programme note refers to

a sort of Leitmotif with which the Introduction begins that recurs frequently throughout the piece. The rest of the work falls roughly into three sections . . . This division into sections is made for the purpose of analysis only. The broad effect is that of introductory matter (in slower tempo), followed by a frequent interchange of quicker and slower elements related to or contrasted with each other, and the predominance of calmer moods towards the end.

A few critics gave it a tepid reception, though when one critic wrote that the work exemplified 'the composer's sympathies with the modern idiom' there was more than a hint that the critic's own sympathies did not lie in that direction.[3] Ten days later Beecham repeated the work at a Hallé concert after which the *Musical Times* critic wrote of the *Fantasy* that it 'ranks quite worthily with the best British music. It was superbly played.' Regrettably both *In Maytime* and the *Fantasy* have long since disappeared, quite likely destroyed by their composer.

In 1914 Gardiner gave up 7 Pembroke Villas and moved to the other side of Holland Park at 1 Hillsleigh Road, which became for a while his London residence, kept concurrently with his Ashampstead cottage. Gradually his attitude towards music and concert-giving was hardening. That his own concerts had not received the fullest support they merited was a decisive factor, and he kept no secret of his feelings about British musical life from Grainger (who by the end of the war was to adopt American citizenship). 'All the little . . . busybodies are giving "English Music" of a sort – the public must be disgusted with music of every description by now', he wrote on 7 February 1915. Grainger had some faith in his public but it was not an attitude with which Gardiner could concur. He continued:

I feel very cynical when I read of such enthusiasm – I cannot share it. And yet it is the only thing that gives meaning to artistic activities on a large scale. And the corollary of that – my lack of such enthusiasm – is that I feel inclined for little hole -&- corner activities – if I am to be active at all: either that, or I shall use what resources I have recklessly, giving concerts in much the same spirit as that in which men marry. 'I take this woman', they say in the marriage service, 'for better or worse' – there is some bravery, or at least some recklessness, & certainly quite a lot of folly about that.

So, despite his despondency and his earlier declaration of 'never again' after the troubles of the 1913 concerts, he once more attempted to continue the Gardiner Series and booked Queen's Hall for three dates in March 1916 in the hope that the war would by then be over. But he still had a deep distrust of such a scheme's worth, writing on 17 September:

Public musical affairs over here are as rotten as ever – it turns out, after all this talk of British Music, that the nation, having been grossly unpatriotic as regards music before the war, now let their patriotism stand in the way of whatever little musical feeling it possesses: on no account, it seems, must 'British' & 'Music' be brought into actual conjunction.

His attitude reached its nadir when writing to Grainger on 17 April 1916:

I almost feel a duty to you to do so, & to proclaim openly, what I have long felt secretly, my apostasy from your faith in the public aspects of music, a faith I may have appeared to share, judging from my own activities. I have been long in reaching my conclusion, but what I feel now I felt indefinitely & partially long before the war. Briefly put, the degradation of English national life & the impossibility of founding any art upon it. That much from the side of the artist – I assert that he can make nothing worth making on that basis. From the other side – the side of the public – a complete insensibility to anything really serious, subtle & profound . . . The somewhat depressing result of these perceptions is that I will never lift a finger again on behalf of music in England, or have my works performed if it means the slightest effort on my part: but the great personal gain I have from this new standpoint is that I have regained my entire liberty to enjoy music as I enjoyed it when I was a child, without any reference, near or far, whatever. I feel like a prisoner released.

Naturally there is nothing worth speaking about in the musical happenings in this country: & the composers seem to be drifting further & further apart from each other, as is only natural when we get older & have no genuine community of civilisation to bind us together. I have been thrilled by one or two things, however, mostly by new orchestral pieces of Von Holst – &, as you refused to produce yours, I have done my own setting of 'The Three Ravens' which was sung by the Oriana, & gave me great pleasure.

In at least one respect he was not alone with his opinions as by 1918 there was mounting criticism of the content of the Promenade Concerts with their bias towards German and Russian music in the weekly Wagner nights, Russian nights, symphony nights (frequently Beethoven), and the 'Popular' nights mainly devoted to foreign works. The outspoken Robin Legge considered that far too little was being done to encourage any potential native musical ability. There was also support from Sir Ernest Palmer who argued that since the concerts were supported by a British public with British money and a British orchestra, it was not too unreasonable to hope for a British night at the Proms.[4] But the reply forthcoming from Messrs Chappell & Co., the proprietors of both Queen's Hall and its orchestra who had taken over the running of the concerts in 1915, supplied the pith of Gardiner's contention. The sad fact was that the concerts were in essence a commercial undertaking and the programmes were a reflection on public preferences, usually for works other than British ones out of which only those by Elgar and Edward German held any attraction. The Prom promoters did not believe in educating the public but instead used the box office returns as an indicator of taste. They also pointed out that with the economic string-encies of war it was hardly the time to indulge the caprices of 'novelties', the current term that in their usage assumed a suggestion of ephemeral value in the works to which it applied. In this respect Wood's hands were tied, and the 'novelties' that found their way into his programmes tended to be slight, shorter pieces that would make little demand on the public's tolerance. Bevis Ellis must have detected this fickle attitude as his concerts which had followed Gardiner's were a blend of British and foreign works. An 'English Night' had in fact been introduced at the Proms in October 1901 yet when the experiment was repeated over a quarter of a century later it led to Vaughan Williams apparently protest-ing against the 'segregation' of British composers.[5] British music has always occupied a rather uneasy position in the concert hall, often for those commercial reasons that had drastically reduced its representation in the war-time Proms.

Gardiner had more to say on the subject of concert promotion when late in the summer of 1916 Philip Heseltine, with the help of composer and critic Cecil Gray, was making tentative preparations for an ambi-tious project of hiring a small theatre and giving a month's season of operas and concerts. As Delius's *A Village Romeo and Juliet* was one opera he intended staging, Heseltine acquainted its composer with his plans, but Delius wisely warned him against such a war-time scheme, adding: 'I know of no artistic musical–dramatical undertaking that has ever come off in England.'[6] Gardiner's reaction was one of cautious anticipation. In a similar vein to Delius, on 30 October 1916 he reminded Heseltine:

You know approximately what my attitude towards the performance of music in England is, & I need not elaborate it . . . If I were giving advice to others about concert giving I could say a lot, from my experience, about practical & worldly measures of inveigling the public. But I feel that as regards all that you had better – or rather may just as well, work out your own – damnation. For you are going to make the public a present – and you are at the same time going to put yourself into antagonism against them. What are they to think & in what mood will they be to accept what you offer them? I feel that for such a situation any small worldly wisdom I could offer would be out of place.

He did put forward some suggestions for the concerts, including *Neptune* from Holst's then unplayed *Planets* suite. 'This is a piece of the most fantastic & subtle description – & he has others as well, many of which I know you would not care for, but "Neptune" deserves a hearing, as much as, or more than, any work you are doing.' He explained how the female voices were to fade away behind the scenes as a door was closed on them – 'a wonderful effect'. Heseltine's scheme, however, came to nothing.

Among the 'little hole -&- corner activities' which Gardiner had referred to when writing to Grainger that were part of his contribution to the war effort, was some teaching at Ludgrove, a boys' preparatory school at Cockfosters which supplied pupils for Eton. Cecil Sharp had served on the staff from 1893 until 1910. Gardiner joined the school in January 1915 and taught singing and gave piano lessons until he left for war service the following year. He also organised the twice-yearly school concerts of songs, choruses and piano pieces, participating himself at least once in a piano duet. While at Ludgrove he specially composed two songs: a sea-chanty *Heave Ho!* and *A Song for Supper Night* that was traditionally sung at the end-of-term prize-giving. His teaching timetable kept him occupied from Tuesday to Thursday of most weeks, leaving him the long weekends free for other activities. During that time he saw something of two friends from Frankfurt days, Herbert Golden and Thomas Holland-Smith. Holland-Smith had also turned to teaching and was combining music and modern languages at a boys' school in Durham.

Later in 1914, with the threat of the German advance, the Deliuses left Grez for the comparative safety of England, arriving there mid-November. Even before the war there had been indications of the dreadful illness that was later to afflict Delius, and he had undergone some treatment in Switzerland and Germany. Now Delius's nerves had been seriously affected by the experience of war and he was for a while subject to slight attacks. For much of the time Beecham put the Deliuses up at Grove Mill House which he had leased just outside Watford. In June 1915 Gardiner planned to spend a night there and then take them the next day to Ashampstead if Delius was in a fit state to travel, and he invited Heseltine to join them. But it is not known whether anything came of these arrangements.

During the early summer months Gardiner went through a period of depression, aggravated by a bout of German measles and pleurisy. But by 25 August he was himself again and able to write from Ashampstead to Heseltine: 'It has come at last – an overwhelming flood of music – and I feel certain of myself as I never felt before. The damned London public linger in my memory with a faint unpleasant odour. Meanwhile, I write about all the beautiful things around me, & it seems, as long as I have them, I shall have music.' In fact he felt so creative that it was with great reluctance he returned to teaching at Ludgrove in September, regretting that he could not devote his whole time to composition. On 17 September he wrote to Grainger that he had 'been fearfully hard at work on a new orchestral work which is now finished', and though he did not mention the work by name, it was possibly the *Ballad* for orchestra for which he was to have a waning enthusiasm. He added that 'old Gustav von Holst too has done well & produced three orchestral pieces better even than Beni Mora'. Later in the year he went by train to Thaxted in Essex where Holst was now living: neuritis and short sight had caused him to be rejected as unfit for military service. In November the Deliuses, after having spent most of the summer in Scandinavia, returned to France, though they were later to be again uprooted by war.

Despite the prevailing gloom, for Gardiner 1915 had after all been a reasonably fruitful year. It was in that exultant mood later in the year that he had considered giving further concerts and, besides the revised *Fantasy*, he had received a fair share of performances of other works, notably the *Overture to a Comedy* at Bournemouth again and at Cape Town, the String Quartet in Halifax and Birmingham played by the Catterall Quartet, and with growing popularity *News from Whydah* in Belfast, to mention but a few. When in May Hugh Allen conducted *The Recruit* in Oxford it had been eagerly encored. Gardiner was still closely involved with the Oriana Madrigal Society of which he had become a committee member late in 1914. A work of his usually appeared in each of their concerts and for them, in 1915, he made an arrangement of what he referred to as 'that lamentable ditty' – *God save the King*. But this relatively peaceful existence was not to last.

As, contrary to many expectations, the war dragged on, in January 1916 compulsory military service for single men was introduced (those married were caught in the same net by May), leaving Gardiner no option but to enlist. This terminated his teaching at Ludgrove, for which he received appreciative recognition in the School Notes:

Mr H. Balfour Gardiner, who was good enough to undertake the duties of Music-master in the absence of Mr G.J. Wilkinson, is now acting as Censor 'somewhere in France'. We should like to place it on record how greatly indebted we are to him for all he has done here. He threw himself heart and soul into the life of the school and took endless trouble over the interests of the boys. We, one and all, miss him very greatly, but look forward to his constantly being at Ludgrove in the near future.

While he did not return to teaching after the war he often revisited Ludgrove, especially at prize-giving. It seems from a brief diary entry that in 1916 he may also have intended to give some music lessons at Bradfield College, a stone's throw from Ashampstead, taking an orchestra for an hour on Monday evenings, the Glee Club for an hour on Wednesday evenings, and a choir practice and services on Sundays. Conscription put an end to any such intentions.

On 25 February he attested at Reading and joined the 16th Battalion County of London Regiment (Queen's Westminster Rifles). The next month he was mobilised and sent to Hazeley Down Camp at Winchester. To his friends there was nothing more incongruous than the thought of

Balfour Gardiner in uniform. Delius wrote to Heseltine on 25 April: 'We are having visions of Gardiner in Kaki, walking up & down under a railway bridge with a gun over his shoulder [Delius actually wrote 'soldier': the erratic spellings are his] & whistling Tiperary.' Later he was to learn more of the truth which he passed on to Heseltine on 11 June:

Gardiner wrote me a long letter from Calais – where he is employed reading soldiers' letters 7 hours a day, Sundays included – He enlisted as an ordinary Tommy & had a very hard time of it – drilling in a camp (Hazeley Down). He was lodged in a sort of hut with 37 others – fearful discomfort. He got so confused at last that he could not understand what people were saying to him. However he has been promoted to Sub-Lieut now & he has an easier time of it.

On 8 May 1916 he was discharged on his appointment to a temporary commission, becoming deputy assistant censor in Calais and Boulogne until June 1917. From France he wrote to Grainger on 1 September 1916:

I think I wrote to you about a month after I joined the Army as a private. It was an unforgettable time & I never learnt to appreciate the kindness of my fellow countrymen as I did amongst the hardships of Hazeley Down Camp. In May I got a commission and was sent out as Censor to Calais, where I spent three months reading soldiers' letters. You may be interested to know that the Australians, judged by what they write, are the most intelligent & wideawake of all our troops in the field, though I came to the conclusion that like all Colonials they are hopelessly undisciplined. I didn't like the Canadians at all. The peoples of the United Kingdom exhibit a surprising variety of intelligence & temperament. But the greatest surprise came when I started reading German prisoners' of war correspondence three weeks ago at Boulogne, where I am now stationed. They are almost unbelievably illiterate & seem to take no interest in anything but their own immediate wants. Even their 'grüsse ü' Küsse' are purely conventional. No passionate love letters such as you get from the English (in spite of the fact that they know that a third person will read them!).

In France he was at least able to indulge one of his pleasures by ringing the changes of wines he consumed at meals. He corresponded with close friends but longed for leave. 'I dream of many English villages', he wrote in his notebook on 17 July. At other times improvements to his Ashampstead cottage would be in his thoughts and he gave instructions for his Hillsleigh Road house in London to be put on the market. War had not entirely obliterated musical thinking; he had begun a little composition under difficult circumstances at Calais, but was then disturbed by his transference to Boulogne. At the end of September his wish for leave was granted, and on his brief return to Ashampstead he looked again at *A Berkshire Idyll* and pencilled on the manuscript: 'October 3 '16. Read this during my week's leave from Boulogne & delighted with some of the material, recalling the joy with which I wrote it.'

Although officially still on duty in France until 24 June 1917, Gardiner left Boulogne at the end of April and the remaining two months were spent at postal censorship at Strand House in London. He used his time there to advantage. He saw a little of Cyril Scott who did all he could to get Gardiner a job that would save him from returning to France. When the opportunity arose he dined with friends, with Norman O'Neill, with Geoffrey Toye, and at least once with Gustav Holst's wife Isobel and the young Imogen. With her artistic flair for such things, Isobel Holst gave Gardiner advice about the alterations and decorations to his cottage which he was gradually furnishing with articles from Hillsleigh Road. Although his London house had been on sale for many months, it was in the meantime available for his friends' use. In December Holst wrote to his friend W.G. Whittaker: 'Balfour Gardiner's house 1 Hillsleigh Rd will be your residence. You'll be alone but perhaps that will bring a relief.'[7] The Deliuses had planned to come again to England earlier in the year and hoped that they might use Gardiner's house in view of the difficulty of renting furnished accommodation in war-time London. But it was to be a little time before they were able to make the crossing.

With this brief spell of renewed living in London, on 28 June Gardiner was elected to the Savage Club of which he remained a member until November 1920. His proposer was Norman O'Neill who had become a member the previous October, and his seconders were the singer Harry Dearth and Landon Ronald. Gardiner was once again represented in that year's Proms, and Henry Wood, who on 11 January 1916 had taken *News from Whydah* to Liverpool, introduced the work to Birmingham on 22 November 1917. Throughout these difficult times Gardiner kept a watchful eye on his investments with the same scrupulous attention he would give to a musical score. War had not lessened his generosity: in December 1917 he gave £100 in Australian War Loans each to Frederic Austin, Norman O'Neill, Kennedy Scott, Gustav Holst, and his chauffeur Cox who had joined the British Expeditionary Force in East Africa. This was followed the next year by a gift of £900 in National War Bonds to Holst. Gardiner's own wealth was at this time substantially increased by the gift from his father of £20,000.

This more agreeable period in London soon ended, for at the end of June he was posted as interpreter to three prisoner-of-war camps in turn: at Pattishall until August, at Richborough until November, and at Kerry in Montgomeryshire (now Powys) for the remainder of the war's duration. The fact that Gardiner, like each of the Frankfurt Group, was fluent in German helped determine this posting, which to his relief prevented him from being stationed abroad again. This appointment suited him far better, as he told Grainger on 28 September 1917:

Since the end of June I have been interpreter at two Prisoner of War Camps, & expect I shall have another change at the end of next month. It is infinitely better than being a Censor, which is the most fearful occupation one can imagine. As an interpreter I am comparatively happy, but of course it is awful being away from one's home & one's friends & never being able to write any music.

Kerry, the last of the three camps at which he was stationed, was in every respect the most satisfactory. In beautiful surroundings not far from the Clun Forest, he was within reasonable reach of Ashampstead when leave came up. He stayed a mile outside the camp at Brook Cottage where he generally took his meals. Rarely in perfect health, he found for once that the colder climate and regular life improved his constitution, rising at eight each morning for a cold bath, a simple breakfast and a brisk walk to the camp. He was constantly concerned about his health, restricting himself to a moderate diet, a chief ingredient being apples, with small quantities of cider and wine. This he tempered with short sharp walks and breathing exercises, fully aware all the time that he smoked too much.

Kerry was a work camp. The German prisoners on arrival in Britain were first sent to a camp at Bala in North Wales from where they were conveyed by rail to Kerry. Here the prisoners, unusually of mixed services, felled about two hundred acres of trees, though no planting was done. Gardiner's task as interpreter was tedious but not too demanding. There was one occasion, later recounted much to the amusement of his friends, when he was required to be on duty while the commanding officer addressed a new intake of prisoners who could speak hardly any English. Trying to put on a humane front while outlining to them the camp routine, the CO was at pains to impress upon them that both he and they were after all only human, that they would be fairly treated, and that despite the conditions things need not be too disagreeable. Balfour Gardiner, having to stand in attendance while this lengthy address continued, became increasingly restless and uncomfortable, colouring in the face as was his habit. And when eventually he was turned to and asked to translate for the captive audience, there came a prompt concise response: 'Der Hauptmann behauptet er sei kein Tintenfisch!' (The CO assures you that he is no octopus!)

Later in 1918 Gardiner learned that Gustav Holst, although unfit for any active war-work, was being posted abroad to Salonika where, as the newly appointed musical organiser for the YMCA, for nine months he would supervise the education of the troops in the Near East soon to be demobilised. Gardiner's reaction was one of typically unpredictable generosity. As a parting gift he gave Holst a private performance of the as yet unperformed *Planets*, about which he had written so enthusiastically to Heseltine. It was indeed a generous gift, for the cost of hiring an orchestra of the size Holst's suite called for, especially in war-time conditions, be excessive. Holst excitedly approached Adrian Boult, who earlier that year had made his name as a conductor through some concerts with the London Symphony Orchestra. 'Adrian, the YMCA are sending me to Salonika quite soon', Gustav explained, 'and Balfour

13   Gustav Holst (left) with Balfour Gardiner in his Ashampstead garden
(date uncertain)

Gardiner, bless his heart, has given me a parting present consisting of Queen's Hall, full of the Queen's Hall Orchestra for the whole of a Sunday morning. So we're going to do *The Planets* and you've got to conduct.'[8] Parts were hastily prepared with the assistance of St Paul's Girls' School (of which Holst had been director of music since 1905) and a select choir of schoolgirls and staff was trained for *Neptune*, while Boult was helped in familiarising himself with the large score by hearing the work played several times in its two-piano arrangement. Those friends who were able to come were invited, and from his Notting-hamshire YMCA camp Holst wrote to Whittaker: 'If you'll be busy on the 29th it's no use inviting you to a special private performance of my *Planets* that morning at Queen's Hall! Balfour is treating me to it. I shall probably go off in 3 or 4 weeks.'[9]

On that memorable morning in September the orchestra had less than two hours for their only rehearsal, from ten until a quarter to twelve. Then after a fifteen minute break they played through the whole work, Boult unleashing *Mars* before an audience of over two hundred. Although the top gallery was not used, many friends and the whole of St Paul's School occupied the first circle, while the choir sat in the stalls until they were required for *Neptune*, when they positioned themselves at one side of the hall near a door through which they walked to obtain that 'wonderful effect' of voices becoming lost in the distance. Many critics and musicians were there too, including Henry Wood. In his self-effacing way Gardiner kept so much in the background that Boult did not even see him that morning. This was the celebrated occasion on which the charwomen working in the hall are said to have downed their mops and brushes and danced to the strains of *Jupiter*.

Holst had in fact six weeks to wait before leaving for Greece, and the beginning of November found him after thirty-six hours' notice travelling across Europe by train to Rome, from where on 6 November he sent postcard greetings to Gardiner at Brook Cottage, Kerry: 'Many happy returns of the day from the most beautiful city I have ever seen. May this be your last birthday in kharki.' (He had yet to see Athens which altered his opinion.) In his absence Norman O'Neill took over the St Paul's School orchestra and so joined his wife Adine on the staff where she had been the head music mistress since 1902. Indeed, it was partly through Adine that Holst had been appointed to St Paul's. Holst's educational work of teaching, lecturing and arranging concerts took him from Salonika to Constantinople. On seeing St Sophia and bearing in mind Isobel and Balfour's shared interest in furnishing and interior decoration, he wrote tongue-in-cheek to his wife of an idea to 'deliver St Sophia and £200,000 (I think that would be enough) to you and Balfour, giving you absolute freedom'.[10] Shortly before sailing home in June 1919 he wrote to Isobel of plans for his return: 'I shall want to see people: – Ralph [Vaughan Williams], Adrian [Boult], Balfour, etc.'[11]

The war twice caused the Deliuses' removal to England. They came again at the beginning of September 1918, staying first at Henry Wood's house and then at a flat in Belsize Park Gardens. When he was able to, Gardiner accompanied them to Queen's Hall concerts. But by 1919 he was becoming frustrated at the prolongation of his military service. From Kerry on 31 March he wrote to Grainger:

All efforts to obtain my demobilization are fruitless. I even heard yesterday that they are looking for interpreters to go to France, so that even when the prisoners leave this country I may have to go with them. I am heartily sick of military life & am longing to get out . . . I am very anxious to see what sort of stuff I shall write after all these years.

It was not until 25 May that he was able to relinquish his commission, retaining the rank of lieutenant, and he immediately set about expressing his joy in a short march for piano, *The Joyful Homecoming*. On 25 June he wrote to Grainger: 'Two days ago I wrote a splendid small march, the most thrilling piano piece I have ever done, though it wants a big martellato piano technique. I want to score it for military band.' In fact he scored it for orchestra in time to conduct it himself at the first night of that year's Proms. He dedicated this exuberant work to Grainger (it is very much of the Grainger idiom and contains a possibly intended suggestion of his *Walking Tune* in the seventh bar), but he was not happy with it later as the ending had given some difficulty and he wished that he had had more time to rework it and strengthen it. He dismissed it by saying 'it was not a great success: it was not written originally for orchestra nor is it written very well for piano: it is a sort of nondescript writing like a reduction from a full score'.[12] This judgment is typical of the way he would often dismiss his own work at a time far removed from the excitement of its conception. Grainger, however, took the work to heart, as he did with the other works Gardiner dedicated to him, and in his own unmistakable style commented in a 'round letter to friends' on 17 February 1947:

The real fact is that THE JOYFUL HOMECOMING is one of mankind's great heart-lay-barements. It voices flawlessly, sweetly yet powerfully, a true-to-type Englishman's feeling on the first day of peace after the 1st German War. It is one of the noblest hero-songs of all time & one of the most once-only-ful (unique) tone-utterances in all tone-art (music). It is GREAT MANKINDHOOD & GREAT SOUL-SPEECH. All thoughts as to whether it was first written for the wretched piano (the tone-box of the town-skirts (suburbs)) or for the almost alike-wretched mixed-band (orchestra) is FLOUNDERING – forgetting the elephant for the gnat!

In 1919 Gardiner sent the manuscript full score to Grainger who made an alteration to the percussion in the last bar with Gardiner's approval. Much later he also made some sketches for an arrangement for strings and 'tuneful percussion', writing out instrumental parts of eleven bars on 22 November 1946 for a 'sound trial' in Montreal, but this version remains incomplete. Gardiner's orchestral version brought in bells at the close, and, with its directness and cheerful nature matching the mood of the time, made sufficient impression on the Prom audience for a repeat to be demanded. It was played again at Bournemouth and Huddersfield, other performances were announced for Bradford and Manchester, but only the piano version exists to this day. Though prone to Gardiner's tendency to overwork a figure particularly in developing a climax, this three-minute piece (example 22) communicates in simple terms much of its composer's feelings on obtaining his release from the army. But it hardly lives up to the hopelessly exaggerated claims Grainger made for it: it is little more than a *succès d'occasion*.

The early months of peace after demobilisation were certainly times for rejoicing, and the jubilation that found expression in *The Joyful Homecoming* concealed for a while the more lasting effects of war. Not for long was Gardiner able to proclaim as he did to Grainger on 25 June: 'The wasted years in the Army have gone by leaving hardly any mark; after three or four days' musical thought I find myself, as regard

Ex. 22

capability & the quality of the stuff, just where I was. Thank goodness nothing has been lost . . . ' He returned to composition with renewed vigour. On 11 September he wrote to Rose Grainger from Ashampstead: 'I seem to be busy all day long. Especially during the last month I have been at work from morning till night (& in the *middle* of the night, too), composing hard: there is very little to show for it, as usual, but I don't care as long as that little is good.' At home there was one strange reminder of his war service: he had acquired some wooden door-labels he had taken a fancy to in the Kerry POW camp, and 'Schlaf' and 'Bad' now hung on a bedroom and the bathroom door in his Ashampstead cottage.

One special homecoming was Gustav Holst's return from the Near East that June. He and Gardiner intended celebrating their reunion, in the company of W.G. Whittaker, with some pleasant walks. But it seems their energetic partner had other ideas. 'Balfour and I had planned a nice gentle fat middle-aged tour for you – Thaxted, Cambridge, Oxford, Burford, Bibury, Ashampstead', Holst protested good-naturedly to Whittaker on 12 July. 'And then you come along with your 600 miles record stunt! *NO.* I can't do it. I haven't a byke or the energy or the will.'[13] Gardiner would have met too strenuous a plan with a look of horror. He had a special remedy for ridding any walk of its physical discomforts: he would have his chauffeur drive them to the start of the finest stretch of the route and arrange to be collected later at a suitable place to be driven back to the comforts of his cottage.

It seems probable that the three did meet in the second week of August, whether for a walk or a bicycle ride, since Holst sent instructions to Whittaker on 30 July from Thaxted: 'After Burford – which is glorious – get on to Oxford. Balfour expects us on the Tuesday [12 August].'[14] Whittaker, who was a few months older than Gardiner, had conducted *News from Whydah* earlier that year in his home town of Newcastle where he had already gained an enviable reputation as a choral trainer. That year Holst began teaching both at University College, Reading, and at the Royal College of Music in London. Reading was conveniently close to Ashampstead and, as Gardiner made occasional trips to London, opportunities for their meeting would be plentiful. In the early years of their friendship Holst travelled much by bicycle and on one occasion arrived at Ashampstead soaked to the skin after cycling through the pouring rain with his trombone on his back. In November Gardiner made a special note to attend one of Holst's lectures in London and also to hear him conduct for the first time three of *The Planets* at Queen's Hall. Since the gift of a private performance, the complete suite had not yet been given publicly.

Peacetime made possible the renewal of two other friendships: with

Benjamin Dale and Edgar Bainton. Both composers had the misfortune to be in Germany at the outbreak of war and were interned at Ruhleben, near Berlin, until 1918 when they were transferred to camps in Holland. Dale returned home just before the Armistice in November 1918, but his health had suffered and for a while he did not settle easily to composition. It was quite possibly at Gardiner's suggestion as a kind of therapy that he made a transcription for piano duet of the Delius orchestral score which Henry Wood had introduced on 11 January 1919, *Eventyr*. Bainton, on the other hand, was in no need of any such restorative but continued in a small way to promote Gardiner's name. He had contributed a brief assessment of his works to the August 1912 issue of *Musical Opinion*. While in Holland he had played *Noel* for piano at an invitation concert given at The Hague on 12 July 1918 by the British interned civilians. Then after his release he gave two identical concerts in Amsterdam and The Hague with the Concertgebouw Orchestra. The *Overture to a Comedy* shared the programme with works by Bridge, Coleridge-Taylor, Delius, Elgar, Grainger and Stanford (the Amsterdam *Algemeen Handelsblad* critic detecting the influence of *Die Meistersinger* on Gardiner's overture). Before the war Bainton had been professor of piano and composition at the Newcastle-upon-Tyne Conservatoire to which he returned after leaving Holland. There he did not miss an opportunity of giving Gardiner's works, including pieces by Scott and Gardiner in a recital in December 1919 and conducting *Shepherd Fennel's Dance* in March 1920. Gardiner in turn was probably responsible for Bainton's *Concerto-Fantasia* for piano and orchestra being played under the composer's direction at a Royal Philharmonic Society concert in 1922. (In other performances the composer was often the soloist.) Much later, in 1934, Bainton went to Australia to take up the appointment of director of the State Conservatoire in Sydney.

There were a few other performances worthy of note in 1919. At an RCM concert on 14 February Stanford conducted *The Recruit* with W. Topliss Green as soloist (possibly the last time the orchestral version was heard). At an Oriana concert in the Aeolian Hall on 10 April Gardiner's two settings of traditional tunes, *The Three Ravens* and *The Hunt is up*, were given, the latter receiving its first performance. The Oriana Madrigal Society was at that time particularly grateful to Gardiner for his continued – if anonymous – support, something to which Kennedy Scott alluded in a *Musical Times* article in October 1920 when he wrote: 'The Society also owes a debt of utmost gratitude to one without whose disinterested help, especially during the past few difficult years, we could hardly have survived. He would dislike public mention of his name, but his brother musicians will know to whom I refer.'[15] Both words and melodies of Gardiner's two part-songs were familiar to the Oriana singers as the settings by Thomas Ravenscroft and John Benet were well established in their repertoire. At the turn of the century Grainger had also set these two tunes and Gardiner had heard him play his version of *The Three Ravens* in 1902. When much later he compared Grainger's with his own he was relieved to find himself free of any 'unconscious plagiarism'; his own had been 'entirely different, not so original in some ways, but with equal harmonic resource', he wrote to Grainger on 20 June 1938.

Gardiner was represented at the 1919 Proms by both the *Overture to a Comedy* and *Shepherd Fennel's Dance*. On 29 November Sir Frederick Bridge conducted the Royal Choral Society in *News from Whydah* and the same month Gardiner was able to make his first post-war visit to Grez. After being away from their home for so long the Deliuses had at last returned to France, taking *en route* a holiday in their beloved Norway, as well as spending some time in Frankfurt where they attended the rehearsals and first performance of *Fennimore and Gerda*. During the year Gardiner had added his name to an artistic group calling itself 'The Plough Club' whose chief aim was to present works of art, whether of a dramatic, musical or literary nature, that were of sufficient merit and originality to commend themselves. Arnold and Clifford Bax served on the committee and Charles Kennedy Scott also became a member. In the months that followed, Kennedy Scott was to see a great deal of Balfour Gardiner who, with his benevolent outlook, embarked on yet another venture.

9 Philharmonic patronage

1919–1922

'I have a certain influence with the Philharmonic now', Balfour Gardiner wrote to Percy Grainger on 25 June 1919, and so began the last phase of his patronage of music. For it was through the Royal Philharmonic Society that he was able to continue the promotion of concerts he had begun in 1912, but this time in a way that brought him less personal hardship and fewer upsets. At the beginning of the war the Society had been in difficulties that were for a while resolved by the appearance of Beecham who, as well as giving considerable financial backing, took charge of the programmes for four seasons from 1914 until 1918. When his support temporarily wavered after the second season and the Society seemed destined for hard times without his artistic and financial assitance, he eventually agreed to continue his association under certain exacting conditions which gave him tighter control over the Society's activities. An agreement was drawn up with Beecham being elected both director and chairman of any meetings he attended, while his right-hand man Donald Baylis was nominated honorary secretary. Between them they had absolute control over the programmes which naturally reflected Beecham's predilections, with British works making a frequent appearance. During Beecham's reign Gardiner's *Fantasy* was given for the first time in its revised version and Delius, Scott, O'Neill and Austin were all represented.

But Beecham's complete control had robbed the Society of its independence and the Board of Directors of any influence: indeed, there had been no board meetings between October 1917 and July 1918. When an approach was made in July 1918 to rectify matters, Beecham immediately resigned, leaving the Society without the financial support it had enjoyed throughout the war years. It was at this juncture that Balfour Gardiner stepped in. Robert Elkin, the Society's historian, has written in *Royal Philharmonic*:

That great patron of music, Mr H. Balfour Gardiner, promised to guarantee £1200, to be called up if necessary after the ordinary guarantors had paid ten per cent of their guarantees, and with the very reasonable proviso that, if he were called upon to pay more than £500, he was to decide the number of concerts to be given at the next season, also the conductors and soloists to be engaged; it being his hope that he would co-operate with the Society not only for the current season but for a number of years. (It may be added here that Mr Balfour Gardiner not only renewed his guarantees but paid out very substantial sums in subsequent years: and that although he retained the right to veto any drastic alteration in the Society's policy which might arise from some unfortunate and unexpected cause, never in fact interfered with the management of the concerts.)[1]

From the autumn of 1919 he regularly attended the director's meetings, probably co-opted in an ex-officio capacity with a voice in the choosing of programmes. One of his first steps was to make his own personal list of works for possible inclusion in the Society's concerts. With the notable absence of his own works, this list contained many by his friends: Cyril Scott's (First) Piano Concerto; Bax's *Spring Fire* and *Nympholept* (neither in fact to be performed in Gardiner's or Bax's lifetime); a symphony and *The Baron of Brackley* by W.H. Bell; several choral and orchestral works by Delius; and others by Grainger, Holst (including *Neptune*) and Poldowski. To these he added works on a wider repertoire, seasoning his suggestions of more familiar pieces with less frequently heard works like Berlioz's *Harold in Italy* and Fauré's *Ballade* for piano and orchestra. Much farther off the beaten track were works by some of Gardiner's contemporaries: van Dieren's *Comedy Overture*, Florent Schmitt's *Hymne à l'été* for three unaccompanied choruses; and, from America, John Alden Carpenter's Piano Concerto and Rubin Goldmark's *Requiem*. Also down for consideration were the Breton composer Paul Ladmirault, the Swiss Othmar Schoeck, and Albert Volkmann, a German composer of an earlier generation who had been much encouraged by Schumann. All these and many more made up a rough list that reflects a musical mind more adventurous and farther reaching than the rather insular restrictions of Gardiner's pre-war British music concerts might suggest. And while only a few of the works he put down found their way into the concerts, and his personal list no doubt underwent many changes and additions, there were few concerts in the three years of his close association that did not contain at least one work in which he would have shown a special interest.

Following Beecham's resignation the concerts were entrusted to Adrian Boult, Albert Coates, Hamilton Harty, Landon Ronald and Geoffrey Toye who shared the conducting in the first three post-war seasons. Gardiner kept in touch with each of them, lunching with Boult, several times playing host to Toye and his wife, and contacting Coates who was responsible for several important Delius performances (a debt acknowledged in the dedication to Coates of the *North Country Sketches*). Although the programmes for the 1919-20 season were largely left to Gardiner to arrange, he did not have the autonomy he had enjoyed with his own concerts. There were too many factors preventing a programme on paper becoming a reality, and as early as 23 October 1919 he wrote to Heseltine: 'I am disgusted with the making of programmes,

& the contretemps they involve.' (Heseltine had offered to write the programme notes but that task had already been allocated. He nevertheless made suggestions for inclusion, van Dieren's name among them.)

Balfour Gardiner's steady financial assistance covered a three-year period up to the end of the 1921-2 season, with a few contributions at a later date. The records show that in 1920 he made three payments to the Society totalling about £650, the next year he gave £610, and the year after £500. This was by no means the limit to his aid. For example, when in 1921 Bell visited England and conducted his own *Symphonic Variations* at a Philharmonic concert on February 24, Gardiner paid for the parts to be copied for that performance.

But it was in the formation of the Philharmonic Choir that he showed the keenest interest. For several months he had given much thought to the matter. From the foundation of the Oriana Madrigal Society Kennedy Scott had proved himself a choral trainer of outstanding ability. He had constantly widened his musical horizons (no doubt partly through Gardiner's encouragement) and tackled works that made increasing demands both technically and numerically on the forces under him. It soon became apparent that the larger-scale works demanded a chorus stronger than the existing Oriana choir, and so by October 1919 the Philharmonic Choir was formed with Kennedy Scott as its conductor. Totalling about three hundred, it had a large professional strengthening, especially in the tenor section, and these expenses were chiefly met by Gardiner who paid out £500 in the first year of its existence. Stainton de B. Taylor, who sang for many years under Kennedy Scott's baton, wrote of Gardiner's patronage:

From the first this far-seeing, generous friend of music was a strong supporter of Scott's, devoting his pecuniary resources to bringing forward the music in which he believed – that of his own countrymen. Delius, Holst, Bax, Dale, Grainger and many others owed much to him, and his help enabled Scott to realise many of his dearest dreams. Gardiner was a prime mover in the foundation of the Philharmonic Choir, which indeed, he personally made financially possible.[2]

He rarely missed an opportunity for his friends' works to be given. To Rose Grainger he wrote on 11 September 1919: 'As well as the Oriana, [Kennedy Scott] is taking on the new Philharmonic Choir which I am supporting, and tomorrow, when I go to town, I shall hear how the Choir is forming. I hope it will be a good one: we have put down *Morning Song in the Jungle* & *Father & Daughter* for performance.'

Gardiner's hope was fully realised. The choir's excellence soon became a by-word in musical circles. Stainton de B. Taylor continued:

If the London critics were at first far from unanimous in their praises it was at least obvious that Kennedy Scott had brought into being a musical instrument of a new and vital importance . . . By 1922 the choir had firmly established itself and was winning almost unstinted praise from even the sternest of the critics. It was commended for its loveliness of tone, for its power to draw and sustain long level lines of choral sound, for its command over every difficulty of technique, for its enthusiasm and staying power.

Its availability now made it possible for choral works to appear more frequently in the Philharmonic concerts. It first came before the public on 26 February 1920. Kennedy Scott conducted a Bach motet and Coates gave the first performance of Delius's *The Song of the High Hills,* completing the evening with Beethoven's Choral Symphony. The choir's second appearance, at the next Philharmonic concert, was a memorable occasion. Kennedy Scott conducted a Bach cantata, the two above-mentioned Grainger items, *News from Whydah*, and orchestral works by Handel and Wagner. But the success of the concert was crowned by the first performance of Holst's *Hymn of Jesus.* Fifteen days earlier this work had two 'run-throughs' with piano accompaniment in an RCM Choral Class concert, and when Holst conducted it on 25 March there was a great demand for an immediate encore. While that was not considered possible the same evening, another performance was nevertheless arranged for 2 June when Coates also repeated *The Song of the High Hills.*

The Delius score was one of many that Balfour Gardiner handled, and Grainger recalled a particular problem which arose when the proofs were later being corrected:

Gardiner kept asking about a kettle-drum passage . . . in which the kettle-drummer, with only 4 drums, was required to play 5 different notes and with no time to tune between them. Gardiner insisted that the passage, as printed, could not be played. But all he got out of Delius was: 'I don't know how he plays them; I only know he *does* play them.' Gardiner was disconsolate: 'The trouble is that the drummer does *not* play the 5th note, but Fred never notices it.'[3]

(There was some justifiable confusion on Gardiner's part for, while the published score in fact specifies two drummers, even so Jelka Delius could write to Grainger on 4 April 1924 that 'Fred wants me to tell you – the score of S. of H.H. only *two* drummers are marked – But that is a mistake, there ought to be *3* . . . ')[4]

Grainger also had much to do with *The Song of the High Hills*: he prepared the chorus for a Delius birthday performance at Frankfurt in 1923; that same year he made an arrangement for two pianos, and on 28 April 1924 he conducted the American première, repeating it two days later, with yet another performance in 1926. Gardiner possessed a copy of Grainger's two-piano version and he requested another so that he and Kennedy Scott could play the work to Delius when they visited him at Grez. The upshot of this collaboration was most satisfactory, as he related to Grainger on 20 March 1926:

I went over to Grez again at Christmas, taking with me Kennedy Scott. We worked for a couple of hours a day at the Song of the High Hills, the second piano part of which reached me in plenty of time . . . We gave old Fred two performances of it, & he was delighted. A further result of this arrangement of yours, you will be glad to hear, is that CKS, having had the advantage of studying & discussing it at Grez, gave a good performance of it in London a couple of weeks ago. The tempi were almost perfect: the chorus perfect, absolutely. The orchestra, on the other hand, left a certain amount to be desired: this is Kennedy Scott's weak point.

Even Jelka Delius had occasion to comment that 'Kennedy Scott is no good as an orchestral conductor tho' unrivalled as a chorus trainer.'[5]

Delius had attended the Philharmonic Choir's first concert. He was clearly impressed with 'that lovely Kennedy Scott chorus'[6] and expressed a desire to hear them sing his *Mass of Life* before he died – even if, as he put it, it meant ending up 'in an urn at Golder's Green'.[7] His rapidly declining health prevented him from hearing them give many performances of his works, including the *Mass* under Paul von Klenau in 1925 and Kennedy Scott in 1928. But his wish was ultimately granted when he was persuaded to cross from France for the 1929 Delius Festival at which Beecham's conducting of the *Mass* with the Philharmonic Choir was a fitting climax to the six concerts.

Through his connections with the Royal Philharmonic Society Gardiner once or twice tried to secure engagements for deserving friends. He had hoped that Grainger would be able to play at one of the 1920-1 concerts and even conduct his *magnum opus*, *The Warriors*. While that did not prove possible owing to Grainger's commitments elsewhere, he was able to assist the violinist Dorothy Lambert (who went under the professional name of Murray Lambert). Six years older than Gardiner, she had occasionally been with him and the Austins on their holidays at Chapel St Leonards on the Lincolnshire coast. She played at Oriana concerts in 1918, 1921 and 1922, and at a Philharmonic concert in January 1921 when she was the soloist in Hamilton Harty's Violin Concerto. Many years later with much gratitude she remembered Gardiner as a 'wonderful friend' in her professional career.

Only once did he use his influence with the Society for his own benefit, and even then in very small measure. At intervals during the war years when in a composing mood he had turned to an orchestral *Ballad*, about which he wrote to Grainger on 31 March 1919:

I generally get tired of my stuff soon after it is finished, but I have constantly thought of this Ballad during my three years' military service & I like it as much as ever – so much so that I want to get it published as soon as ever I have heard it at rehearsal. And as regards this I want your advice. It is unfortunately not a popular work & will not make its way by itself like Shepherd Fennel, and I don't think it is likely to be played much even if it is pushed. It will certainly have no chance whatever if it is *not* pushed, & I must get it brought to the notice of all the prominent conductors as soon as it is printed. How would you set about it if you were in my place? . . . I am so fond of the work that I do not want it to be entirely wasted, & as long as it is published & has a tolerable number of performances that is all I care. There are one or two other works I have the same sort of feeling about. Bax's 'In the Faery Hills', Austin's 'Spring Rhapsody', & your own first version of the 'Hill-song'.

He even contemplated a joint publication of his *Ballad,* those of his friends' works he mentioned that were close to his heart, and a new orchestral score by Delius. This was not mere enthusiasm of the moment as on 11 September he wrote to Rose Grainger:

I have been at the Ballad again . . . This is the 5th or 6th time I have altered it, and it gets considerably better each time – I have come to the conclusion that it must have been *very* bad at first. I shall not score it now, but put it by for six months, or until I am certain there is absolutely no more to be done to it.

The *Ballad* must have been scored at some stage of its early reworking as in the spring of 1919 he took the score and parts to one of Geoffrey Toye's Philharmonic rehearsals for a run-through. But Toye had only twenty-five minutes left at the end of the rehearsal and the orchestra, being tired, was not keen on giving much attention to a work not down for the concert in hand. So Gardiner took the work back to Ashampstead where he reworked the score further.

The *Ballad* remained for a while uppermost in his mind. Writing to Grainger on 14 October 1919 he drew comparison with *The Joyful Homecoming* which was then receiving a handful of performances:

I sometimes think that these are the only pieces of mine that will ever have, or deserve to have, a success – those that are done in a few hours & come to one in a wave of enthusiasm, not those that one labours at for months. All the same, I am longing for the recognition of one of my more important works, the *Ballad* for example, that I have toiled at, on or off, these last four years. I think I have got it really good by now.

Before leaving for France to visit Delius, he noted a reminder to take the score to the RCM on 27 November to be considered for a Patron's Fund rehearsal at which selected new scores were now given a public run-through instead of the more formal concert that had been the practice before the war. The *Ballad for Orchestra* was one of four works accepted for a two-hour rehearsal followed by a complete run-through on the morning of 27 February 1920, with either the composer or Adrian Boult conducting the London Symphony Orchestra; since then the score has disappeared. To get any nearer to the missing work one must read what one can into the *Times* brief report that 'Mr Balfour Gardiner's ballad for orchestra moves rather heavily, but thinks and dreams as it goes', and that of the *Morning Post* which found it

a characteristic piece of work of the right quality, since its idiom is thoroughly British, and its expression charged with feeling both for expression and colour.

The rehearsal of it should be of help to the composer, since it must have made it clear to him that condensation is required. Shortened the piece will prove as representative as anything this composer has written, which is saying much.[8]

It is in keeping with the quixotic side to Gardiner's nature that a work for which he had shown such enthusiasm should be allowed to fade away while his attention was drawn to the work of others.

Delius came over to England in February to attend several important performances of his works including *The Song of the High Hills*, the Double Concerto, and his opera *A Village Romeo and Juliet*. He stayed first with the O'Neills for about a fortnight and then for several days at Ashampstead with Gardiner, including one 'delightful afternoon'[9] spent in Oxford. He was back at Grez towards the end of March. Gardiner and Kennedy Scott took a holiday together in Spain that spring, returning near the beginning of May. Spain, as mentioned before, was a country for which Gardiner felt a strong attachment and it had been very much in his musical thoughts. Earlier that year he had been working on the most striking and least conventional of his piano pieces, *Salamanca*. He wrote to Grainger on 8 May: 'I am turning my thoughts more towards piano & small combinations at present. My liking for the orchestra & indeed my capability for writing for it, seems to be on the wane.'

After the full orchestra, in *Salamanca* he began to explore the more limited potential of the piano. While its title might suggest pleasant memories of that Spanish city, the substance of the piece is far from relaxed, and surviving sketches give a fascinating clue to its origin. '25.2.20 At night: from a dream. Salamanca. Waters under a bridge (Thought also of 'cellos & D♭ doing it divisi)', he wrote above the first sketch, and as was often his habit he worked on much of it by night. The work took shape quickly and, as befits many a dream, the finished piece is moody, sombre, dark-hued. In it he has forsaken melodic line for sonority, harmony for dissonance. The opening moves slowly in three unison lines, the upper two being two octaves apart (becoming the bass line in example 23). The music occasionally goes into three staves, and brief but rapidly oscillating figures play an important part (example 23).

He was clearly fascinated by the effects he found possible to bring off, relishing the stark sonorities offset by dissonant clashes. One tender figure *piano dolcissimo* he singled out – 'This chord sounds ravishing!' (example 24). The ending, with both the conflict and tonality unresolved, dies away with soft irregular spread chords suggesting the rippling waters of the work's inspiration. He himself described the work in a letter to Grainger on 8 May 1920 as 'very serious, difficult & unlike anything I have ever done', and while not all his fellow composers seemed to share his opinion, he thought it his best piano piece to date. It explores, on a smaller canvas, a turbulent vista similar to the 'tragic landscape' of Bax's *Winter Waters* for piano (1915).

Ex. 23

Ex. 24

His Spanish holiday was a great tonic: he declared it the most wonderful he had ever had in his life. But with his frequently indifferent health he complained that year of mild heart trouble which caused him further restlessness. He attempted to cut down on his smoking and restrict himself to a meagre allowance of one pipe and cigar a day with occasional days of complete abstention, but his craving for tobacco proved stronger than his will. Soon after his return from Spain he felt less well and lapsed once more into an unmusical mood.

On 19 October *The Three Ravens* provided an unconventional opening to the Liverpool Philharmonic Society's first concert of the season when Dr Pollitt conducted the part-song before Landon Ronald took over the main orchestral part of the programme. Gardiner's name was certainly not new to Liverpool as *News from Whydah* had twice appeared in their Philharmonic programmes, once with Henry Wood and more recently under Pollitt's baton. The next month Gardiner journeyed north by train to Newcastle to attend a special concert on 20 November, mainly devoted to his unaccompanied choral works. W.G. Whittaker conducted *The Stage Coach*, *The Hunt is up*, *The Three Ravens*, and the first performance of a Masefield setting, *An Old Song Re-sung*. There must have been some doubt as to whether Gardiner would make the effort to be present for, although one cannot be absolutely sure that he is referring to this and not an earlier occasion, Holst had written to Whittaker on 26 April: 'Certainly I would ask Balfour. If he doesn't want to come he'll say so (he does not love the North!) but in any case he will like being asked especially if you type the letter! Your script grows more wonderful each time.'[10] Gardiner showed his gratitude to Whittaker for performing his works by dedicating to him a group of five piano pieces published in 1922 under the general title of *Shenadoah*. Perhaps intentionally, in some places the sparser textures and quasi-folksong elements draw the set geographically closer to Whittaker's beloved Northumbrian region.

Towards the end of 1920 Gardiner was more active. He checked the proofs of Holst's *Beni Mora* (first performed at his 1912 concerts) for publication the following year, he attended the first London performance of Arnold Bax's symphonic poem *November Woods* at a Philharmonic concert on 16 December, and meanwhile he was collaborating with Arnold's brother Clifford in two very differrent works. The first was a song, *Rybbesdale*, a setting of an old English text adapted by Clifford. Begun that November, it had to wait a year and a half for its completion. This vigorous song, in contradiction to Gardiner's too frequent moods of despondency, exudes great confidence. Its bold sweeping lines enjoy much freedom of metre (see example 3, p. 40) and it displays the assurance one finds in Peter Warlock when in a boisterous mood. The other collaboration concerned Clifford Bax's play for children, *Old King Cole*, for which Balfour Gardiner started to compose the music that December. This three-act play makes much use of familiar nursery rhymes like *Jack and Jill*, *Humpty Dumpty*, and *Ride a Cock Horse*. Gardiner used again the traditional tune of *London Bridge* but in a version simpler than the one found in his *Five Pieces* for piano published in 1911. The piano score occupied him all December and the same month he began scoring some of it for a small orchestra of flute, clarinet, bassoon, trumpet, horn, drums and percussion and five strings. Unfortunately the scoring does not appear to have been completed. It is not known whether any performances took place, but the manuscript piano score has survived.

As well as *Salamanca*, that year saw the publication of a Gardiner piano piece that would surely grace any recitalist's programme as a short but effective encore, leaving an audience eagerly enquiring its composer's name. Though short in length, the *Second Prelude* is of considerable charm and strength, its gentle opening figure returning at the end richly harmonised (example 25) and building to a powerful yet finely controlled climax.

Ex. 25

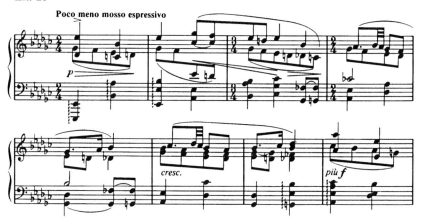

Early in 1921 the musical world was deeply shocked to hear of the accidental death of Gervase Elwes on 12 January in Boston, USA, where he had fallen from the station platform and been several times struck on the head by a departing train. Elwes had been especially renowned for his oratorio singing, notably the name part in Elgar's *Dream of Gerontius*. His memory was dear to the Frankfurt Group and to Roger Quilter in particular who wrote: 'I feel suddenly as if my life and my work had lost their significance.'[11] Cyril Scott and Percy Grainger shared this sense of loss, and in a brief tribute Balfour Gardiner paid his respects to a great singer: 'I regarded him as the embodiment of a certain ideal I have always cherished. I shall always remember him with affection and with something like reverence.'[12]

That month Gardiner wrote to the Philharmonic directors, once again offering to make up the programmes for the coming season. On the last day in March he took a month's holiday in the Pyrenees and Spain, missing a performance on 13 April of *Shepherd Fennel's Dance* which opened the Bournemouth Festival of English Music. Neither was he present on his return at a reception held at the Grafton Galleries, London, in honour of Rachmaninov. Many prominent musicians were there for a programme of works by living English composers, in which

Herbert Heyner sang *The Stranger's Song.* Gardiner generally avoided official functions, at which he felt ill-at-ease. He preferred instead the private company of friends like Gustav Holst. Shortly after his return from Spain they had tea together in Reading, and in July Gustav stayed at Ashampstead for a couple of days, being collected from University College by Cox the chauffeur and driven to Balfour's cottage. They were probably together again in September at Hereford where Holst was conducting his *Hymn of Jesus* at the Three Choirs Festival. In between a rehearsal on the fifth and the concert on the morning of the eighth, Gardiner planned a fleeting visit to Kerry where he had been stationed for much of his war service. Then on 22 October he visited Holst at St Paul's Girls' School in Hammersmith. One of the Holst scores he had been looking at that year was *Hecuba's Lament* for contralto, chorus and orchestra, a work he had hoped to have performed before the First World War dashed such concert plans, and it is likely that he was now helping prepare it for publication the following year.

Throughout the autumn he was feeling remarkably well and thankful to be free from any ailments. He took to cycling and walking again and attempted further restraint in his smoking to preserve his present euphoria. At the end of the year he gratefully accepted the dedication of Quilter's *As You Like It* suite. The Frankfurt Group were not now the constant companions they had once been, especially as Grainger had taken up residence in America, and during 1920 and 1921 Cyril Scott had been touring America. Nevertheless they did not sever the bonds of close friendship, something that Grainger particularly strove to preserve. Such mutual dedications strengthened the links and Gardiner returned Quilter's compliment by dedicating to him *A Sailors' Piece* for piano, doubtless in part a private joke for the obvious similarity it bears to the *Gumsuckers March* from Grainger's *In a Nutshell* suite.

In the last quarter of 1921 Gardiner was an interested observer of another's efforts at concert promotion. The 28-year-old Eugene Goossens had found financial backing for a series of four concerts of modern music he was to conduct at Queen's Hall. The works to be played were by no means exclusively British, though of Gardiner's intimate circle Cyril Scott, Bax and Holst were well represented by their *Aubade, The Garden of Fand* and *Beni Mora* respectively. The Goossens series was representative of the much-changed musical climate in England, the most exciting new element being the current vogue for Stravinsky whose name had first come to the fore with the pre-war Diaghilev seasons of Russian ballet in London. In June that year Goossens had given the first concert performance in England of *Le sacre du printemps* to a full Queen's Hall, with the composer in the dress circle, and he repeated it at the last of his four concerts on 12 December which Gardiner attended, dining beforehand with Arnold Bax. The names of Malipiero, Satie, Milhaud, Roussel, Poulenc, de Falla, Debussy, Ravel and Honegger lent a distinctively Continental flavour to the programmes, and this influence from abroad, particularly of those composers including Stravinsky who were centred on Paris, was apparent in the music of the youngest English composer represented, Arthur Bliss. There was the daring inclusion of Schoenberg's *Five Orchestral Pieces* which nine years previously had been hissed at the Proms, but so as not 'to gild the pill of overmuch contemporary music, and to bolster the sagging subscription list'[13] Goossens included several less demanding scores by Bach, Rossini, Rimsky-Korsakov and Richard Strauss, and at the last moment substituted Brahms's First Symphony for Stravinsky's *Song of the Nightingale*. But even so he noted a response to his own concerts similar to that which had greeted Gardiner's, that 'while the pit and gallery were thronged, circle and stalls showed depressingly empty spaces'.[14] He even considered bringing the series to a premature end, but was dissuaded from doing so by friends. Nevertheless it was apparent, as Gardiner had observed, that with rising prices after the war there was no increase in audiences but quite the reverse, with the result that the financial loss on concerts was greater than ever.

In 1922 Gardiner was elected an honorary member of the Royal Academy of Music. He was as busy as ever entertaining friends, including the O'Neills, Holst, and Arnold Bax, who in May brought with him John Ireland whose recently completed symphonic rhapsody *Mai-Dun* had featured in the final concert of Goossens' series. At that time Grainger sent a six-handed piano arrangement of *The Warriors* to Gardiner who managed to persuade Bax, Austin and Harriet Cohen to play the work through so that he could pass on advice to its composer. But that year was to be overhung with sorrow. The first blow came in April when Grainger's mother, after a sharp deterioration in her mental health, committed suicide, plunging fourteen storeys from a New York apartment to her death.

10 'None shall revive the flame
that perisheth . . .'
1922–1924

At the time of his mother's death Percy Grainger was giving a concert in Los Angeles, and on his way back by train, fearing that even he might himself die before reaching New York, he wrote Balfour Gardiner a lengthy letter acquainting him with his financial position and requesting that he become his executor. In this emotional state he also asked Gardiner to see to the publication of all his compositions to 'place me as Australia's first great composer and make Australia's and *my mother's name* shine bright'.[1] For over two years Gardiner had already been negotiating with English publishers on Grainger's behalf. 'If I can be of any help to you over here with publishers I will gladly do what I can', he had offered on 25 July 1919, and he continued to assist in this way, if somewhat diffidently, as he had asked Grainger on 15 December the same year: '. . . give me definite instructions & do not merely tell me to make the best terms possible, as I am very bad at bargaining and always let people get the better of me'. The tragedy deepened their friendship. For his part Grainger tried to shake off the grief by throwing himself into hard work, and in August he sailed from America to Scandinavia where after folk-song collecting in Denmark he embarked on a five-week concert tour of Norway.

There was also sadness from another quarter. Delius was now showing visible signs of syphilis which he had contracted many years before, with oncoming blindness and paralysis beginning to make their mark. For several years he was to seek a cure in Germany. As far back as 1910 he had entered a Swiss sanatorium where a doctor diagnosed that his central nervous system was affected. Now at the beginning of 1922 he visited a sanatorium in Wiesbaden from where he wrote on 28 March to Heseltine: 'Balfour Gardiner just writes me that he would love to go and see me at Wiesbaden but cannot bear to travel without a companion, and Bax and Austin cannot go. I shall write him at once & suggest he should invite you.' As it turned out the two did not make the journey together, but in September Gardiner crossed to Norway and joined the Deliuses at their mountain chalet near the little village of Lesjaskog, in Gudbrandsdalen. When he saw Delius he was utterly shocked by the impact of his friend's deteriorating condition. Sailing home to England much later, he wrote to Grainger:

14 Percy Grainger, in many respects the most outstanding member of the
Frankfurt Group, with his mother Rose not long before her death in
April 1922: a photograph sent to Balfour Gardiner and inscribed,
'Loving New Year wishes to dear old Balfour from us both [signed]
Percy Jan 1922'

145

All you told me about your dear mother saddened me unspeakably, and the revelation about Delius was a great blow. I find now I do not thoroughly get over these things: the memories of friends killed in the war, and of those who have suffered or are still suffering during their lifetime, leave their mark on me. But I will no longer speak of these things: one must carry on with a pretence of wearing a brave heart & with unapparent grief. (9 September 1922)

While staying with Delius at Lesjaskog, Gardiner worked on what was to be his last large-scale score, *Philomela*. This was a setting for tenor soloist, female chorus and orchestra of Matthew Arnold's poem of the same name, which evokes the Greek legend of King Tereus, his wife Procne and her sister Philomela. After dishonouring her, Tereus cut out Philomela's tongue so that she could not tell his wife of his misconduct. But Philomela made the truth known by embroidering her tale onto a peplos which she sent to Procne – 'the too clear web, and thy dumb sister's shame'. Procne took revenge by cutting up her son and serving it to the king. With Tereus in pursuit, all three were changed by the Gods into birds, Philomela (literally the lover of song) becoming the classical nightingale. In this beautiful and haunting work, it was a masterly stroke to give the dumb Philomela expression through the chorus's occasional wordless exclamations of 'ei-aa', sharply accentuating the passion and pain predominant in the text. Just as Grainger had attempted to 'wrench the listener's heart' through his music, so in *Philomela* there is an almost unbearable poignancy approaching that of another work in which a bird has become the personification of human sorrow and suffering, *Sea Drift*.

With *Philomela*, as in the similarly proportioned *April* of 1913, it is hardly surprising with someone so intimately associated with the works of Delius to be able to detect signs of the older man's influence. As early as 12 February 1908 one finds Gardiner thanking Delius for a copy of *A Mass of Life* and adding: 'I am reading it with great interest, & I hope profit, as I am trying to do a choral work myself', that work probably being *A Corymbus for Autumn*. There were certainly times when they discussed music together, for Gardiner admitted to Grainger that he had altered one chord in his own setting of *The Three Ravens* on Delius's advice. Grainger's music they also discussed. 'He was quick in noting any harmonic weakness', Gardiner wrote on 11 April 1943. 'He once criticised your *Father and Daughter* very sharply, saying that the music was quite in variance with the tragic words.'

Quite how much criticism and advice Delius gave to Gardiner one cannot tell; whether it went beyond the occasional comment passed either on glancing at a score or hearing it being tried out on the piano, or whether indeed, as is rather questionable, Gardiner was in the habit of freely bringing forward his compositions in Delius's presence. With their

146

15   Frederick and Jelka Delius in Norway, *c.* 1921

similar musical outlook and their common harmonic language, this influence was more one of example than the kind to excite imitation. Gardiner did not drink so deeply of the Delian wine as to write unconsciously 'second-hand' Delius as a few like Moeran and Warlock came close to; never inviting the direct comparison with a specific Delius work as does C.W. Orr's song *Soldier from the Wars Returning* with the 'sad waters of separation' from *Songs of Sunset*. The admirable pointing of woodwind in both *April* and *Philomela* is perhaps an unspoken acknowledgement of Delius's mastery in that sphere, while the use of wordless voices in parts of *Philomela* may be attributed to either Delius's or Grainger's example. Grainger, after employing 'wordless syllables' in such works as his *Brigg Fair* and *Irish Tune from County Derry*, claimed to have influenced Delius[2] who used them to notable effect to express some visionary state of ecstasy in *A Mass of Life* and *The Song of the High Hills*; in the former a Nietzschean dance of Life, and in the latter a paean of Nature worship. Even in *An Arabesque*, *Philomela*'s closest Delian counterpart, for two bars the chorus are required to sing to 'Ah' as an enlightening commentary on a mystical moment of enchantment within the text.

In *Philomela* the key-note is not rapture but pain, the first bar of example 26 providing the pattern for later repeated cries of 'ei-aa'. The work begins after a one-bar flourish with the tenor soloist whose opening line is immediately taken up and developed by the women's voices (example 27). One other important idea (example 28) becomes the grief-laden phrase with which the work ends, to the dying wordless cries of the chorus. The scoring throughout underlines the classical and pastoral elements in the text, for example the cor anglais commentary on the

Ex. 26

148

Ex. 27

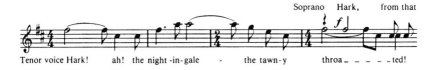

Ex. 28

'wanderer from a Grecian shore' and, at a mention of the English countryside with 'its cool trees, and night, and the sweet, tranquil Thames',
an almost Holstian moment as flutes, clarinets, celesta and harp
alternate on two chords. Like the rapturous *April*, the melancholy *Philomela* is a work of consummate mastery and striking individuality, and
its almost total neglect is an unaccountable loss.

From Lesjaskog Gardiner went on to Christiania (now Oslo) where
quite unexpectedly at the Grand Hotel he met Grainger who had just
started his Norwegian tour. It was their first meeting for eight years, and
when they saw each other after so long an interval, Gardiner threw up his
arms in a characteristic gesture (that could apply equally in moments of
scorn), declaring, 'How young!' Much to Grainger's delight he decided
to accompany him on the tour, a decision that touched Grainger deeply,
and he later lovingly referred to Gardiner as the only one of his friends
who was willing to go anywhere to be with him after his mother's death.
The tour proved how much a creature of habit Gardiner was. Grainger's
recitals generally began at eight o'clock each evening. But Gardiner was
accustomed to having his evening meal at that precise time and would not
take it any earlier. As the hotel dinners were usually over by six-thirty,
special arrangements had to be made for him to be served in his own
room at eight. Consequently he regularly missed three-quarters of each
recital, though he insisted on purchasing a ticket and would afterwards
apologise profusely to Grainger for being late. Gardiner prided himself
on his punctuality and frowned on anyone who did not adhere to

appointed schedules. He was once persuaded by Oxford friends to go with them to the cinema, but when after five minutes the film had not begun at the advertised time he summoned the manager and had words with him.

Grainger's athleticism was much in evidence on the tour. One day, while Gardiner covered the distance to the next town on their itinerary by carriage, Grainger trotted alongside. In one town they were photographed together, a rare moment as Gardiner normally shunned the camera, considering himself with typical self-deprecation to be 'hideous'. When after ten days they reached Flekkefjord on the South-West coast, Gardiner suddenly decided to take the post-boat back along the coast to Christiania and make his way via Germany and France to Dover. Grainger tried in vain to point out to him that if he stayed on for another two days he would be able to take a much better boat from Bergen which would get him home more quickly. But, with his mind made up, Gardiner could not be shaken from his resolve. When he waved good-bye to Percy as the boat drew away from Flekkefjord, there were tears in Balfour's eyes.

The journey home that he had chosen in the whim of a moment did not turn out to be a pleasant one. The social scars of war were plainly visible everywhere and his racial prejudices, much in keeping with Grainger's, came to the fore. He wrote to Grainger on 29 September while sailing home:

After all the rattling, jolting, swaying, pitching & tossing to which I have been subjected, I feel as if I should like to sit in my garden without moving for a month. At Hamburg I was compelled to wait about three hours in a room with an appalling collection of emigrants, some of whom looked more like animals dressed up than like human beings. I never felt racial affinities and repulsions so keenly. The Jewish element is the most distressing, and is of course just as prominent among first-class passengers as any other: but the low-type Germans are pretty bad also. I longed to be back among Scandinavians again.

Writing of that tour, Grainger said that Balfour Gardiner was 'a sweet companion. I could have been happy spending part of each year with him, joining with him in concert giving and other musical policies and hearing the detailed criticisms of my and other music.'[3] Gardiner's critical observations could often be extremely frank, even blunt. On the evening of their surprise meeting in Christiania, Grainger had accepted a prior invitation to the American consul's house and he induced Gardiner to go with him, rather against his will. Grainger wrote in his anecdotes:

The Consul's wife knew about Country Gardens & asked me to play it, which I did. Balfour had not heard C.G. When I came to where the bass is fragmentary (because the left hand is looking after the tenor voice too) Balfour jumped up & said, 'How awful!' much to the embarrassment of the Consul's wife, who had no conception, of course, of the outspokenness of composers to each other. Balfour explained that all such fragmentary, incomplete voices (the continuations of which are imagined but never heard) were the bane of piano music.[4]

Not all such candour was accepted with equal grace. After the tour Balfour Gardiner wrote to Grainger on 22 October, expressing his dislike of the way Percy made use in his scores of certain effects such as whistles, the muted trumpet, and the harmonium. 'These sounds are, to people like Delius & myself, ghastly: in fact, everybody I know is agreed about it', he wrote. Referring to the harmonium, he drew an analogy with 'a little undersized man, poorly dressed & not smelling too sweet, who is trying to "worm his way" into your favour', and in its tone he found a 'meanness coupled with persistency, & a certain nastiness'. The muted trumpet he considered 'a noble tone deliberately debased, therefore expressive of irony, cynicism, and the like'. Whistling had for him 'the psychic character of coarseness', and a combination of all three effects would make him feel 'terribly uncomfortable' and arouse 'the wildest antagonism'. Such outspokeness naturally rankled with Grainger for some time, particularly when Gardiner added: 'So often, of leat, has my intense enjoyment of your music . . . been marred by the thought that the instrumentation would spoil it for me.' There was perhaps a note of atonement when he concluded: 'You see I am terribly touchy – a red-faced old gentleman this evening, very grumpy – and what makes it worse, I cannot give you an efficient substitute.'

The old practice of playing each other the works they were engaged on had not ceased. Work in progress during the previous summer had been Gardiner's most extended and arguably his finest piano piece, *Michael-church*. During 1922 he reworked parts of it and the next month while staying with Delius at Lesjaskog he wrote out a final copy in ink. But later, at Grainger's suggestion, he lengthened the middle section (page six of the published score). He had also wanted to extend the *meno mosso* section on page ten (example 29). 'I remember one day going quite mad about those tramping chords', he wrote to Grainger on 11 December 1923, 'wandering off into remote keys & piling up masses on masses of sound. If only one could realise those ideals! But I, at least, run on a very short chain, and am always dragged back by petty practical considerations.' In itself almost a miniature nature poem, rich in ideas and with recurring bell-like images, this optimistic piece starts with a toccata-like opening (example 30), and on its course takes in an expressive pastoral interlude (example 31), the first two bars of which briefly return at the close as a fond reminiscence. *Michaelchurch* was published in 1923.

Back at Ashampstead after his Norwegian holiday, Gardiner continued to work at *Philomela*. The peace of his environment was an added stimulus to work. 'The soft lights & outlines of the English country – everything melting –; the queer houses & hovels, the strange people, have

Ex. 29

the quality of a dream & romance after the glaring distinctness of every-thing in Germany, Denmark, Norway & Sweden', he wrote to Grainger on 10 October. 'This, I feel, is the really inspiring country. Here, there are few facts: one can think & dream as one likes, and one's thoughts & dreams are always helped. Elsewhere, devastating, oppressive, hard reality, a death-like finality which permits of no further possibilities.'

As with *A Berkshire Idyll*, it was once again in direct response to his surroundings that, in between days spent working at *Philomela*, he composed his last song, *The Quiet Garden*. The verses he had selected of the Canadian poet Frank Prewett could have hardly matched more closely his mood at the time:

> If I might have two rows of trees
> And a quiet space between
> Where stirred none, or the faintest, breeze
> And the grass stood thick and green

The song unfolds at a restful, leisurely pace in perfect accord with the aspirations of the final verse:

> Then would I take my days in ease
> And watch the butterflies
> Pensive between the rows of trees
> Parade their newest dyes.

Marked *tranquillo*, the music relies less on the melodic line, which occasionally merely alternates between two notes a tone apart, than on its inner pulse which may be likened to the peaceful flow of a river, the gentle shifts of harmony like the changing shades of sunlight filtering through the leaves on a summer's day (example 32).

Ex. 30

Ex. 31

And it was in his own Ashampstead garden, surely the inspiration of that idyllic song, that one morning at the beginning of December he left off pruning his lime trees to read news from Grainger of a short visit he was making to England early that month. On 4 December Balfour Gardiner made a point of hearing Albert Coates conduct the first performance of Bax's First Symphony at Queen's Hall ('it shakes a Promethean fist at heaven' was how one critic described that crisis-ridden work), and three days later he and Percy Grainger met once more at Roger Quilter's. That evening, with Frederic Austin, the three Frankfurt friends dined together before hearing the Philharmonic Choir sing

Ex. 32

Delius's *The Song of the High Hills*. Much farther off, on the 28th in the Belgrade Opera House, Thomas Dunhill introduced *Shepherd Fennel's Dance* to a Slav audience as part of an English music concert. This brought forth a strange comment from a local critic: 'Curious, for us, was the *Shepherd Fennel's Dance* of Balfour Gardiner, which represents the merry festivities of rural life in England. We felt how far off we are from this restrained English joy.'

After the composition of his last two solo songs, the ebullient *Rybbesdale* and the contemplative *The Quiet Garden*, both of which John Coates sang at Chelsea Town Hall on 23 January 1923, very little else was to be forthcoming from his pen. He would look through his old music notebooks in the hope of finding something worth recovering. Early in November he had found 'some splendid notes' for an orchestral work started in 1912 and he decided to go on with it. After several days of work it was put aside again until July 1924. 'After many months, thought again of the old orchestral piece I had worked at with such enthusiasm in Nov '22', he then pencilled on his sketches. 'Decided to continue it, but must first set out in order as much of it as I consider should be retained.' But as with many a work, it progressed no further. *Shenadoah (and other pieces)* for piano, begun around November 1921 and published in 1922, were partly reworkings of old sketches, the fifth piece originating from 1907. For separate publication in America he named the first two *Jesmond* and *Melcombe*, though in the original sketches *Jesmond* was at first called *Mafeking* (or 'Mafficking!' as he once wrote with Elgarian relish). The title of the set of five was to have been *Joy*, but this was changed in favour of *Shenadoah* because of the inclusion of the richly harmonised fourth piece which, while not based on the traditional sea-chanty with a similar title, derives from a kindred mould.

He dabbled now and then at works on a larger canvas. In 1921 he had sketched a few fragments of a piano concerto, and there was the constant challenge of a symphony. On 27 October 1921 he wrote in his music-book:

Elements in a piano piece I was thinking about led me to turn to the old last movement for a symphony, on which I worked Jan and Feb last year. I had almost forgotten it. I wish I could finish this movement. It would be a technical achievement, & parts of it that I have already are so good. It certainly wants a new second subject: the present one is very bad & there is a monotony of rhythm in the first part: it is as if I were goading myself on.

But old habits, especially bad ones, are hard to shake off and the following July the tone was more one of despair: 'Is not this sort of symphonic stuff wholly impossible to write without falling into all the clap trap of regular symphonic movements?' He could fall back on his technical re-source, but the well of inspiration was fast drying up. Furthermore his time was too much taken up by other interests not directly relating to composition. To friends he would shrug off his problems with such re-marks as: 'It's all so silly. I mean, these old tunes – either they go up or they go down. Why can't they do something different?' As the conductor Guy Warrack, a friend for many years, commented, it is difficult to con-ceive of a tune going sideways.

Early in 1923 Gardiner reacted with typical kindness to an incident which, though less tragic than Rose Grainger's death, was for a while to have serious consequence. On 11 February Gustav Holst, taking a re-hearsal at University College, Reading, fell from the rostrum and struck his head. The effects of that fall were to tell for two years. Gardiner immediately offered to take over Holst's teaching duties both at Reading and at the RCM. In his diary he made a note to contact W. Probert-Jones, one of Holst's pupils:

Gustav ordered 14 days entire rest. I am doing harmony & composition, will he take orchestra & choir. (The music will be Locke's Macbeth – Mr Ford's pupil will take the bass solo.) Beethoven's 1st Symphony, would Probert Jones choose some unaccompanied choral music fit for out of door singing – Gustav suggests one or two ballets, but leaves it entirely to him.

For his own harmony class he scribbled, with a touch of humour: 'Play them modern music & explain it!' He only stood in for Holst for a short period, not long enough for the fact to be recorded officially by either college, but among the students with whom he had brief contact were Maurice Jacobson, Edmund Rubbra and Guy Warrack. Holst's fourteen days' rest proved rather optimistic as later that year recurring pains in the head necessitated a much longer period of recuperation and he was compelled to take a year's complete rest. He resigned his post at Reading that year (where he was succeeded by Benjamin Dale) and at the RCM in 1924.

Holst's *Hecuba's Lament* (one of the works Gardiner had hoped to present in his projected third series of concerts in 1914) received its first London performance at Queen's Hall on March 14, Kennedy Scott conducting the Philharmonic Choir in a concert that also included *April* and *Sea Drift*. Several days later Scott and Gardiner left for a holiday in Spain. But after the glorious holiday of three years earlier, this one turned out a disaster as illness landed Gardiner in a German hospital in Madrid for a whole week. Clemens von Franckenstein, a friend since Frankfurt times, had joined them for a while in Spain, and it seems that he became the recipient of one of Balfour Gardiner's frequent and generous gifts of money. At the time Gardiner was also paying a weekly sum of eight pounds into Holst's account, just a small portion of the many kindnesses he was to show towards his fellow composer. Grainger was obviously aware of this extraordinary generosity for after Gardiner's death he wrote that 'Balfour's deeds in connection with Gustav Holst will go down in history as the great acts of a great man'.[5] Such gifts would vary from cash amounts, ordinary savings certificates, to investments in companies in which he himself had special holdings. Rather than make donations to charitable causes, he generally preferred to help the individual wherever he detected the special need, and where possible in kind instead of just cash. Needless to say, this would always be done with the utmost humility and reticence.

No finer example of the way in which he used to selfless advantage what Arnold Bax once referred to as Balfour Gardiner's 'Medici-an munificence'[6] could be found than in the case of Delius, who as a result of the war was in financial straits. With so many of his important works in the hands of German and Austrian publishing houses and the royalties from them effectively frozen, he was not receiving the return to which he was entitled. Furthermore his continual quest for a cure and medical treatment in Germany was becoming increasingly costly and was draining his capital. It seemed at one point that he might even have to sell his house at Grez to make ends meet. Balfour Gardiner quietly intervened and offered to buy the house on the understanding that Delius and Jelka would continue to live there until the death of the surviving occupant. A contract was drawn up in November 1923 and Gardiner paid the Deliuses a large sum (a brief diary entry merely records 'Policy on Grez-sur-Loing – 70,000 [francs] to Delius'), so relieving them of their immediate financial worries. Through the love of his own cottage and the seclusion it afforded him, Gardiner would have been sensitive to the anguish that a separation from Grez would have caused Delius. Both men were autocrats and while Gardiner had neither the disdainful bearing nor the hardness of character that Delius possessed, they had certain things in common: they shared a liking for the finer comforts of life in which both were connoisseurs. Purchasing the house at Grez was in itself an act of preservation – of the house and the style of life associated with it.

That year there was a poor summer. In August Gardiner went up to Kerry once more from where he wrote on the 29th to Grainger: 'I have again got to work on "Philomela" which I was struggling with in Norway, nearly a year ago, & am now certain that it will be completed, and also that it will be successful . . . I have no doubt that I have chosen exactly the right medium . . .' Other days he left free to entertain visitors at Ashampstead: the Toyes, the Milfords, the Holsts and Dale. In between his guests on 18 September he finished the score of *Philomela* but almost at once found alterations to be made and transposed the whole work down a semitone. This was done by 30 September. It had been a struggle ('after many years' was written at the end of the score) but he had faith in it. Yet the hoped-for success of which he had written was not to be and, sadly, he was never to hear a performance of what is perhaps the most passionate of his scores.

Delius was in London that September to attend the rehearsals and the first night of James Elroy Flecker's *Hassan* for which he had written the incidental music. Gardiner, who disliked travelling under the slightest adverse conditions, had not been to see him earlier that year at Frankfurt. The occupation of the Ruhr had made travel very difficult in Germany and so he had missed the celebrations there for what was mistakenly believed to be Delius's sixtieth birthday. (The error was corrected when Heseltine, Delius's biographer, checked the birth date at Somerset

House and found him to be a year older than was generally supposed.) On this September visit to England Delius spent an evening with Gardiner who, though he much enjoyed *Hassan*, was far more disturbed by the change he now saw in his friend. He wrote to Grainger on 2 October:

The performance, the production and above all the music were excellent, and Fred was delighted. I was distressed however to see him in such a truly pitiable condition – much worse than he was in Norway a year ago. I sincerely hope that he will get better living at Grez, and I am glad to be able to tell you that he has taken a very sensible step and done a thing I never thought he would do and that is, has bought a small motor car so that he can get about the country.

Delius's condition was indeed serious. The strength in his limbs was gradually disappearing; from his hands so that he had to dictate letters to his wife Jelka, and from his legs which he was exercising in vain to strengthen, so that he had more frequently to be either carried or confined to a wheelchair. After treatment in Oeynhausen, Westphalia, and a last holiday in Norway, the Deliuses went by car to Rapallo in Italy for the winter months. There they rented a villa perched high above the bay. But the elements were not kind and they found it terribly cold at times. By mid-January the weather had improved and Gardiner hoped to visit them with Arnold Bax. On 14 January 1924 Jelka sent a postcard: 'Delighted to see you & Bax here beginning of Feb. The weather is heavenly now and we are sitting in the sun on our verandah. We are quite comfortable and have at last found a piano, an old, old little Broadwood but Fred needed one to work with.' Gardiner and Bax went out to Rapallo together and Jelka wrote on 24 February to Grainger of their visit: 'They were both very nice – but stayed rather far away on the other side of the Rapallo bay, so that thin little Bax always looked exhausted when they got here – Balfour doing exercise on principle.'

One evening in April Bax again took John Ireland over to Gardiner's, and though over the years he was an infrequent visitor Gardiner and Ireland remained on friendly terms. Gustav Holst was then taking a year's rest after a nervous breakdown and Gardiner visited him that month at Thaxted. During the summer he saw Cyril Scott for the first time for many years, informing Grainger on 24 November that he had 'found him very young & boyish, & just the same, in every way, as he was years ago. I have not seen Roger lately.' That year Gardiner gratefully accepted the dedication by Heseltine of a group of three songs, the second set of *Peterisms*. Otherwise much of the time he was kept busy with repairs and alterations to his properties, and he frequently travelled to Dorset where he had shown interest in a farm. For getting to Oxford and back he often used his motor-cycle, a 650 c.c. belt-driven Triumph, from which he took a nasty fall on Applepie Hill at Compton, knocking out four teeth in the process. Covered in bruises, he was slowly recovering when he slipped downstairs and badly sprained an arm.

But more serious were internal bruises of a very different nature. His earlier disillusionment with the public's attitude to British music, his continual difficulties and lack of confidence in his own composing ability, and his increasing interest in non-musical activities were all heralding a crisis. The previous December he had written to Grainger: 'I have had a dreadful period of barrenness since finishing Philomela, and have not been so consistently unmusical for a long time.' Now, a year later, the first signs that the psychological moment had been reached came in a letter he wrote to Grainger on 21 December 1924:

But, as usual, I shall disappoint you, though I feel vexed & ashamed about it. To begin with, it looks doubtful whether I am ever going to write any music again, ever, on any terms: I am too much disheartened now by continual failure. I set out with great enthusiasm and write twenty or thirty bars: after that it is worry, first with one small point & then with others, till the whole edifice collapses under a weight of misery. I am ill for days after – The other reason is that I am hardly ever keen enough on old work to do anything more to it. My one & only chance of writing anything now seems to be a happy period of three or four hours in which I get a section outlined, complete in itself. To this I would add others, & so in time build up a work. But as I say, I am disheartened, & hardly like to try. Indeed for some time past, I have deliberately put music aside and engaged in other pursuits, & on the whole I am happier. Or perhaps I ought to say I do not get the days & days of misery I used to get: on the other hand the exaltation of living in a world of music is something to forego than which there is nothing better on earth or in heaven: I feel as if I were an outcast from Paradise. However, in a few weeks' time I shall again find myself without my other, substituted, occupation, & I will then turn again to music, and see whether, after all, I cannot achieve something.

There was another equally important reason for this despondency. Each age is a time of changing values and the rift of a world war was cause to such a change. A post-war air of austerity had crept into music and Gardiner felt increasingly out of sympathy with this mood, if not out of place. Others sensed this change. Even in 1924, after a performance of Elgar's Second Symphony which nowadays is seen to epitomise the drawing to an end of the Edwardian era, a critic could write that 'it brings back the essence of our pre-war life'. With remarkable perception Edwin Evans put his finger on this change in musical climate when he wrote in an article on Benjamin Dale which appeared in the May 1919 issue of *The Musical Times*:

It is unlikely that any English composers who are now students will, on reaching maturity, retain as much allegiance as [Dale] has done to a tradition which has lost contact with actuality. It is doubtful whether the somewhat aristocratic distinction of which his style furnishes an excellent example, will characterise our post-war music. The present trend of musical psychology favours ruggedness rather than polished utterance, and the cult of beautiful phrases is giving way to a search for greater veracity. It is at least probable that those composers who have passed through vivid personal experiences in the present war will be among the foremost to give us this element of uncompromising truth in their music.[7]

The most representative of the immediate pre-war generation of British composers was Elgar, whose Muse, after a late autumnal flowering in the Cello Concerto and the three chamber works, was now virtually silent. In his remaining, barren years he seems occasionally to have been at odds with this new musical climate. Basil Maine has recounted how 'during one of the early performances of Walton's Viola Concerto, given at the Three Choirs Festival, Elgar was seen pacing up and down behind the orchestra gallery and deploring that such music should be thought fit for a stringed instrument'.[8] Frank Bridge was one of the few British composers successfully to straddle the war divide, with a transition of style from the evocative pastoral *Summer* (1914-15) to the tough problematic Piano Sonata of 1921-4 (with a strong undercurrent of Alban Berg) and gritty orchestral scores like *Oration* (1930) and *Phantasm* (1931). In the inner conflict of the works in his final phase, Bridge seems to be wrestling with the emotional and psychological upheaval the war had created. Among the young British composers in the early 1920s, the chief protagonists of this trend towards 'ruggedness' were Walton and Bliss, whose seeming discordant strains showed their composers pricking up an interested ear to such influences from abroad as jazz, Stravinsky and the Parisian ferment of musical activity, all of which were helping to reshape the syntax of contemporary musical language. But even the efforts of Walton and Bliss were mild in comparison with Continental developments: 1924 was mid-way between the completion of Berg's *Wozzeck* and the commencement of *Lulu*. Musically Britain seemed to lag several steps behind the rest of Europe. Out of the Royal Philharmonic Society's five concerts in 1924, the only non-British twentieth-century work performed was the suite from *The Firebird* of 1909-10, a choice that hardly acknowledged the directions Stravinsky was currently taking, and that year's Promenade concerts contained no new works at all. 1924 marked the end of the noble line of Sibelius symphonies and the completion of Prokofiev's abrasive Second. One wonders what Balfour Gardiner might have made of Webern's distillation of that form in his Opus 21 four years later, or for that matter how he regarded that concept of atonality (or pantonality), first put forward by Webern's teacher Schoenberg as long ago as 1908, that seemed to encapsulate the very antithesis to all accepted notions of how music ought to sound. He would surely have turned to phrases more forceful even than 'terribly uncomfortable' and 'acute mental distress' with which to express his reactions to such products from the new frontiers of music composition.

Privately Gardiner advanced the theory that a man ceases to be musical at a certain age, and he felt that he had reached that age.[9] But this was more than likely a rationalisation of his own condition. His cultural roots were too firmly embedded in pre-war tradition. When once asked in what style of music he wrote, he answered casually, 'Oh, the style of 1902, I suppose.'[10] Trying to define the cause for his dislike of some of Grainger's instrumentation about which he had expressed his views so openly, he wrote on 5 April 1923: 'The difference between [Delius and my] point of view and yours is due to the fact that we are bound by certain traditions of culture & association from which you are entirely free.' In this changing musical climate there was little place now for the full-blooded romantic. Music for him, as he once said, should be an 'intoxication', something that would lift him out of this world, with none of the harsh severity that was edging into the music of the twenties. He could not adapt and therefore withdrew. There is a poignant significance, indeed almost a curious presentiment, in these lines from the song *Ah, Sweet Those Eyes* (unattributed, but with strong echoes of W.E. Henley) composed on his eighteenth birthday:

> Ah, sweet those eyes, that used to be so tender,
> Are grown so cold, as bitter cold as death:
> The burnt-out ashes fall into the fender,
> None shall revive the flame that perisheth.
> . . .
> 'Twere better, love, to leave the ashes burning
> Than wait too late till they are burnt away . . .

11 'My substituted occupation . . .'

1919–1927

Of those 'other pursuits' that were gradually displacing music from the centre of Balfour Gardiner's attention, the chief claimant on his time was architecture in which he had long shown an interest. As far back as 1902 there is evidence of him sketching plans for houses, and his methodical mind rose well to the challenge of finding the optimal utilisation of space. On holidays, too, he would sometimes note down an architectural detail that appealed to him. Before the war he had been too involved in music to have sufficient time to spare, but the first signs of his taking a serious interest came immediately after the war.

A diary entry for January 1919 contains the following proposal for submission to the Bradfield Rural District Council (in whose province Ashampstead lay):

(1) RDC give me particulars of accommodation required and price of a cottage with similar accommodation erected by them

(2) HBG submits his design for approval & undertakes to pay them the difference on the cottage he builds & a cottage of similar accommodation built by the RDC on condition that

    (a) no addition may be made to the cottage, or no other building of any description erected on the site

    (b) no advertisement or disfigurement of any sort to be allowed on the premises, HBG to be the sole judge of what is disfigurement or not

    (c) right of access for the purpose of inspection

(3) The RDC to own the cottage & site & take over all liabilities with regard to them

No official record exists of such an agreement being reached (which may anyway have been too binding for the council to stomach), though Gardiner's architect friend Basil Sutton was responsible for some post-war council houses in Ashampstead in which Gardiner may have been partly involved. However, he went ahead with a building programme of his own.

In addition to his own cottage, Gardiner already possessed another in the village which he was letting. Then in December 1920 he employed a builder to start erecting two houses. Built much according to Gardiner's own design, the pair were called Stubbles I & II. He planned to use the first house for his guests, to let the second for three years and then perhaps enlarge it, by which time he hoped a further house would be under construction. But by the following summer the start on the third house had been delayed – 'having spent so much money on cottages, to allow myself time to recuperate', he gave as the reason. The third house was in fact never built, but in the meantime there were other schemes afoot including the many alterations that had been in his mind during the war to his own cottage. An outbuilding was converted to provide accommodation for his housekeeper, and a guest room in the cottage he had specially padded to obliterate the sound of his piano from the adjacent music room reached by a separate staircase. In one of his rooms a painting of Grez by Jelka Delius now took pride of place.

With the coming of peacetime Gardiner had been able to resume his friendship with Basil Sutton whose practical experience and knowledge of architecture were now to prove invaluable. Both men possessed highly individual tastes, and their friendship, which spanned many years, developed into almost a partnership. Both had a keen interest in restoring old buildings and in 1921, while at the peak of his Ashampstead activities, Gardiner's curiosity was aroused by a property just over the Berkshire border in the village of Childrey, near Wantage. This building, Cantorist House, was an ideal subject for their restoration work. Once a priory and reputedly dating from 1492, it was situated next to a Norman church from which there was rumoured to be an underground passage leading to the house. To complete the romantic picture, the house even today is said to be haunted by a beautiful lady in a blue veil and seen on different occasions by at least two of its occupants.

Gardiner purchased Cantorist House in 1922 together with some land opposite on which four old cottages stood. These he let for a while, though ten years later they had to be demolished. Cantorist House, built partly of Cotswold stone, was L-shaped: a farm-house adjoined a malt house with a small cottage at its end. The restoration work inside was extensive, the exterior remaining little altered. One unusual aspect of the conversion was a mock tower erected in the courtyard where cart sheds had once stood. Solid oak doors with wooden latches and an elegant oak staircase were typical features of their work. Perhaps not wishing to make too many concessions to modernity, Gardiner was reluctant to install electricity, and a curious distinguishing mark of his designs was the habit of embedding a claret bottle, base outwards, in the apex of a gable. No detail was too minute for his attention and he enthusiastically addressed his mind to everything inside and outside, from plumbing to planting. But nothing about the conversion was as curious as one feature that an impish sense of humour must have impelled Gardiner to add. In what was once the malt house he had had the original attics removed, leaving a high-ceilinged drawing room with exposed beams. From one of those oak beams the central portion was cut out and on the protruding butts he had carved the faces of two friends who were at enmity, thus forcing them to stare at each other for eternity.

Gardiner kept a constant eye on the work at Childrey, and when the restoration was nearing completion in December 1923 he offered the house to Norman O'Neill for £75 per annum if he would take it for a minimum period of three years. Norman and Adine had indeed been looking for a country house to use as an occasional break from their busy London life, but Norman had set his heart on an Elizabethan farm-house in Surrey which they could not afford. A gift from Gardiner and some assistance from Adine's mother made the purchase possible. Gardiner meanwhile let Cantorist House and in 1925 bought forty-six acres of adjacent land.

Then in 1932 the least expected happened: he presented the house and grounds to the Chancery of Liverpool Cathedral. As a professed non-believer the gift was clearly not made on any religious impulse but instead out of sympathy for that massive Gothic structure that even until quite recently has shamefully advertised its lack of completion. The Anglican Cathedral of Liverpool, whose foundation stone had been laid way back in 1904 by King Edward VII, was designed by Sir Gilbert Scott. When it was consecrated in July 1924 in the presence of King George V and Queen Mary, the building was only about a third completed. The cost of the completed portion had been nearly three-quarters of a million pounds, with further millions expected to be spent. In March 1925 Gardiner signed an agreement giving the Cathedral £1,750, to be paid in amounts of £250 each March for seven years. When this gift had run its course he crowned it with the further gift of Cantorist House. But as the years passed and the Cathedral remained in a state of incompletion Gardiner lost interest. Cantorist House did not long remain the property of the Chancery of Liverpool Cathedral as it was sold back into private hands. In recent years many additions have been made to both the house and its grounds, yet although the interior has undergone considerable alteration the exterior facade remains much as it was after the Gardiner–Sutton conversion.

Besides Liverpool Cathedral, Gardiner's architectural sympathies found another ecclesiastical edifice as the object of his charity. This was the spacious Thaxted church in which in 1916 Gustav Holst had held the first of his Whitsun festivals. By the mid-twenties that Essex church was in great need of re-roofing as it frequently leaked. Pails had to be placed at the foot of the pillars in the aisle to collect the dripping water. A donation of £1,000 from Gardiner in 1925 made it possible to have the roof re-leaded.

Meanwhile the Gardiner-Sutton partnership continued to flourish.

Some six miles south of Childrey is the village of Upper Lambourn, John Betjeman's 'leathery Lambourne',[1] now a thriving centre of horse-training, liberally scattered with paddocks and stud farms. There Sutton was responsible for rescuing and restoring several fine old cottages, some of which had utilised the individual sarsen stone, and such was the respect in which he was held by the local inhabitants that the village was sometimes referred to as 'Sutton's village'. The work was again a joint venture, though this time Gardiner probably took little part in the planning but instead advanced money for the derelict and decaying premises to be purchased, renovated and sold. Two of the finest examples of Sutton's work in Upper Lambourn are Sarcens Cottage and Cruck Cottage (itself the subject of a detailed *Country Life* article on Sutton's restorations in the October 1927 issue). Gardiner showed an interest in the Old Manor and the Old Malt House which both received similar treatment at Sutton's hands and in this way Gardiner generally made work available for Sutton during the difficult inter-war slump. He also offered to finance Sutton's son through an engineering course, but this generous offer was not taken up and Sutton's only son died during the Second World War. The partnership was to be called upon once more when – to the surprise and dismay of his friends – Gardiner decided to leave Ashampstead and build himself a house in Dorset.

Such diversions, whilst robbing his own music of the time he might otherwise have spent on it, in no way lessened the attention and concern he showed for his friends' welfare. At the beginning of April 1925 he lunched with Roger Quilter and ten days later went with Kennedy Scott to visit Delius at Cassel where he was undergoing further treatment. Jelka's hopes had been falsely raised the previous year: '[The doctor] calls Fred's disease sclerosis multiplese & he thinks it is an after-disease of malignant influenza', she had written to a friend. 'Well, thank God we came here before it was all too late!'[2]

But to Gardiner's eyes Delius was a sad and depressing spectacle. 'He tries to walk', he wrote to Grainger on 30 April, 'but even with support can hardly manage it. He cannot use his hands to eat, & everything has to be done for him, feeding, shaving, dressing, & imagine he has to be helped even for the commonest physical necessities.' Although he had originally intended staying for only two or three days, Gardiner remained at Cassel for a whole week and spent much of the time correcting proofs of the full score of Delius's opera *Fennimore and Gerda*. Kennedy Scott stayed for three days, helping to carry the emaciated Delius between his hotel room and the dining room. Yet even in such a pathetic state he seemed to Scott as mentally alive as ever: 'There was plenty of life in his talk – pungent observations were always forthcoming.'[3] Soon after their departure Frederic Austin also paid Delius a visit. As Delius's eyes were too weak for him to manage the task himself, Gardiner undertook to complete the proof-reading, and from Cassel he went on to Munich for Clemens von Franckenstein's fiftieth birthday celebrations, which included a production of Clé's opera *Li-Tai-Pé*. Back in England, from May onwards he spent his time either in Dorset, in Oxford, entertaining at Ashampstead with the occasional game of tennis, or walking with Sutton.

Gardiner also put the finishing touches to his last piano composition which was published that year. This was the *Fantasia* for the left hand, dedicated to Douglas Fox, who before the war had been organist at Keble College, Oxford. For his war service Fox had joined the 4th Gloucester Regiment and in August 1917, on a second tour of duty in France, lost his right arm. In 1918 he was appointed director of music at Bradfield College, and Gardiner, living so close, came to hear of him. In October 1921 Gardiner began sketching out a toccata for the left hand, but when it was nearly finished he put it aside for three years, returning to it early in 1925. He then invited Fox to come and play it through and was surprised by the sonorities that one hand alone could produce. He made several alterations in February and on returning from his visit to Delius sent a copy to Fox on 7 May. As in the case of the admittedly superior works written for the similarly afflicted Austrian pianist Paul Wittgenstein, Gardiner's was one of several pieces expressly written for Fox. Amongst those other composers to recognise Fox's need were R.O. Beachcroft, Philip Browne, Lionel Ovenden, Ernest Walker and Frank Bridge. While momentarily reminiscent of Grieg's *Solitary Traveller* in the short central *tranquillo* section which plays briefly with three wistful ideas (examples 33 a, b & c), Gardiner's *Fantasia* is nevertheless a striking piece calling for considerable strength in the one hand, although, as the score states, it is equally playable by two.

Moments like these spent on composition were becoming rarer. New ideas were scarce and there was little compulsion to devote himself to fresh work. That year Gardiner relinquished all formal associations with the Oriana Madrigal Society and drifted farther away from music. Only through friends it seems was his interest kept alive. Delius's fortunes were meanwhile cruelly fluctuating. In the early summer months of 1925 he and Jelka were at last home at Grez after all their unsuccessful trips to Germany. They still had faith in their doctor at Cassel. But in July the terrible blow fell – blindness. Jelka could hardly bring herself to write of it to friends. Within three years it was total. So began the long final descent. Musicians rallied round and made frequent trips to Grez, keeping music alive in the Delius household. Gardiner crossed in August, Grainger had sailed from America, and together they entertained the ailing Delius with sessions of two-piano works. Gardiner had taken with

Ex. 33

him Grainger's arrangement of *Dance Rhapsody No. 1*, Heseltine's arrangements of *North Country Sketches* for piano duet and *Brigg Fair* for two pianos, as well as Grieg's *Norwegian Dances* and *Symphonic Dances. The Song of the High Hills* was also in their impromptu repertoire. They were joined too by the celebrated Russian cellist Alexandre Barjansky who played Delius's Cello Sonata on his visit. Jelka was able to write with delight on 16 August to Heseltine: 'Barjansky and the two pianos are going all the time.'

Barjansky's sculptress wife Catherine had vivid memories of their staying at Grez, recalling in particular one incident which shows Delius had lost little of his independence of spirit:

Sometimes musicians like Percy Grainger and Balfour Gardiner came from London. Then there would be discussions and disputes about music. On one such occasion Mr Gardiner, an old bachelor with white hair, a red face, and baby-blue eyes, very English and very stubborn, spoke so violently against jazz that his face became twice as red as usual. He nearly suffocated with anger. There was a brief silence after his long and fiery monologue, and then Mr Delius's clear voice said: 'Jelka, we have some jazz records. I'd like to hear some of them.' And Mr Gardiner, who had loved him nearly all his life, listened quietly.[4]

167

While crossing the Atlantic on board the *SS De Grasse*, Grainger had prepared a two-piano arrangement of Gardiner's *English Dance* which they played together at Grez. But Gardiner was still dissatisfied with the old work. They had only got half-way through it when he broke off, exclaiming, 'It won't do, Percy, it's no good.' Back in England he worked at it again between September and December, and even returned to it as late as 1928. He rewrote the beginning of the *Dance* but met with further difficulties as he went on. From Ashampstead he wrote to Grainger on 7 October:

I have finished the introduction to the English Dance, but cannot get on with the Dance itself: it baffles me, and I am already stale. I think it wants new material, something to break what you once called 'the fatal jigginess of English composers'. I am taking my time, as I want to make the old work really good, & I never want to start anything fresh so long as I live. Composition means for me much more misery than happiness, anxiety, ill-health, & the mentality of an idiot – all sorts of odds & ends buzzing about in my head without any meaning from morning till night. I hate it!

The heading to the sketches – 'Reworking old English Dance (for PG)' – suggests that a sense of duty had made him persist with this work in return for the trouble its dedicatee had taken in arranging it for piano. There was a feeling of being in Grainger's debt in more than one way for, while Gardiner would do nothing to promote his own music, Grainger, who was ever the Frankfurt Group's propagandist, had done some campaigning on his behalf by including his works in American recitals. In December 1920, for example, he had played *De Profundis* and *Humoresque* at Carnegie Hall, proclaiming Gardiner in a more than generous programme note as 'one of the most original and outstanding of British composers'. Grainger did nothing by halves. Then in January 1925 his Carnegie Hall recital had contained four of Gardiner's works including *Michaelchurch*. Grainger's programme note was again most sympathetic: 'Balfour Gardiner maintains always his own individualistic utterance, free alike from old-fogyism & extreme modernist experimentalism. He never writes without genuine emotional & musical inspiration & his thematic invention is direct, trenchant & personal.'

In October 1925 Gardiner experienced another 'wave of enthusiasm' that now occurred all too rarely. One evening in an idle moment there came an idea that fired his dwindling interest in music and composition. He returned to it each day after tea-time until it was written out in short score. He wrote to Grainger on 14 November about this brief phase of excitement:

About the middle of October I got rather tired of the English Dance & had another experience similar to the Shepherd Fennel one years ago. I was strumming idly when I got hold of a vulgar waltz theme that suddenly grew, & in three weeks I have finished the whole of the little work, 39 pages of score & a piano duet arrangement. I have now put it aside & shall try to forget it, so that when I come to it fresh I shall be able to judge whether it has any musical value. The one thing I know for certain about it is that it is extraordinarily vulgar; a sentimental waltz theme increasing in tempo till it gets three times as fast as any waltz that has ever been written, big, quite passionate climaxes & a sentimental slow end. I wish I could handle serious material with the same certainty & keenness. My scoring has improved enormously.

He had recently been reading through Cecil Forsyth's text-book on orchestration and as a result now thought his bassoon parts more effective. He felt too that it was in this kind of music that he had more resource than in any other. Considering the feverish state of composition of this concert waltz and similar works like *Shepherd Fennel's Dance* and *The Joyful Homecoming*, how truly had he observed in his diary as far back as July 1901: 'I have noticed that in my more musical moments, common forms of commonplace sentiment are raised to a higher plane by my own exaltation of spirit (for example, a harmonic point in a hymn-tune).' Whether there had been an unconscious influence of Ravel's *La Valse* is hard to tell. He affixed a temporary title to the sketches, *Café Milani '95*, but his enthusiasm was short-lived as they are all that remain. This work went the way of the earlier *Ballad* for orchestra.

Gardiner had intended going to Grez during November, this time with the pianist Evlyn Howard-Jones, whose interpretations of Delius's piano works their composer so much admired. When the time came Howard-Jones found himself unable to go, but Gardiner nevertheless left for France on the 12th, spending the night at Folkestone and arriving at Grez the next day. His intention on that visit was to interest Delius in publishing his *Air and Dance*, a short work for string orchestra dating from 1915 about which Jelka had written a month earlier to Heseltine:

Unfortunately Fred cannot make up his mind now to publish the little string orch. piece, as he does not quite like the end and in his present state sees no prospect of altering it himself. We expect Balfour G. and H. Jones beginning of Nov. for a few days. I will get them to play it to him again and try to arrange it.

While at Grez Gardiner wrote to Grainger that he was hopeful of interesting Delius in preparing the *Air and Dance* for publication. But it had to wait yet a few years. In 1929 Heseltine copied the full score in his own hand and the work was not published until 1931.

Balfour Gardiner's visits to Grez were always most welcome, even more so now in view of Delius's declining health, though, as Jelka informed Grainger, his deeply felt compassion for Delius's condition was inclined to make him feel uneasy when in the presence of his friend's suffering. On 8 December she wrote:

[Fred] thoro'ly enjoyed Balfour's visit. Only he always brought the conversation back to Champagne and wine. Poor Balfour was in such an embarrassing situation: He tried to act according to your letter – but he is so true and frank – he managed it but badly. His embarrassment made him all the more lovable . . . You would have been amused to see Balfour so delighted with the Gramophone.

Delius had recently obtained four records of Spanish songs for voice and guitar to which they both listened with great enjoyment.

As was so often the case, Gardiner's visit was but a brief one as he had decided to come again very soon with Kennedy Scott and spend Christmas at Grez. The religious symbolism and the festive trappings of Christmas meant little more to him than they did to Delius. Gardiner never celebrated the season in the customary fashion, complaining that it made him feel miserable. 'I am always glad when Christmas is over', he wrote much later to Grainger on 27 December 1938, 'with its unpleasant combination of business, correspondence, religion, and, in spite of "festivities", colossal dulness.' This did not, however, prevent him from giving presents to his friends and servants, and with him that year he took to Grez a little foot-warmer for Delius, chocolates for Jelka, and even a gift for their nurse or 'Bruder' in the shape of a muffler. As Delius had so frequently to be carried about the house, it had been necessary to employ a male nurse. These nurses came from a religious order in Cassel, and it was no easy matter to find one who suited Delius's very demanding requirements. Furthermore, the order which supplied the 'Bruders' would move them around at intervals, and, as their present one had proved so admirable for the task, Jelka was anxious not to lose him. As usual Balfour Gardiner came to the rescue. 'Our "Bruder" has permission to stay with us until March the First', Jelka wrote to Grainger on 8 December. 'But Balfour has written to his Clergyman and offered to pay an Ersatz-Mann liberally, so as to make it possible that this Bruder stays here.' Gardiner duly sent 2,000 marks to Cassel to retain the nurse's services.

Over Christmas Gardiner and Kennedy Scott were busy at Grez playing four-hand piano arrangements, including *The Song of the High Hills* and *Dance Rhapsody No. 1*. Delius's sister Clare was also staying in the house and she remembered their visit:

One evening at Grez particularly stands out in my memory . . . Balfour Gardiner and Kennedy Scott both came together on one occasion, and we had some glorious music which Fred thoroughly enjoyed. One evening I sang some of Fred's songs to Kennedy Scott's accompaniment, which was so beautiful that the singing of the songs was a special delight to me.[5]

Of those they performed *I-Brasil* was the song Kennedy Scott liked best.[6]

By 1926 Gustav Holst had recovered from the after-effects of his fall three years ago and was already back at teaching and conducting. In January he was a guest at Ashampstead. It was possibly at about this time that Gardiner asked him to keep an eye open for any young musicians who might be in need of financial assistance. While with the passing of years the actual number of persons who in this way became the object of Gardiner's philanthropy is obscure, one known individual was Stanley Bulley, a young man then of twenty-three who came from Plymouth where his father was a retired Royal Marine. Bulley studied the viola and organ at the RCM from 1927 until 1929 and Gardiner's generosity was for a long while shrouded in anonymity. Sums of money were paid into Bulley's account without any mention of the donor's name, the first deposit probably being one of fifty pounds banked towards the end of 1926. Holst acted as a go-between, handling any correspondence between the two. Ignorant of his benefactor's identity, Bulley would resort to addressing his letters of profound gratitude to the 'Dear Great Unknown'. This arrangement continued for several years until at the suggestion of one of them the blanket of secrecy was lifted and a meeting arranged. Their earliest known encounter was on 10 July 1935 when Bulley had supper at the flat Gardiner then owned in Oxford. Perhaps Holst's death in May 1934, robbing them of their intermediary, brought about the meeting. Bulley later went to Vancouver where he became the organist of Christ Church Cathedral.

Gardiner had also arranged that over the period from September 1926 until May 1927 a bi-monthly payment of two hundred pounds was made to Holst – a grand total of one thousand pounds to bring comfort to Holst's comparatively frugal existence. While indeed it is possible that some of that money may have been directed towards students like Bulley whom Gardiner was patronising, a portion was spent on something close to his heart – restoring old buildings. The Holsts were then living four miles from Thaxted in a Tudor farm-house at Brook End, which they rented from Lady Warwick from 1925 to 1928. As well as making various essential improvements, Isobel Holst had a barn converted into a music-room, a change in which Gardiner would have shown interest, from an architectural point of view if not a musical one.

There were also changes to his own Ashampstead property. With much delight he was installing a wine-cellar 'which I shall stock with all sorts of beautiful wines, to increase the health & happiness of friends & myself', he told Grainger on 20 March, equipping it also with a lift. He would trifle with odd ideas, such as a contraption of fish-shaped figures he constructed to indicate the level in his water tank. Then there was a weather–vane bearing his own initials in musical notation. But this stood at odds with the cold wind that was blowing through his musical life. His despairing attitude remained unaltered and concert-going seemed to aggravate his frustration. On 20 March 1926 he had written in that same letter to Grainger (who just over a month later conducted *Shepherd Fennel's Dance* in Los Angeles) in tones that were becoming increasingly familiar:

Never again shall I work when I am in the slightest degree stale or indisposed, for such work means worry, worry means ill-health, ill-health means unhappiness & I have had enough of all this to last me my lifetime. I am now, thank goodness, about as well & as happy as I believe it possible for me to be: & having got to this enviable state, never again will I go back to the wretchedness I experienced during my years of music. Composition may still be possible, occasionally, & sometimes I think that certain moments during its process may be worth months of unhappiness. As for performance & the concert world, I have done with it forever. Two or three times during the past winter I have been to rehearsals, & they have left me in a state of nervousness & disgust absolutely indescribable.

That he could continually regard his own works with strong disapproval was nothing new. In December 1923 he had written to Grainger: 'It always seemed quite incredible to me that people should like my stuff as well as they said they did; to myself it always seems fourth or fifth rate'; and years on in September 1936 there is the same fusion of excessive self-criticism and utter humility: 'They seem to me merely the honest efforts of a decent but not very original musician.' Yet he had not forsaken all interest in music. Some paternal instinct stood in the way of a total withdrawal. Since 1922 he had struck up a firm friendship with the composer Patrick Hadley whose scores he occasionally examined. He was friendly with two rising young conductors, Guy Warrack and Richard Austin, the son of his old friend Frederic Austin. He was also showing a god-fatherly concern for the musical future of another younger composer, Robin Milford, about which he consulted Holst. When he went to Grez in August 1926 he was busy checking the proofs of Delius's *Appalachia* and *Sea Drift*, the miniature scores of which were engraved in 1927 and 1928. His apparent distaste for performances did not prevent him from attending several concerts and operas on his visit to Germany in December. Returning to Frankfurt, Wiesbaden, Mainz and Cronberg put him in a reminiscent mood, thinking back over twenty-five years to his student days there. And, despite those protestations to Grainger, he attended a few concerts in 1927. He took an interest in Guy Warrack's concerts when he was in charge of the Oxford Orchestral Society, just as he did much later when Richard Austin took over the Bournemouth Municipal Orchestra. He showed Guy Warrack some of Robin Milford's scores and dined with Robin and his father, Humphrey Milford, on 24 February before hearing a Royal Philharmonic Society concert. The programme betrays his reason for going: Frank Bridge was conducting Delius's Violin Concerto and Bax's *In the Faery Hills*, one of Gardiner's favourites.

Robin Milford was married on 16 July and he and his wife were often guests at Ashampstead. Balfour Gardiner gave them a small car and a beautiful summerhouse in which their young boy Barnaby spent many happy hours until he was tragically killed at the age of five. Gardiner had

even advanced money for their son's education,and of the many kindnesses shown over the years Kirstie Milford has written:

He always took the greatest interest in Robin's music & gave unstintingly of his
carefully considered advice . . . I can recall happy visits to his cottage at Ashampstead, where one might arrive on a winter's day to find him waiting to greet us at
his front door, waving a lamp, the wind blowing his white hair into a halo round
his jolly beaming red face, & then the entry into his sweet-smelling old home & a
log fire in one's bedroom. He would give hours of his time to studying Robin's
compositions, & would then go through them in detail with him.[7]

16   Percy Grainger and his fiancée Ella Viola Ström with Balfour Gardiner
in Delius's garden at Grez, August 1927

His devotion to Delius continued unabated. While still working on
corrections to *Sea Drift* he went with Kennedy Scott on 11 April 1927 to
hear Beecham conduct the work at Queen's Hall so that he could then
consult Delius about certain details in the score before its publication.
On 10 May he crossed to France for the brief first visit of three that year.
He went again on 12 August and stayed longer than usual, for about three
weeks. Percy Grainger arrived with his Swedish wife-to-be, Ella Ström,
whom he had met at the conclusion of his recent Australian tour. With
Percy there were more 'two-piano bouts' to entertain Delius, their
repertoire on this occasion including *On Hearing the First Cuckoo in
Spring* and *Summer Night on the River*.
  There were at this time one or two Delius projects in the air with which
Gardiner was in some way connected. His friend Geoffrey Toye was

recording some of the orchestral works for the Columbia Graphophone Company and Gardiner liaised with Delius and his publishers over the recording agreements. There were also plans to issue piano rolls of some Delius works, and as Grainger was an exclusive recording artist for the Aeolian Company who produced the Duo-Art rolls he was likely a key figure behind the scheme. Indeed, for them with Ralph Leopold he recorded four-handed arrangements of *Brigg Fair* and *North Country Sketches*, and it was probably through his good offices that Delius was lent a player-piano. About August 1927 Gardiner pencilled a note to 'set *Song before Sunrise & Cuckoo* for pianola' and for Frederic Austin and himself to 'play *2nd Dance Rhapsody* for Duo-Art'. Just how far these recording plans progressed is not clear, but when Gardiner and Austin visited Grez over Christmas, Jelka was able to write to Grainger[8] of their struggles and triumphs with the Duo-Art piano and the rolls Grainger and Gardiner had made for it from Delius's works. Balfour Gardiner's roll, which contained *On Hearing the First Cuckoo in Spring*, would only play very loudly a piece of Balfour's which Jelka referred to as an unspecified 'Dance'. But at least they found it possible through the player-piano process to introduce Frederic Austin to the *North Country Sketches*. During their visit Gardiner and Austin also played piano-duet versions of *Song before Sunrise* and *Dance Rhapsody No. 2* which they had perhaps been unable to record satisfactorily for the Duo-Art system.

The rolls they played that Christmas may well have been the equivalent of disc 'test pressings' or 'experimental takes' as by the following May, after receiving rolls of Grainger's *The Warriors* (dedicated to Delius), Jelka wrote to Percy that they 'had not yet received the real rolls of Brigg Fair and N.C. Sk. or *any* of Dance Rhapsody No. 2 and Fred would so much love to have them soon as they might fetch away the D.A. Piano . . .' Such rolls would surely have given Delius much pleasure during the hiatuses between musicians' visits. But, despite the mention of further proposals for a Duo-Art Delius biographic double roll with Howard-Jones playing, perhaps in consequence of the Wall Street crash the two works that Grainger had recorded were the only ones to be issued commercially.

Another unfulfilled project was for Gardiner to make an arrangement for two pianos of Delius's *Paris*. Julius Buths, a pioneering champion of Delius's music in Germany, had already completed a two-piano version in 1903. But he had worked from an early copy which did not include the alterations incorporated into the full score published in 1909. During October 1927 Gardiner set about working on *Paris* in his Ashampstead garden. But he was not to complete it.[9] There were other grander schemes on the horizon and his mind, once so much at rest in Berkshire, was now being drawn towards Dorset.

12 'If I might have two rows of trees . . .'

1927-1933

To the south-east of Shaftesbury – Hardy's 'Shaston' – and straddling the Dorset-Wiltshire border lies Cranborne Chase, which in the novelist's own words was 'a truly venerable tract of land, one of the few remaining woodlands in England of undoubted primeval date'.[1] It was on the slopes of The Chase that Tess of the d'Urbevilles became 'a maiden no more'. Once a vast woodland area with a perimeter of over eighty miles and the haunt of innumerable deer, it was disafforested in the 1830s in an attempt to put an end to a variety of illegal activities for which it so conveniently provided a haven. Poachers, thieves, smugglers and murderers found easy shelter within its secluded interior. It gradually fell to the axe and the plough, leaving but a vestige of its former glory.

Balfour Gardiner's close association with this corner of Wessex began in 1924 when, for a little less than £2,000, he purchased the seventy-five-acre Gore Farm on a ridge of the North Dorset Downs crossed by The Chase. For reasons not known he had offered the tenancy of the farm to a friend, Hugh Freeman. The farm was then more-or-less derelict and as his friend had little capital Gardiner generously allowed him to occupy it rent free and advanced some money for stock and farming implements. Each year he gave Freeman an additional hundred pounds. He took considerable trouble to make the farm-house comfortable, furnishing it with items from his Ashampstead cottages. By 1927 his capital outlay on the farm, including the loan of £600 and gifts of £300, was nearly £3,000. But Freeman's venture into agriculture had not proved a success and, as if the kindness he had already been shown were not enough, he looked to Gardiner for some assistance with the farming. For once the request was declined. He felt he had done quite enough to set Freeman up with both a home and a livelihood and they parted after a disagreement, leaving Gardiner with a farm on his hands.

Meanwhile locally there had been a significant turn of events. In the valley below Gore Farm and to the south are the villages of Fontmell Magna and Iwerne Minster which had once formed manorial estates that in the early 1920s had been allowed to lapse into a very poor condition. The higher land in particular, overrun by a much increased rabbit population, had become derelict, and through lack of care the district was in ecological terms fast becoming a wilderness. In 1925 Fontmell Magna, which had been part of the estate owned by Sir Richard Glyn, was split up and in May of the following year auctioned in lots. This gave Balfour Gardiner the opportunity to embark on the most ambitious of his schemes, one which led ultimately to an achievement comparable to his patronage of contemporary British music. He saw a chance of putting new life into the dispirited countryside through re-afforestation, clothing the barren slopes of the coombs and downs with trees. This project would not only radically alter the landscape, but it would also provide much needed employment at a time of economic depression. Gardiner's wealth, time and energy had found a new and worthy outlet.

Gardiner first took to tree planting on a very small scale at Ashampstead where he learnt the beginner's mistake of placing trees too close together. His initial attempts had apparently been influenced by a Professor Hiley from Oxford. With such limited experience this new project was indeed an ambitious one. He was approaching fifty and the scale of the undertaking was too vast for him alone. So he sought assistance from his nephew Rolf, then twenty-four years of age. Rolf's interests at the time lay chiefly abroad where he had much to do with youth groups in Northern Europe. He was closely involved with the starting of the Musikheim at Frankfurt/Oder and with the Meihof at Oosterbeck in Holland, and many similar projects connected with adult educational establishments elsewhere on the Continent. Perhaps Balfour saw it as a way of getting his nephew to settle down in England; certainly his proposal came almost as an ultimatum. In September 1927 he offered him Gore Farm, adding that he would himself pay for the tree planting and for the employment of a head forester if Rolf would share in the venture.

Balfour's and Rolf's ideas for Gore Farm, while not born of like minds, shared sufficient common ground for the partnership to prosper. Whereas Balfour was concerned with revitalising the landscape, Rolf also saw the chance of establishing a regional rural centre on the lines of schemes with which he had been associated abroad. In those bleak times, while prophesying the possible breakdown of industrial civilisation,he also firmly believed in the concept of local economy, returning to the land and living off it with reasonable self-sufficiency. It was therefore essential that people should be educated in waning rural skills, and Rolf's plans were not limited to conservation alone but embraced social and cultural aspects as well, in which music-making, folk-dancing and rural crafts all played important parts. He planned 'work camps' to establish and disseminate such values. In this respect he was regarded by many as a visionary with the tenacity to see his ideas through, and Gore Farm was his opportunity of putting them into practice. He outlined the plan to D.H. Lawrence whom he had met for the first time the previous year.

Lawrence expressed a longing to share in the scheme, and, though he was to take no active part, it was nonetheless Lawrence's sympathy that encouraged Rolf to accept his uncle's offer.

Straightway Balfour set about installing a Mr Boden in Gore Farm as head forester for a year rent free as soon as Freeman had vacated the premises. But whether out of carelessness or malice on the part of the out-going tenant, everything with the exception of the farm-house was gutted by fire and Rolf spent from April until October 1928 rebuilding the farm with local labour and local flint. Meanwhile the previous September tree planting had begun in earnest, and in time between them Balfour and Rolf re-organised, purchased and pieced together 1,500 acres of the original Glyn Estate, later to become known as the Springhead Estate, 900 acres being wooded and the remainder farmland. Gradually the bare fields were forested, the soil restored and the water-table raised, and it is some measure of their achievement that over a period of forty years three million trees were planted on the chalk downs of the north-western reach of Cranborne Chase. The opening lines of Balfour Gardiner's song *The Quiet Garden* had proved to be a prophetic understatement – 'If I might have two rows of trees'.

It was soon apparent that Ashampstead was too distant for Balfour Gardiner to keep watch on his forestry work, and so in November 1927 he offered £2,100 for Hill Farm which lay a short distance along the ridge from Gore Farm between Ashmore and Fontmell Magna, with a view surveying the then bare landscape. Hill Farm, like Cantorist House, was L-shaped: a barn for corn and a shed for cattle in winter. With Sutton's assistance, Gardiner designed his own house on that site. And while that was under way, the following year he also took a flat in Oxford at 59A Cornmarket Street which, as his guests could on occasion hardly fail to notice, was situated directly over a restaurant. Surprisingly Gardiner seemed to tolerate the frequent intrusion of food smells. Now, with his Ashampstead cottage, a flat in Oxford and his frequent journeys to Dorset, he found it desirable to employ a valet, and he could have found none better for the post than a prim, dapper and lithe Essex man, Hubert Adams, the perfect gentleman's gentleman, who had so admirably carried out his employment with Gustav Holst for four and a half years. His loyal service had been particularly appreciated during Holst's period of recuperation at Thaxted in 1924. In her father's biography, Imogen Holst has written that Adams 'combined, with incredible efficiency, the role of cook, valet and guardian. He was an artist to his fingertips.'[2] At the end of Adams's term of service Gustav Holst had written thanking him: 'It is largely owing to you that I was able to get well and strong again so soon and so easily and I am most grateful.' Gardiner had known him from the time he was working for Holst and

177

had complete confidence in him, a trust that was fully rewarded. Adams was a superb cook and remained devoted and loyal to the end.

While much involved in his Dorset schemes, Gardiner snatched two breaks from work towards the end of 1927. He paid a brief visit to Kerry in September, and in December he was in France and Germany, spending a few days in Frankfurt. For the third time that year he called in at Grez, taking with him Christmas presents including some for Delius's servants: handkerchiefs alike for Madame Grespier the housekeeper and cook, Hildegarde the Saxon maid, and the German nurse for whom Gardiner was paying. From his return in January he was frequently in Dorset, staying either at a local farm or at the Grosvenor Hotel in Shaftesbury while with Basil Sutton he supervised the building of his new house. At the same time he kept a close watch on the tree planting now in progress, once more gaining valuable experience from a beginner's errors.

Fontmell Hill House, as it became known, adhered to the L-shaped plan of the original farm buildings, and its most prominent feature was a spacious dining hall with a minstrels' gallery that in a change of mind was converted into a bedroom. Specially imported Barcelona tiles were set into the floor and staircase in the entrance hall, yet for all its obvious comforts the house had a certain monastic ring about it. Once more Gardiner preferred to be without electricity, and his own bedroom was devoid of plumbing, so that each morning a large bowl of cold water had to be filled from a tap on the landing and carried into his room. He gave his chauffeur Cox and his family a cottage in Fontmell Magna and a car as well for their convenience. As one of his employees remembered, 'he liked his staff to be as comfortable as himself' and had three houses in the village either built or converted for their use. When a bath ordered for his own house turned out to be larger than he wanted, instead of sending it back in exchange for a smaller one he gave it to one of his employees for his own cottage which could then boast the largest bath in the village. His life-style was one of modest and unaffected affluence. As Edgar Bainton's daughter Helen remembered (here probably looking back on the Ashampstead days before his move to Dorset):

Balfour Gardiner liked what might be described as simple elegance, and everything in his home, though completely unostentatious, was nonetheless much more grand than anything to which we were accustomed. One day he decided to take us for a river picnic. This necessitated a car drive to the river, where we took a punt to the picnic spot. Arnold Bax was with us on that occasion, and I remember how glamorous he and Balfour looked in their white flannels as they stood up in the boat propelling us along. On arrival at our destination the luncheon basket was unpacked: a snowy white cloth was spread upon the ground; cold chicken and salad were placed upon dishes; a bottle of hock next appeared – Balfour's cellar was renowned – then gooseberry pie and cream. We were seated upon the ground having partaken of this gargantuan feast when Balfour said in his naïve and gentle manner: 'Picnics are all very well in their way, but I really *do* prefer eating at home with Phyllis to wait on one!'[3]

Gardiner very quickly endeared himself to those who worked for him in Dorset. At a time when work was scarce and wages low, he offered generous employment and paid his workmen a shilling or two above the average weekly wage. Apart from his permanent personal staff of house-keeper, gardener and chauffeur, there were at times up to thirty men employed in the woods. As at Ashampstead he continued for a few years to keep pigs, and bee-keeping remained a special hobby. But the woods called for most of his attention when he was down in Dorset.

In March 1928 there came a pleasant surprise with the present of Norman O'Neill's *Two Shakespearean Sketches* for orchestra, published not in full score but as a piano conductor's score and bearing a printed dedication. 'Dear Balfour', Norman had inscribed the copy, 'I have been so bold as to dedicate these little pieces to you. This is the nearest approach to a score permitted by the modern conditions!' In June Gardiner spent three days with Holst who in turn stayed three days in August at the new Oxford flat. At the beginning of October he invited Richard Austin, Guy Warrack and Basil Sutton to join him as his guests for a three weeks' holiday in Spain. He broke his return journey to look in at Grez where there was a new arrival in the household.

Delius had accepted the offer by a twenty-two-year-old Yorkshireman, Eric Fenby, to take on the seemingly impossible task of amanuensis to the incapacitated composer. The miraculous success of their musical partnership is now well known, but at first Gardiner held out little hope that Fenby's assistance would accomplish anything worthwhile. He told him that Delius would never be able to dictate music as he was incapable of making a firm decision, a failing that Fenby was soon to recognise. But Gardiner's predictions were fortunately proved wrong. During his previous stays at Grez he had been working on a two-piano arrangement of Delius's *A Poem of Life and Love*, an orchestral score dating from 1918 that had been put aside. Delius wanted to hear it, to see if it was good and whether anything might be made of it. The arrangement was unfinished by the time of Fenby's arrival at Grez that October, and his first task there was to complete it. This he had not quite done when Gardiner came again *en route* for home after his Spanish holiday, but between them they finished the transcription and several times played the work through to Delius. When he left for England Gardiner still had doubts whether anything would come of it. But in due course the best material was extracted from the score and used as the basis of a new work, *A Song of Summer*, which was then sent to Gardiner for his inspection. 'I was astonished at what I found', he wrote to Jelka after receiving a parcel containing the manuscript. 'I thought there would be numerous sketches all pieced together, with some parts scored and others not, and a great mass of material for me to deal with. Instead, I find a short work practically completed and ready for the copyist. All that

17 In holiday mood: (left to right) Richard Austin, Charles Kennedy Scott,
Balfour Gardiner, and Frederic Austin

remains for me to do is to go over the score in detail and suggest minor improvements.'[4] Fenby found Gardiner's interest and encouragement invaluable and a great incentive, especially after the latter's initial doubts as to whether the partnership would prosper. Before Gardiner's arrival, Delius had spoken of him to Fenby, saying that he was one of his oldest friends and one of the very few whom he trusted and admired implicitly. 'You will like Balfour', he had said. Fenby did, in everything except what he called his intolerable musical pessimism.[5]

Gardiner was soon back in Dorset for those months best suited to tree planting – from October to March while the trees are dormant. In November Arnold Bax visited Fontmell Hill and with Gardiner's persuasion planted a few trees on a poor stretch of downland that was named Arnold's Plantation. Gustav Holst similarly had a plot named after him. 'Well, you see', Gardiner later explained to Fenby, 'I have some doubts about the survival of my friends' music. But they were so dear to me that I really feel that I must try and perpetuate my regard for them as men in more permanent means.'

The move from Berkshire to Dorset was a gradual one. Towards the end of 1928 he gave notice to his Ashampstead tenants and started to plan in detail the scope of his forestry work. He considered purchasing land to the value of £10,000 per annum over a period of five years by withdrawing the same amount from his capital without increasing his already substantial investments. 'I should not scruple to buy any land I want', he wrote in his diary on 5 January 1929, and this he could well afford as by the end of 1926 his capital had stood at a little under £200,000 with an annual income after tax of about £10,000. As far as music was concerned, his concert-going was now more irregular, though when Barjansky came to London in January 1929 to play Delius's Cello Concerto with Barbirolli his interest was awakened, and in July he made a special point of listening in to a broadcast of W.H. Bell's *South African Symphony* so that he could write an account of the performance to its composer.

But on a more practical level were the suggestions he wrote to Delius on 21 March 1929 for a concert suite to be made out of the *Hassan* music. For a person who professed to have finished with music his proposals show all the workings of an astute, experienced musical mind:

Use the existing material and existing instrumentation as far as possible, and arrange the suite for *small orchestra, small chorus,* and *soloists.* There is a large quantity of most attractive music, and there ought to be no difficulty in making a suite that would be a useful addition to the repertoire of small choral societies.

I should proceed thus:

(1) Get Eric Fenby to play over the whole of the music in its existing form, and first pick out the numbers that will stand by themselves: these can form the backbone of the new suite.

(2) You will then have to consider questions of contrast, alternating long numbers with short ones, instrumental numbers with numbers in which the chorus is employed, quiet with noisy ones and so on.

(3) The problem may then arise of joining up small sections in order to make a sufficiently long movement.

(4) When the suite is arranged, a new score should be written out, eliminating all the errors in the old one.

(5) A new version for piano must then be made: it will be possible for the publisher to use many of the existing plates, thus saving the heavy expense of engraving fresh ones.

(6) Printed parts for the chorus probably exist already, and if that is so, all that will be needed is to use the old plates but alter the title and binding.

(7) Fresh orchestral parts will have to be made and carefully corrected.

(8) Negotiations will have to be undertaken with the publisher regarding the new suite, performing rights and mechanical reproduction rights not being forgotten.

I think that is all.

Although a suite was extracted from the *Hassan* music, Gardiner's suggestion of including a small chorus and soloists was not, it seems, taken up, despite Jelka's statement in a letter to Norman O'Neill a month later that 'Fred has just made a glorious orchestral suite with chorus of the *Hassan* music, with the aid of Eric Fenby.'[6] The resulting suite was arranged only for orchestra, though Delius later was not entirely satisfied with the omission of voices which indeed seem such an essential constituent of the complete score.

Percy and Ella Grainger were married the previous August in typically unorthodox fashion on the stage of the Hollywood Bowl at the conclusion of a concert conducted by Percy and before a large paying audience. They came to England in the summer of 1929 and Gardiner met them a short time after at Grez. The arrangements were then well in hand for the Delius Festival to be held later that year in London under Beecham's direction, but with Gardiner's strong dislike of Beecham it was understood that he would not attend the festival, which tactfully was not mentioned in his presence. His curiously inconsistent attitude to concerts showed itself again when a festival of British music was given that July at Harrogate. Frederic Austin, Norman O'Neill, Roger Quilter and Cyril Scott all appeared as composer–conductors. Grainger's works were conducted by Basil Cameron who was assisted by Grainger in the organisation of the three-day festival. And although his *Shepherd Fennel's Dance* was included, Gardiner let it be known that he would neither take part nor attend himself. 'I have been now telling you for years that I dislike music, & that it worries & depresses me & I cannot understand why you do not believe me', he wrote to Grainger on 26 May. Nevertheless he was obviously troubled by his self-imposed absence, and his next letter on 11 June is a sad and touching document:

Music, for me, was always a personal matter. I loved it for its own sake, and the worst time I ever had in my life was when I realised it was slipping from my grasp. I did not give it up without a struggle, but being compelled to give it up in the end, I was not content, & never can be content, with any substitute, such as the exercise of my musical critical faculty or the pursuit of music for ulterior motives such as my pride, my reputation, or whatever slight value it may have in English musical life. To consider it a religion, or an obligation, when the spirit is gone, is merely futile and false, and I, at any rate, am not content with shams, though I see very plainly, after my own catastrophe, that other musicians are . . . Music has been the best thing I have known in life. Like youth, it has left me.

The sentiment of the penultimate sentence echoes closely that expressed by Delius to Heseltine in January 1913 when he wrote: 'The greatest pleasure and satisfaction I have experienced in life has been through music, in making it and in hearing it, and in living it.'[7]

Delius came over in October for the festival held in his honour and stayed in London at the Langham Hotel. Gardiner went to see him there, taking Patrick Hadley with him. Hadley was an admirer of Delius and while a student at the RCM had conducted the college orchestra in *On Hearing the First Cuckoo in Spring*. Gardiner thought highly of Hadley's compositions and once spoke of him to Delius as one of the few people still writing beautiful music. In November he had a short holiday in Cork and the following March he took Hadley to Grez for the first time. Gardiner had ordered a barrel of French wine for the Deliuses and decided that he, Hadley and Fenby should between them bottle, cork and wire it. He gave special instructions for the barrel to be placed in an outhouse so that the operation could be carried out while they looked on to the garden and the spring landscape. Seventy bottles were eventually transferred to Delius's wine cellar.

Although on his visits he would often spend much of the morning attending to his own financial affairs, Gardiner delighted in tackling various jobs at Grez, and Jelka suggested that they next cut down a large unsightly branch overhanging the water's edge. In *Delius As I Knew Him* Fenby has left a memorable account[8] of their attempts at manoeuvring a rowing-boat into position beneath the offending branch while contending with a strong river current. First there was the sight of poor Balfour 'gyrating helplessly in mid-stream, and battling with one oar against the strong current about fifty yards down the river' until eventually the burly local inn-keeper had to come to the rescue of all three as they struggled to escape the dangers of a nearby weir.

Fenby observed that, as was his habit, no sooner had Balfour Gardiner arrived at Grez than he began to talk about leaving. This spirit of unrest and the frequent need of change may in part have been responsible for his giving up Ashampstead. Just as Delius's river-side garden at Grez had been enshrined in his *In a Summer Garden*, so too had Gardiner's in *The Quiet Garden*. (Indeed, Gardiner might have had both gardens in his mind as one can almost sense the River Loing lazily flowing through that tranquil song.) He could hardly have found a more restful spot than Ashampstead. Why then did he give it up? One reason he let slip himself: 'My Muse left me at Ashampstead.' His cottage held too many associations with his active years as a composer as well as memories of the anxieties he had suffered. As he confided to a close friend in his last years: 'I have just been reading through some old diaries, and when I see what I suffered through music I am glad I don't have anything more to do with it.'[9] It was forestry, not music, that now occupied his mind and the move to Dorset was symbolic of that change. When in need of an alternative environment there would be his Oxford flat.

There were minor irritations as well that hastened the final decision. In 1921 Ellen, his housekeeper for fifteen years, left him and he was never satisfied with any of the successive replacements. He complained that whenever he returned to Ashampstead he would find either his housekeeper or housemaid ill. Jelka Delius sensed his restlessness and indecision and wrote to Grainger on 4 November 1929:

We have not seen Balfour since the spring and I fear he is not very happy. He wants to sell Ashampstead, and then again not, and now again he has put it in the agent's hands. I think, giving up music like that *entirely* (and he with no women either) must be so dreary. And planting all these little trees, that may wither again – it does not nourish the Soul; consequently he is not well. I suppose you heard that his grand piano fell thro' the ceiling into the room underneath, and *that*, he said, was the end of music for *him*.

What had actually happened was that a fire had broken out beneath his music room and had so weakened the ceiling of the room below that he got some workmen to lower his piano through the floor to the ground level. 'Aw, it's escaped!' he remarked in a lighter mood.

His leaving Ashampstead caused a great feeling of loss amongst his friends who had many happy memories of days spent at the cottage. Patrick Hadley and Arnold Bax paid their last visit in July, and both were moved to write to Gardiner with mixed feelings of gratitude and loss. Hadley wrote:

The profound happiness I always feel at Ashampstead was this time over-shadowed with sadness. One has of course no right to allow oneself to get so upset by an affair which is so manifestly not one's own business, yet one's feelings sometimes become so poignant that it is impossible to refrain from expressing them. As we drove away it was terrible to think that this would be the last time – almost too much to bear. Speaking for myself (Arnold, I know, shares these sentiments, to say nothing of others whom we haven't seen) I can say with deep conviction that there is nowhere I look forward to going to with pleasure anything like comparable to that I feel in looking forward to going to Ashampstead: I have a strange affection for the place: it is vividly associated in our minds with you, and you with it. Now a severance is about to take place, which one could never imagine conceivable. It would be useless to say that there will be times when you will regret it because there is only one judge of that, and that is you! But dear me, well I've been trying not to think of it, but it will pursue me . . .   (11 July 1930)

Bax's friendship spanned many more years, and he looked back over their times together in the quiet comfort of the cottage and its garden:

I must thank you again for these lovely days – so full of sunlight and gaiety – and more than this, I must try to tell you of all my gratitude for your unfailing friendship and generosity through all the twenty-one Ashampstead years. When I crossed the lawn to the gate this morning I simply dared not realise that I might never see the dear place again. I suppose I know and love Ashampstead and the cottage more intimately than anyone except yourself, and to me the place has always been a refuge in adverse times, and a beautiful stressing of all the fleeting happiness of this uncertain life. But I think you know how I have loved it – or anyway guessed – (and this in spite of my general indifference to *any* local habitation). Indeed all of me that is English has always thought of the dear little cottage and its garden as *home*. I do thank you from my heart for all the serene happiness you have allowed me to enjoy through these long years. (11 July 1930)

Unfortunately Gardiner's early days at Fontmell Hill were not trouble-free. He experienced a near disaster. Whether due to a failing in the design or to inefficiency on the part of the local builder, an unusually heavy rainfall played havoc with the building and for a whole week water forced an entry through every possible crevice and crack in the structure. Ironically this coincided with an attack of influenza that carried

Gardiner to his bed. He was unwittingly plunged into the midst of the troubles. For days his workmen, armed with pails, worked like mariners, bailing out the flooded floors. When he was able to, Gardiner withdrew to Ashampstead in disgust, determined to give up the new house. But after a while sanity prevailed; he had the building covered with rough-cast to make it at least water-tight, and he returned, convinced that its appearance had been completely ruined. He was never to be really happy with the house. By March 1931 the move was complete. The Stubbles cottages he also put on the market and was near to selling them when, in a generous change of mind, he gave them instead to the younger Austins.

For his holiday in April that year he chose Italy and Yugoslavia and invited Frederic Austin and Norman O'Neill as his guests. He also extended an invitation to Clemens von Franckenstein, offering to pay his hotel and travel expenses and asking him to bring a friend. But instead, as it turned out, the three met Clé in Munich on their return journey. As always Gardiner planned the holiday with meticulous care and even had some lessons in Serbian beforehand. Adine O'Neill and her daughter Yvonne dined with them at the Gare de Lyon in Paris before seeing them off on their train to Milan. This may have been the occasion on which Gardiner, having planned to dine before leaving, had carefully consulted the railway timetable in advance to ensure they had sufficient time without hurrying their meal. But when a railway official informed him nearer the hour of their departure that the time of their train had been changed and they would have to make other eating arrangements, Gardiner was furious and expressed his feelings accordingly. However, after further checking it was found that a mistake had been made and the original plans could stand. But Gardiner, by then resigned to the idea that a change of plan would be necessary, once more exploded with anger.

A typical touch to his holiday planning was that he would, if possible, arrange to arrive at Venice under a full moon. Norman O'Neill was not fond of 'sight-seeing holidays' but when the party emerged from the railway station onto a moonlit Grand Canal he was enchanted. From Venice they crossed to Yugoslavia and cruised down the Dalmatian Coast. They returned by way of Salzburg to Munich where they were Clé's guests. As Intendant at the Munich Opera House he gave them seats for *Gianni Schicchi*, *The Nutcracker* and *Rosenkavalier*. From there the party split, with Gardiner and Austin going on to the Black Forest and then to Grez. This was the last holiday Gardiner took with O'Neill. 'Norman enjoyed the trip enormously', he later wrote. 'I think I may say he was one of the best travelling companions I ever knew, good-humoured, accommodating, with no tiresome ideas about the necessity of seeing all the "sights" and so on.'[10] Austin similarly treasured the holiday and shared Gardiner's feeling of post-war decay:

New sights and sounds, ideal weather, and three long-intimate and congenial friends – what more delightful holiday could be imagined?' It was also, alas, to be a last golden aftermath of the happy years in which we, with other kindred creative spirits, had lived and worked, before the First World War had touched everything we had known with its disintegrating finger.[11]

Even with the problems of settling into Fontmell Hill Gardiner's patronage and generosity remained largely unaffected. He continued his earlier support for the Philharmonic Choir by offering them two hundred pounds each October for a three-year period. Nor did his gifts diminish the following year, as he recorded with some surprise: 'Apparently I gave away £2,600 in 1932, and Cantorist!' For a while his trips to Grez became less frequent. On 17 March 1932 Jelka wrote to Grainger: 'Balfour comes so rarely and then so hurriedly – just a meteor – that one can never do a thing. Then Balfour is in such a state about the £ having sunk, that he dare not leave England on account of the loss!!' Nevertheless he was abroad in June, first at Sondershausen and then he crossed to Stockholm to meet up with Percy and Ella Grainger once more. There too he joined Arnold Bax and Harriet Cohen who were on their way to visit Sibelius in Finland. They stayed a few days in Stockholm where, as Cohen remembered, Gardiner delighted them 'with quite incredible stories about Percy Grainger, of whom he was inordinately fond'.[12] Harriet Cohen was not one of Gardiner's favourite women. He had to endure one uncomfortable evening alone with her in a restaurant when her attentions to other men dining at nearby tables caused him embarrassment, irritation, and finally disgust. He accompanied Bax and Cohen on the steamer crossing to Finland, but then parted company to visit his brother Alan and his wife Hedi who were staying with Hedi's relations. He later rejoined Bax and Cohen for a drive through the Savo province.

Holst had made his last visit to Ashampstead in September 1930 and the following year he was twice a guest at the Oxford flat. In January 1932 he left for America to take up an appointment as lecturer in composition at Harvard University. But in March he was seriously ill with an attack of haemorrhagic gastritis. On his recovery he returned home in June and spent a night in Gardiner's flat in August. Sadly, he was to suffer from poor health for the remaining two years of his life. Gardiner's own health by comparison was for a while remarkably good, his only complaint being eczema which periodically troubled him.

His companions abroad in 1933 were Arnold Bax and Patrick Hadley. His plans this time needed very careful consideration. While he and Bax had few restraints on their time, Hadley was teaching at the RCM. More seriously, Hadley had an artificial leg (which in a boisterous mood he would sometimes take off and brandish wildly in the air). This made any arduous walking quite out of the question and Gardiner took considerable trouble to devise an itinerary that would impose the least strain on his companion. In April the three toured Greece and Yugoslavia by boat, train and car. Bax and Hadley often went together to Fontmell Hill and, much as Gardiner loved their friendship, he found entertaining as ever very exhausting, especially when his guests showed a fondness for consuming spirits into the small hours. One night he left them with a decanter of whisky ('firewater', as he called it) and was amazed the next morning to find it empty. 'But aw! is it possible, Adams?' he enquired of his faithful valet. Gardiner's hospitality, though freely given, was not to be solicited, and Bax came dangerously near to doing so after one particularly enjoyable weekend. While thanking Gardiner, he had expressed the hope that it might be repeated soon. From a wary Gardiner came the rejoinder *sotto voce*, 'Er, yes, Arnold, at not too frequent intervals.' Arnold's brother Clifford was a less regular visitor to Fontmell. Both Bax brothers were keen cricketers and during one of their infrequent joint visits all the guests were organised by them into a game of cricket in which Gardiner actually participated, regarding the whole thing as a huge joke.

In July 1933 there came an invitation from Grainger, asking Gardiner to accompany him to Australia where he had an exacting concert tour awaiting him. But this offer was not taken up. The confines of an ocean liner would probably have made Gardiner restless and the long sea voyage would keep him too long away from his forestry work. He was anyway finding travelling more tiring and now preferred the relative comfort of trains to long car journeys; his trips to Grez in recent years were all made by rail. So in September Percy and Ella Grainger sailed for Australia without his companionship.

Other friends meanwhile continued to be the object of his unexpected generosity. When a couple who had been former neighbours at Sutton Scotney were in some difficulties, Gardiner offered to pay for the wife's operation and nursing expenses and told her husband that he would give them £1,250 towards a house they desired. In October 1932 Clemens von Franckenstein's son Eugen had begun studying at Weimar, and Gardiner sent Clé 5,800 marks to cover the fees of the three-year course. There were other gifts, including a donation of £100 to the Berkshire Hospital. But even such kindnesses could not alleviate the deep sorrow that centred on three of his closest friends in the coming tragic year.

13 'This is a terrible time . . .'

1934-1936

No year was more tragic for British music than 1934 which for Balfour Gardiner also brought deep personal grief. A dark shadow had earlier been cast by the death of Philip Heseltine in December 1930 under circumstances that suggested the likelihood of suicide, and Gardiner was one of many musicians to contribute to a memorial concert held the following February in the Wigmore Hall. But now in the first six months of 1934 were announced the deaths of Elgar, O'Neill, Holst and Delius. His acquaintance with Elgar had been but a brief one during the 1912 concerts. Despite their presidential offices in connection with the Oriana Madrigal Society there had been little personal contact. Gardiner even once talked of purposely avoiding Elgar behind cathedral pillars at a Three Choirs Festival,and when the question later arose of a title for the revision of a movement from his early string quintet, he instructed Grainger: 'Avoid Introduction and Allegro or anything that reminds me of Elgar.'[1]

But the loss of three close friends was a heavy blow. Norman O'Neill's death was the least expected. Crossing a road on the way to conduct a rehearsal of his music at Broadcasting House on 12 February, he was struck on the head by the mirror of a passing vehicle. At the time the injury did not seem too serious, but blood poisoning set in and the following evening he collapsed and took to his bed. A little later he was admitted to a nursing home. On 22 February Gardiner requested Adine O'Neill: 'Give Norman my love as soon as he is able to receive messages, and my best wishes for his recovery.' But, despite an operation and a blood transfusion, he died on 3 March. Among their last communications had been a letter Balfour wrote the previous Christmas, thanking Norman for some 1820 Cognac. 'I am afraid I shall have to enjoy it selfishly', he had added, 'for I find that if I offer Cognac to friends they just lap it up like water.'

Holst had been ill again at Christmas 1932 and he spent several spells in an Ealing nursing home. By summer there had been some improvement, and he and Isobel together visited Gardiner, probably for the last time, in July 1933. With typical concern Balfour had enquired beforehand from Isobel about the diet Gustav was then restricted to. Towards the end of that year and in the months that followed Holst spent most of

188

his time in another nursing home, at Windsor. In the afternoon of 30 January 1934, after lunching with a friend in London, Gardiner visited him on what was probably the last occasion they saw each other. Two days after his visit he wrote offering to pay for two months' clinic fees. In May Holst underwent a major operation which he did not survive, dying two days later on the 25th. With the loss of such a close friend the least Gardiner felt he could do was pay for all the nursing and operation expenses himself.

Hardly had this second blow fallen when, in little more than a fortnight, there came the loss of yet another friend. Apart from the grief that any death incurs, in Delius's case it was much aggravated by legal entanglements that were to upset Gardiner profoundly. With Delius's rapidly declining health the drama at Grez had been heightened in May 1934 by Jelka Delius undergoing an operation for cancer. 'This is a terrible time – Norman's death, Gustav's death, and now this serious news about Jelka', Gardiner wrote to Delius on 26 May. Much later he filled in the details for Grainger who was then in Australia:

I must tell you that after eleven days' illness Jelka was hurried away to hospital in Fontainebleau, and had 11 cm. cut out of her abdomen before her eyes (the operation lasted 2 hours & she only had local anaesthetics). Another day's delay, and she would have died! Fred, of course, was in a terrible state, thinking that she would die before him, and telegraphed to me to come over & arrange to be executor of his will. It is almost incredible that they should have gone on for years & years without making provision for the possibility of Jelka's dying first. When I arrived I found Fred too weak to do anything but tell me his wishes; the formalities of making a will would have been too much for him. After a couple of days I returned to England. Jelka was already home again, and although very ill, was practically out of danger. Fred might have lingered on for months. But as soon as I had got back to Oxford I found a telegram saying 'Fred worse': a few hours later came a telegram 'Delius dead'. I had already made preparations to return to Grez. It was an awful time. In all I made six journeys between France and England & another two in September. Happily, Jelka has recovered. I gave what help I could about her affairs, but I can do no more, nor is it necessary that I should tell you all about them. They have made things about as difficult as it is possible to make them, with a will in French though they are English citizens, and banking accounts in Fontainebleau, London, Geneva & Frankfurt!

(28 December 1934)

For someone as ingenuous as Gardiner matters were indeed difficult, and the interpretation of Delius's dying wishes proved to be a bone of contention and the cause of the upset to follow. After receiving a telegram from Fenby informing him of Jelka's successful operation, Gardiner had written to Delius on 26 May:

Now that Jelka is out of danger, as I assume from the reassuring tone of Eric's telegram, would it not be better to wait a little time before I take over the executorship of your will? I do not know what the present arrangements are, but I think it would be wise to let them stand as they are for a little time – at least until we have had time to discuss the matter. This is best done verbally, but I am so busy at present that I cannot get away: in July I shall be able to, that is, in only about six weeks from now.

But the worsening situation made an earlier visit to Grez imperative, and on 7 June, only three days before Delius's death, Gardiner was in France noting down in his pocket-book details for a codicil to the existing will in accordance with Delius's wishes. There was to be grateful recognition of Fenby's services: he was to receive £1,000 and take charge of the music. Instructions were given that there was to be no religious ceremony for the burial, a vault was to be made for Delius and Jelka to lie in the churchyard, and the wine cellar was to be left to Kennedy Scott and Frederic Austin, the furniture having already been promised to Gardiner. Then came the crucial clause:

Everything to Jelka for her life & then when everything is paid out residue of estate & royalties to be used in expense of a yearly concert with Phil [harmonic] . . . & Beecham as conductor – one work of D [elius] in every concert & the rest of the concert made up by compositions of young English composers who merit public performance. Society to be presided over by Beecham who is to choose a committee who will arrange the programmes.

Gardiner was only able to stay for two days, but his brief presence was a consolation both to Delius and to Fenby, who has written in *Delius As I Knew Him* that 'the companionship, understanding, and advice which he gave me during those days made it possible for me to go on alone'.[2] He returned to England, promising to come back to Grez should there be any serious change. A day or two later Jelka was able to leave the hospital and join Delius at his bedside. The end came very soon and with incredible pain. He truly lived up to the creed of his own *Requiem* – 'I honour the man who can love life, yet without base fear can die.' On the morning of Sunday 10 June Fenby telegraphed the news to Gardiner who once again crossed to France, this time to be at the graveside as Delius's coffin was temporarily laid in the Grez churchyard. But, as the wishes that Delius had confided on his death-bed to him had yet to be ratified by law, the troubles were only beginning. The issue at stake was the concert scheme.

However uncharacteristic of Delius the idea may appear, the seed had been sown as long ago as August 1918 when he drew up a will with Gardiner, Grainger and Heseltine as executors, specifying that, in the event of the simultaneous deaths of himself and Jelka, a fund was to be created from which awards of two hundred pounds a year were to be made to young British composers. In its now enlarged form as an annual concert yet to be legally proven, Gardiner was most anxious that Jelka would ensure its recognition under the terms of her own will. As both he and Fenby had originally been asked to act as her executors, he ac-

190

cordingly wrote to Fenby on 20 June: 'It is most desirable that Jelka's will should be made before you go to England. I shall bring a draft with me next Tuesday, but of course completion is impossible till she has made up her mind about the trustees for the concert scheme.'

Matters were very much complicated by the fact that, as Jelka knew only too well, Gardiner would never confer with or even speak to Beecham who was, of course, to be the co-ordinator of the concert plan. Furthermore she had the impression that the wishes which Delius had expressed to both Gardiner and Fenby were intended only in the case of her predecease, something which at the time had seemed a likelihood. She felt there was some misunderstanding for, while after her return from hospital Delius, as was his habit, had left all decision-making to her, Gardiner nonetheless still felt obliged to follow his wishes explicitly. On 28 August she wrote to Fenby: 'I have made my testament in French and I sent a copy of it to Balfour who thought it very good. But, of course, I can modify it any day and make it in England. But I must really speak to Beecham before settling anything definite.'

At the beginning of October Gardiner took Hadley to Grez. Following Delius's death the household finances were in the melting pot and so he lent Jelka five hundred pounds to help her in the interim. Later that month she was well enough to cross to England where she made arrangements for Delius's reinterment at Limpsfield in Surrey. She also attended a performance at Queen's Hall of *A Mass of Life* conducted by Beecham. After the concert, at Adine O'Neill's, she discussed the concert scheme with Beecham who argued that its aims were already being largely fulfilled by the Patron's Fund at the RCM and suggested instead that Delius's royalties could be used more practically under the guidance of a trust formed to perpetuate his name. When Gardiner heard of this he was deeply hurt and on 14 December wrote to Fenby:

Jelka no doubt acquainted you with the terms of her French will. I thought it was final, but to my astonishment she wrote to me about a fortnight ago saying that Beecham's solicitors has sent her the draft of a fresh will for her consideration and that the concert scheme, so clearly described to us by Fred, has been abandoned.

Gardiner was left with little alternative but to resign as executor. Later that same month Jelka told Fenby:

I have been thro' quite a lot of rather painful correspondence with Balfour about the testament. It was, as you know, impossible to arrange those concerts, as Beecham was dead against it . . . As Balfour had said so often that he would as well *not* be an executor, and as he is quite decided never again to have anything to do with Beecham it is quite impossible anyhow to have him in the affair. Besides he is no 'homme d'affaires'.

The trust set up in place of the concert scheme consisted of a legal trustee, a bank trustee, and Beecham and Frederic Austin acting as musical advisers. While in hindsight it can now be judged as the more beneficial course to adopt, for Gardiner it represented an abdication of responsibility by failing to honour his promise to the dying Delius. 'I gave Fred a solemn undertaking to do this and he died in confidence that I would keep my promise', he explained to Fenby on 30 December. He therefore withdrew, bitterly disillusioned.

These differences in no way impaired his affection for Jelka. 'Meanwhile the dear thing has actually been making a tea-cloth for me', he added in his letter to Fenby, 'as if she had not enough to do already.' But such problems were taking toll of her health, and when in May 1935 Delius's body was taken from Grez for burial at Limpsfield, it seemed doubtful whether she would be able to make the crossing as well. However, an ambulance was arranged to take her to Paris where Fenby, who had specially returned to Grez to witness the exhumation, saw her on to the train for Boulogne. She spent the night in a Dover hotel where two nurses and another ambulance met her for the last stage of the journey to London. Adine O'Neill was to look after her during her stay, but Jelka contracted pneumonia on the Channel crossing and was not well enough to attend the funeral service at Limpsfield on 26 May, when many musicians, including Balfour Gardiner, paid their last respects to Delius. Instead she was admitted to a nursing home in Kensington where she died within two days. When she herself was laid to rest alongside her husband, among those friends in the Delius circle present were Adine O'Neill, Kennedy Scott, Hadley, Fenby, Barjansky, Howard-Jones, and Balfour Gardiner, who had himself covered the expenses of her journey and medical care.

There remained the final chapter in his Delius friendship – disposing of the house at Grez. Barjansky among others had suggested that it might be maintained in Delius's memory, but Gardiner felt that as a museum or some such similar idea it would attract little interest. He wrote to Grainger in April 1936:

I did give some thought to keeping the place as a museum, and if you had been in Europe and able to arrange it, I might possibly have considered it further. But it would have been simply for your own personal satisfaction. I must confess that I do not see eye to eye with you about museums, reputations, and so on.

With his forestry work in Dorset it would have been an added responsibility and too distant to be under his constant supervision. So in July he gave instructions for its sale to be set in motion, initially asking 225,000 francs. But the house was not sold until May 1936, to Dr A.R. Merle d'Aubigné, by which time he had had to lower the price to 120,000 francs. With the 'Front Populaire' then at the head of the French government, he feared difficulties with the sterling conversion and so stipulated that it should be paid in English pounds.

With Jelka's death there were a few debts and settlements that Gardiner, although no longer her executor, nonetheless felt obliged to attend to as best he could. Many of those friends in the Delius circle had not been remembered in Jelka's will. He could only suppose that she had intended giving them presents during her life–time had she lived longer. As an artist in her own right, on her death she left many of her own canvases, and Gardiner tried to put matters right by purchasing some of them to give to those friends who had been forgotten. The paintings were valued in Paris for an insignificant sum and Gardiner bought them in most cases for as little as two pounds each and distributed about a dozen between the violinist May Harrison, Kennedy Scott, Frederic Austin, Adine O'Neill, Patrick Hadley and Percy Grainger. Gardiner also generously looked after Marthe Grespier, the devoted cook and housekeeper, whom he kept on at Grez until the house was sold.

Although in April 1935 he had taken a short holiday with Hadley in the South East of France, after more than a year of worries and bereavements he was in need of a rest. He was back again on the Continent in July after Jelka's death to assess the situation at Grez, and later that year he went into a nursing home for the removal of a bursa from his leg, which left him lame for a while. Then towards the end of the year such an accumulation of troubles precipitated a breakdown and once more he was confined to bed, this time with angina pectoris. He had complained of heart pains for many years and he now realised that in future he would have to lead a quieter life. In the circumstances, his doctor thought it inadvisable for him to sleep alone at Fontmell Hill. Up till now his housekeeper had lived in a cottage a short distance below from where she could be summoned in an emergency by a system of bells. So that help could be closer at hand when required, especially in the event of bad weather, it was decided that an annexe should be added to the house, providing accommodation for the housekeeper.

If a multitude of personal worries had brought about his breakdown, there was at least some consolation to be drawn from the pleasure and satisfaction his forestry work was bringing him. After a disagreement with his former head forester, in January 1933 he appointed a new man, James Winskill, and at the end of 1934 he was able to write to Grainger:

The planting is going on splendidly. My nephew Rolf and I will in a few years' time have changed the aspect of the countryside with afforestation and agriculture. When I went there a few years ago it was a scene of desolation, but now the trees are growing up and the fields are cultivated, a joy to behold.

(28 December 1934)

Rolf Gardiner had married in September 1932 and now lived at the foot of the downs at Springhead, Fontmell Magna. From 1934 until the outbreak of the Second World War he ran work camps at Gore Farm and at Springhead in pursuance of his idea for a Wessex centre. These camps, usually held at mid-winter, Easter, and harvest time, drew a variety of people including miners, unemployed workmen, and students from abroad, and work on the land was combined with forms of recreation – singing, mime and folk-dancing. Balfour Gardiner had little to do with the work camps. When staying at Fontmell Hill he was once invited to Gore Farm for a camp breakfast but became disgruntled when a lengthy Latin grace in complicated counterpoint had first to be sung before he could sit down to scrambled eggs – by then stone cold. He good-humouredly dismissed much of the ritual that surrounded Rolf's activities. He would laugh at the idea of a bishop being asked to bless the plough and, to a connoisseur of wines, drinking a toast at dinner-time in water from the local spring seemed an odd custom.

In May 1936 Balfour Gardiner took two days' holiday in Cork. For the rest of the year he saw much of Grainger who, after his extended concert tour in Australia and New Zealand during which he had given forty-eight performances of Gardiner's piano pieces, had sailed in May from America with Ella his wife, and they both visited Fontmell Hill in June. The following month Gardiner called on them at their cottage in Pevensey Bay, Sussex. From there he and Grainger walked over to Hurstmonceux Castle, with Gardiner giving vent to his views on badly planned country houses. 'Instead of thinking the whole thing properly from the start', he told Grainger, 'they build an inadequate house to begin with and then they add on a coal shed here, and a tool shed there until the final result is utterly shapeless.' He could give the impression of rarely being satisfied, for when they passed a house for which he expressed a liking, in the same breath he referred to his own as 'the ugliest house in all England'. While they rested a while and gazed across the Sussex countryside, Grainger explained to him the Free Music he was experimenting with, how its 'curving tone-lines would be like the curving shapes of clouds and tree-tops, and the stir in its form-urges like stream drifts in the air and in the sea'. In a thoughtful moment Gardiner commented, 'Stick to your trees and clouds and currents. They will bring you less disappointment than human-beings.'[3]

In September Percy and Ella Grainger, Cyril Scott and Balfour Gardiner took a holiday together in France. The political upheavals in Spain had put crossing the Pyrenees out of the question, so they kept to the French side of the border, staying for much of the time at Argelès and Lourdes. As usual Gardiner made all the necessary travel arrangements and planned to leave London on the 25th. But Grainger particularly wanted to hear for the first time Delius's *A Mass of Life* which was being performed that day at the Norwich Triennial Festival, Beecham conducting, so he arranged to join the others at Lourdes. On the homeward journey after the holiday Gardiner looked in at Grez and paid his respects to Madame Grespier. But he felt no inclination to see Delius's house. 'It is strange', he wrote afterwards to Fenby, 'that Grez, which we were so intimately bound up with, should leave us so little, now that Fred & Jelka are dead: I doubt whether I shall ever go back there.'

The four met together once more in October at Fontmell Hill. Cyril Scott's *Festival Overture* (a reworking of an early overture winning him a *Daily Telegraph* prize) and Gardiner's *Overture to a Comedy* were both down for performance at Bournemouth. Richard Austin was in charge of the Municipal Orchestra, and as it was only an hour's drive away Gardiner went over for at least one or two rehearsals. Despite his 'having done' with music, he was also revising his early string quintet, but this renewal of contact with the musical world threw him into dejection. He wrote on 25 October to Grainger: 'The result of listening to Cyril's overture & my own, and having to think of this string quintet movement is that I am quite restless and unhappy and more than ever glad that I turned my back on composition and on music generally.' At the end of the month Grainger was taking part in a BBC broadcast of his own works, but Gardiner could not bring himself to attend even the rehearsals and on 4 November once again apologised profusely for his absence: 'I really get irritated, and my nerves at present, owing to many visitors & much business, are frayed already.' He could not face any more irritation by having to listen to music. On 29 October he had pleaded:

If I were still musical, there would be but little excuse, but shall I *never*, although I have been saying it over & over again for more than ten years - quite openly, honestly, sincerely - convince you that my musical feeling has gone, and that I detest music and get nervous and unhappy when I hear it? . . . It is really not my fault, but the great grief of my life that music has forsaken me. Life changes, death comes, and comes sometimes piecemeal, as in the case of my music. That part of me is dead.

He had slipped completely out of touch with contemporary British music, even with the latest music of his friends. He admitted to knowing none of the late works of Delius (except *A Song of Summer* and a violin sonata), none of Bax's recent compositions, and none of Vaughan Williams's excepting the Fourth Symphony which he had heard 'by chance'. As for Lambert and Walton, he had once or twice switched on the radio out of curiosity, only to turn it off immediately.

Partly because of Gardiner's unwillingness to attend the BBC rehearsals and bearing in mind his earlier criticisms, Grainger felt a distinct coolness on his friend's part towards his music. Perhaps age had blunted their acceptance of such frank admissions for Grainger went so far as to suggest that Gardiner had never liked his compositions, something that the facts prove to be very far from the truth as Gardiner had frequently shown unbounded enthusiasm for many of Grainger's scores. 'They, and Cyril's, were the profoundest influences at the most impressionable period of my life', he assured Grainger in November, 'though of course owing to their smaller bulk & scope they could not win over Wagner and Tchaikovsky.' But Grainger was not entirely convinced and as late as 1947 wrote to his friends: 'I feel that all the judgements that have been passed on me & my tone-works by tone-wrights such as Delius & Balfour Gardiner are wholly misleading . . .'[4]

It seemed improbable that someone so steeped in music would be able to make a total renunciation, so Gardiner's looking again at the early quintet had not come as a complete surprise. 'How we hanker after our old works!' he once exclaimed to Grainger.[5] In February 1932 he began reworking the last movement but it was a slow process. He had little confidence in improving the work. 'It is really too poor for performance, though there are one or two passages I like & would be glad to rescue', he wrote on 9 September 1936. 'However the attempt would be futile; I have neither the technical skill nor the imagination to place them in a worthy setting, so they must just perish. This is perhaps the fate of 999 out of every 1000 good musical ideas ever thought of, and we still have enough to go on with.'

Yet he did complete the work, in Oxford, on 11 November that year, calling it a *Movement for Strings in C minor*, with the final movement of the original quintet as its basis. Grainger wanted to arrange the finished work for full string orchestra to which Gardiner at first objected on the grounds that there was nothing for double-basses to do. He argued that the weight and depth given by the basses of a string orchestra called for quite another sort of writing. All the same Grainger prepared an edited version for publication, making the work playable by any number of strings up to a full complement including basses. He outlined the deployment of the extra strings in a detailed preface, and the music was printed as a facsimile score on eight staves, five for the original solo instruments and a further three (in smaller script) for third violin, second cello and double-bass parts when a full string orchestra was being used. Grainger loved this 'string 5-some' in which he felt Gardiner's 'lovely, lovable being-type is all stored up . . . just as summer sun is stored up in the bee's honey'.[6] He was the work's dedicatee, a compliment reciprocated by the dedication to Gardiner of his settings of two traditional tunes they had both independently arranged, *The Three Ravens* and *Sir Eglamore*, as well as *Hill-Song No. 2*. Way back in May 1911 Grainger had had a run-through of this last work in its wind-band version in a small hall off the Tottenham Court Road in London quite possibly hired at Gardiner's expense; another version, incorporating parts for brass and percussion, was played in the second of the 1913 concerts.

The outbreak of war postponed publication of the *Movement for Strings* until 1949 when it was issued by Schott & Co., largely at Grainger's expense. Gardiner wanted all the royalties to go to Grainger but foresaw difficulties and so suggested that to avoid any administrative confusion 10 per cent should be assigned to himself, generously adding that should his share amount to any significant sum he would repay it to Grainger. In its expanded 'elastically-scored' version, the *Movement for Strings* is a splendid addition to the string orchestra repertoire. The gravity of the introduction, built mainly on evenly-stressed chords, is soon swept aside by an uprush of strings plunging into an *allegro*. Reminders of the opening intrude, but these give way to one of the loveliest moments in all of Gardiner's music as the mood relaxes to a song-like melody no less poignant for the similarity it bears to Wagner's *Siegfried Idyll* with its falling fifth, and constructed in fact from the same six initial notes (example 34: solo viola, the quintet version). It was

Ex. 34

an unerring judgment on Grainger's part to realise the potential of this revised quintet version and to make of it such a fine and very English work despite the obvious influences of Wagner and Tchaikovsky.

The *Movement for Strings* was completed at 39 Belsyre Court, the new Oxford flat Gardiner moved into during the summer. One in a recently erected block of flats, this was a considerable improvement on his previous accommodation in the city. Here he made his other home and he now led two lives – as a forester in Dorset and a gentleman of leisure (and only occasionally a composer) in Oxford. He rarely spent more than three to four weeks at a time at Fontmell Hill, and Christmas was always passed (but not celebrated) in Oxford. For a while he studiously avoided having a telephone, an appliance he disliked – when necessary he resorted to the telegraph – and even when one was eventually installed it was almost exclusively left to his valet Adams to handle. Adams was more-or-less permanently stationed in Oxford, attending to the upkeep of the flat which was always at the disposal of friends. Anyone, even an employee, passing through Oxford was welcome to call at the flat where a meal would be provided. Hubert Adams had a twin brother Hugh who regularly visited him there and was free to stay at the flat in Gardiner's absence, and when Gardiner happened to be at home he would put Hugh up at the Randolph hotel at his own expense.

In 1936 Eric Fenby's now classic account of his years spent with Delius was published. Not long after Delius's death in 1934 Gardiner had been approached by a publisher with a view to a biography. With little confidence in his own writing ability – 'hardly a sentence that I write comes easily, and often I have to leave my thought overstated or understated or altogether inaccurate'[7] – he turned the offer down, suggesting Fenby in his place. When *Delius As I Knew Him* appeared, Gardiner was delighted with it. He did have one reservation – the portrait it included by James Gunn of the composer in his last years he found too painful. Despite the reservations he had about his own fluency with the pen, it is much to be regretted that Gardiner never committed to paper any reminiscences of Delius and that he did not live long enough to contribute to Hubert Foss's revision of Heseltine's Delius biography and so add his anecdotes to those of Grainger, Kennedy Scott and Quilter. The Beecham–Wood enmity has already been touched on. When Wood's autobiography *My Life of Music* appeared in 1938, its author is reputed to have said to Benjamin Dale with unconcealed delight: 'What do you think of that? Four hundred and ninety-five pages – and not a single reference to Beecham!'[8] Unfortunately, when Beecham's supposedly authoritative biography of Delius appeared in 1959, Balfour Gardiner received similarly scant treatment – one brief mention that spoke nothing of the years of devoted friendship.

Two years after the publication of Fenby's book came for Gardiner the unexpected pleasure of being asked to accept the dedication of Imogen Holst's biography of her father. As with the Delius book, he was much impressed by both its clarity and the sympathetic treatment of its subject. He must have had some satisfaction in the thought that the 'lives' of two of his closest friends could have been in no safer hands.

14 'We are growing old . . .'
1937–1950

With the approach in 1937 of his sixtieth birthday, Balfour Gardiner gave serious thought to the disposal of his property in the event of his death. Feeling that the preservation of his music for posterity was of little consequence, he had held on to a handful of manuscripts that were of some significance to him, while the rest – the greater number – he had some years earlier relegated to the incinerator. The woodlands were now his chief concern for the future. While he firmly believed in the good work of the Forestry Commission and felt inclined to leave much to them, he also considered forming a company to which he could leave his Dorset property, with his nephew Rolf as the chief share-holder. As it turned out, he bought two devastated woods in Cranborne Chase which he presented to the Forestry Commission, promising as well to buy more land as a further gift for them. The two areas he gave became known as 'Gardiner's Forest' and 'Balfour's Wood'. In time he made over to his nephew the remainder of his land which formed the bulk of the Spring-head Estate under Rolf's management. Meanwhile Balfour continued to take an active part in tree planting, perhaps at least deriving solace from the knowledge that his forestry work would attain some permanence after his death even if his compositions might not endure.

He was abroad in April, touring through France, Italy and Yugoslavia, since Spain had been thrown into civil war. As well as his usual guests at Fontmell Hill that year, including Frederic Austin and Kennedy Scott, there were two special reunions: in January with W.H. Bell and his wife on a visit from South Africa, and in June with Clemens von Franckenstein. In September he felt fit enough for some hill-walking in South Wales that came as a great relief after his recent lameness. Exactly a year later he was back in the Welsh hills and proud of being able to climb to two thousand feet with little exertion. In May 1938 he took an eighteen-day holiday once again in Italy and Yugoslavia and his guests were Richard Austin and his cellist wife Leily Howell. But that year the weather was poor for much of the time and they consequently sat 'too many weary hours in the coach'. With summer came another typically benevolent gesture when Gardiner offered Richard Austin generous provisions should he feel compelled to resign his conducting post at Bournemouth. Under the shadow of imminent war the economies of the day had forced the Bournemouth Corporation to make drastic cuts in the size of their Municipal Orchestra. When further war-time cuts later reduced it to a body of only twenty-four players, Austin felt there was little alternative but to resign, and Gardiner kept to his word.

Gardiner had planned to take Patrick Hadley to the Pyrenees before the year was spent, but his intended guest had recently been appointed professor of music at Cambridge and could not spare the time, leaving Gardiner without a travelling companion and unwilling to make the trip alone. The following year the ominous political noises in Germany were momentarily forgotten in the pleasure of two last holidays before war engulfed Europe. In April 1939 he crossed to Ireland where he was met by Arnold Bax. Together they travelled by train to Kenmare to join 'Jack' Moeran, a frequent companion of Bax's in Ireland. County Kerry was a favourite retreat of Moeran's and the inspiration of his lyrical violin concerto, then as yet unborn, and of those stormy climaxes in his symphony first performed the previous January. Gardiner spent nearly ten days in Kerry and Cork, returning home in the first week of May.

Meanwhile, in America Percy Grainger had sensed the real threat of war and, wishing to greet his friends for what could be the last time, sailed the Atlantic with Ella, and early in June they were with Gardiner at his Oxford flat. The Graingers then left for a walking tour of the Telemark region of Norway in the company of their good friends, the Norwegian composer Sparre Olsen and his wife. When they had completed the tour, Grainger thought that Gardiner would have enjoyed it so much that he suggested repeating it with him. So in July Gardiner sailed from Newcastle and the five did the trip again, this time in reverse and at a more leisurely pace to suit their older companion. Grainger had already introduced Olsen to Gardiner's compositions. 'He is such a fine and lovely person and his music reflects his personality', he told the Olsens. They did indeed like him. 'We liked him right away. He was agreeable and considerate', wrote Olsen. 'Gardiner was older than the rest of us and did not care much for hiking. He lost his heart completely to Seljord where he felt like remaining for the rest of his life. "Why are we leaving?" he said. "It is not possible to find something more beautiful".'[1]

Gardiner also took to Olsen, as a man but not as a composer. When Grainger showed him some of Olsen's works for chorus, his only comment was: 'It's terribly poor stuff, isn't it? It's too bad that such a delightful chap should write such poor music.'[2] It seems that Grainger derived much pleasure from extracting some outspoken opinions from Gardiner of his fellow composers, and this Norwegian holiday had provided him with such an opportunity. In his anecdotes Grainger wrote:

Balfour would seem to lose his art-heart to a given tone-wright for a few years, only to turn against that man and his work in the end. Maybe it was some self-awareness of his aesthetic fickleness that made him unwilling to state his judgements upon his fellow tone-wrights. He tried to wriggle out of doing so if he could (especially with me where he could see that I was mischievously trying to wheedle derogatory statements out of him) . . . But on that trip from Notodden to Bergen . . . I caught Balfour off-guard. That was the morning we saw him striding along with great strides in the rain, his bald head shining wet . . . Later the same morning we had a long rough bus drive from Roldal to Hardanger I think. We were thrown up and down like pan-cakes in a pan and in the middle of this mind-addling jolt I slipped a quick askment at Balfour. 'What do you think of Vaughan Williams' music?' And like a shot out of a gun before he had time to hide behind caution came Balfour's answer: 'Vaughan Williams is a miserable composer.' Those words were my reward for the whole trip.

Ten years later Gardiner enlarged upon his hasty judgment in a letter to Grainger: 'VW is one of the composers I definitely avoid – I find nothing but dreariness in him, & I am not in the slightest influenced by all the boosting he gets from the press.'[3] To him 'Old Vaughan' was 'the dullest composer since Dvořák', an opinion hard to square with those moments of apocalyptic vision in *Sancta Civitas* and *Job* contrasting strongly with the more familiar pastoral vein which makes many a Vaughan Williams score instantly recognisable. Bax once tried to defend RVW by humming a theme from the *Pastoral* Symphony, but Gardiner immediately burst in, 'Aw, but Arnold, how unpleasant!' Considering how he had championed Vaughan Williams's music before

18   Balfour Gardiner, Percy Grainger and Sparre Olsen at Haukeliseter,
Norway, in July 1939

the Great War, this reaction supports Grainger's claim that Gardiner lost his affection for certain composers' works. He cited Scott's and his own as further examples of music that had slipped from favour. Grainger sensed too that Gardiner liked less the later music of Bax and Holst. 'There's Arnold writing all these old symphonies', he once commented good-humouredly. 'He's rapidly outstripping Beethoven and soon he'll have only that formidable couple Mozart and Haydn to compete with!'[4] He thought Holst's see-sawing back and forth on two chords 'a most terrible habit . . . it ruins all his music'.[5] The musicologist E.J. Dent was dubbed 'the old Pelican' and there was no reverence lost on 'old Bach and that congregation'. But his special scorn was reserved for 'that desolating old monkey' – Beethoven. Attending one of Richard Austin's Bournemouth concerts at which Edwin Fischer was playing the *Emperor* Concerto, Gardiner went round at the end of the concert and greeted the pianist: 'Really, Herr Fischer, you must agree, this concerto is nothing but the work of a madman!'[6]

Of those composers for whose music he showed any liking, Wagner and Tchaikovsky remained his models. For the rest, Grainger fortunately provided a few clues to Gardiner's preferences when he wrote in his anecdotes:

I was amazed when he told me he did not really enjoy Bach or any old music. I certainly never heard him say a good word of the Haydn, Mozart, Beethoven period, or for Chopin. What music did I hear him discuss as if it were real and vital to him? Tchaikovsky, Ravel, Debussy and the music of his friends. Perhaps he liked many other composers also, such as Wagner, Strauss, Bizet, but I just cannot remember him talking about them. But about Cyril, Bax, Holst, myself, and later about Denis Blood he was crazy. He wrote out, or threatened to write out, a full score of my *Wraith of Odin* about 1905 just to have it, but he was surpassingly fickle in his musical in-lovenesses . . .

With his love of Wagner and dislike of Beethoven, his tastes shared at least some common ground with Delius who once wrote: 'When at the age of 23 I heard *Tristan* I was perfectly overcome – also when I heard *Lohengrin* as a schoolboy. Beethoven always left me cold & reserved . . .'[7] They both had some liking for Spanish music, probably stronger in Gardiner's case with his love of that country, and he was consequently delighted, travelling to Salamanca on one Spanish holiday, to discover that the Spanish conductor Fernandez Arbos (orchestrator of Albeniz's *Iberia*) was in the same railway carriage. He also once had a passion for Charpentier's opera *Louise* after hearing it in Paris before the Great War.

Gardiner's sometimes startling pronouncements were not, of course, exclusively concerned with music. In *Inland Far* Clifford Bax wrote of him as having no patience with the past and, while at the same time not necessarily admiring and approving the present, living in the delusion . . . that the new is of necessity better than the old, and that the twentieth century is more enlightened than any other. In consequence, when I visit him (and that is as often as possible) I am aware that I must take nothing for granted. No bump of veneration disfigures that rosy cranium. If I appeal to authority, the flash of choler in his blue eyes is followed by a thunder of protestation. If I so much as mention Aristotle, Plato, or Marcus Aurelius, he becomes as restive as a man who is about to be unconsentingly chloroformed. 'Really, really!' he expostulates. 'These Greeks and Romans . . . dreadful old creatures.'[8]

One evening in Palma, on that pre-war Spanish holiday with Holst and the Bax brothers, the conversation had turned to women. As usual Gardiner's opinion was sought. 'You must leave me out of it', he replied, ruefully shaking his head. 'They're incomprehensible to me. I should feel more at home with an Eskimo.' 'What makes them so foreign?' someone asked. 'I don't know', he muttered. 'I never shall. And such an extraordinary shape . . . I can't see that women have anything to do with civilisation . . .'[9] One anecdote that for many years affectionately gained currency amongst his friends (Norman O'Neill would laugh at its retelling) concerns Balfour Gardiner and Arnold Bax crossing Switzerland by train. Towards sunset Balfour looked out on the Alps whose outline suddenly suggested to him the shape of the female anatomy. Without warning he jumped up and exclaimed, 'Aw, Arnold, I must go to bed. I've seen some most regrettable shapes!' and peremptorily pulled down the blinds.[10]

While Gardiner's attitude towards women remained a private joke amongst his friends, it was no secret from them that he was, like Quilter, homosexual, and though this instinct was largely repressed it remained an anxiety to his closest friends and was disquieting for Gardiner himself, no doubt contributing much to his general restlessness. His music betrays no evidence of this troubled condition, never striking that plaintive yet detached note one may with hindsight perhaps knowingly detect in Quilter's (as for example in the only memorable moment in his opera *Love at the Inn*, the slight but compelling quasi-folk-song *If Love Should Pass Me By*). Nonetheless in Gardiner's case one cannot overlook the questionable textual choice of the *April* verses by Edward Carpenter, author of *The Intermediate Sex*, with all their attendant implications. It is also surely highly significant that the piano prelude subtitled *De Profundis* should have been published (and presumably composed and so named) in the very year that extracts from Oscar Wilde's *De Profundis* first appeared, a commitment of some courage on Gardiner's part in view of the sensation caused by the publication of Wilde's 'letter' if the allusion was, as one assumes, intended.

Gardiner enjoyed young company, especially among the undergraduates he befriended at Oxford, and from that number he was to form at least one notably close attachment in his last years. But with women it was another matter. For a while it was allegedly his habit after rising each morning to say to himself: 'Thank God I am not a woman and not an American.'[11] Grainger remembered an instance during the rehearsal of women's voices for Bax's *Enchanted Summer* in 1912 when Gardiner had apparently been taken with a girl they called 'the nightingale' who had a small solo part. 'What do you think of the nightingale?' he had asked Grainger. 'I was just on the verge of proposing to her last night!'[12] But of marriage he could be scornful. Much disillusionment stemmed from the failures of Arnold and Clifford Bax's marriages, and when Grainger told him that he was himself considering marriage, Gardiner's comment was hardly encouraging: 'You once spoke of taking a voyage in a sailor's ship. Wouldn't this be a good time to do it!'[13] Bashford wrote of Gardiner adopting the view that woman was by nature a huntress and attributed the latter's bachelorhood to this fact. Certainly one story goes that he once came close to forming an attachment until he suspected the woman in question of being after his money ('nearly snared by a goose', as he put it himself). Marriage would anyway be a serious encroachment on his independence. As he wrote in December 1922 to Grainger just after sending him a telegram: 'A lovely afternoon, with a leaden sky, and the air warm & heavy: I praised God all the way home on my bike that I was neither married, nor lived in any other country but England.' With the wives of his composer acquaintances he was able to form strong friendships: with Jelka Delius, Isobel Holst, Adine O'Neill and Helen Bainton ('a favourite of mine'). On the intellectual plane he found the basis for a mutual understanding with such women of character and any qualms he had were allayed. But whatever his private views on marriage may have been, these were well concealed by his generosity which on at least two occasions extended to a car as a wedding present.

When once again in his life-time war was declared on Germany, there was little of the optimism so prevalent in 1914. 'I wonder what sort of world we shall have at the end of it?' Gardiner mused to Grainger in December 1939, and less than a year later in October 1940 he wrote: 'I shall go on planting this season for a generation that I hope will be happier than this one.' With a thought to the coming dangers Grainger had invited him to leave war-time England for the States where they could share a less threatened existence at his homes in New York and Springfield, Missouri. But Gardiner declined the offer. 'I should not go to the USA even if things got very bad', he told

Percy in July 1940. 'My interests and duties lie here.' He was worried about the austere times that lay ahead, 'but I should not be so sorry for myself as for the men I have to throw out of employment', he added.

The early war months were clouded by the death of his father, during a game of chess and at the age of ninety-six, on 2 February 1940. He died, as he had lived, a wealthy man with an estate valued at £380,000 and leaving Upton House, his Hampshire home, to his younger son Alan at Balfour's express wish. A clause in his will clarifies this bequest:

Having been able to make the foregoing gift to my son Alan without making an equivalent gift to my said dear elder son Henry Balfour through the unselfish and spontaneous intimation that he would be content if his brother received at my death a share of my property larger than the share taken by himself although in all my dealings with my sons I have hitherto endeavoured to treat them in an equal manner and further that he did not desire to live in the house which I have built at Wonston, I desire to record my warm appreciation of his action and the affection which he has shewn towards myself and his brother.

This show of generosity would seem to give the lie to the suggestion that Balfour had once held Alan responsible for their mother's untimely death,[14] or else it was an act of expiation. The house and its contents went to Alan and the remainder of their father's real and personal estate not already disposed of in legacies and annuities was divided between the brothers. Hitherto Balfour's main sources of income were his substantial shareholdings in Bradbury Greatorex and the family company, then called the Cholo Tea and Tobacco Estates, of which he was a director, though at the end of 1942, subsequent to his father's death, he resigned the directorship which had been his chief reason for having to make occasional journeys to London.

In the first half of 1940 Balfour Gardiner was again laid low, with 'severe illness', but he had recovered sufficiently by June to entertain Hadley, Arnold Bax and Kennedy Scott during the month at Fontmell Hill. Kennedy Scott had earlier contracted tuberculosis from which he was then making a remarkable recovery. While he was widely acclaimed as a choral trainer, he was little known as the composer of a setting of the morality play *Everyman* which was to remain unperformed until his centenary year, although the vocal score had been published by Oxford University Press in 1936, with Gardiner as a codedicatee of Part One. This sizeable work was now undergoing some revisions of orchestration and in the following year Gardiner assisted by scoring a few pages himself.

In September 1940, while staying at Robin Milford's near Newbury, Gardiner made the brief acquaintance of another prominent composer of Milford's and Hadley's generation. This was Gerald Finzi who, with his wife, went over to the Milfords to meet Gardiner. They found him an enchanting old man and for Finzi, who was then nearly forty, it was indeed like meeting a mythical person, surrounded as he was by stories of his generosity and his championing of British music in that long-past pre-1914 era. Even in that brief meeting Finzi had been much impressed with Gardiner's critical faculty and felt that

though never a great composer he was an exceedingly able one, with freshness and individuality. If one had tried to back a winner amongst the young men who were born between 1870–1880 one would have backed him before Vaughan Williams or Holst as far as early promise was concerned. He is a ruddy faced old bachelor adoring children & with an individual wit & delight-fully perverse ideas.[15]

Gardiner's very individual humour was one feature that especially en-deared him to his friends. His was not a subtle humour but of an almost childlike nature with touches of absurdity about it. One story he never tired of repeating concerned a friend running to catch a tram in Paris. 'Tout complêt!' shouted the conductor as the vehicle started to move away. 'Two can play at that!' the friend retaliated, and swung himself aboard.[16]

If the war years brought discomforts and inconveniences there were unexpected compensations. In Oxford, as if to combat the subdued mood elsewhere, a flourishing artistic life sprang up among the under-graduates. The Slade School of Art had been evacuated there from London, and music was kept alive by those not swept away by the serv-ices. Gardiner made many friends in the undergraduate circle and his interest in music was reawakened. This renewal of interest sadly did not bring forth any original work. After the *Movement for Strings* there was nothing to break the silence. But his technical resource did not die so easily and it now found a new outlet through Denis Blood, an organ scholar at Hertford College whom he befriended. With a hint of excitement at this musical rebirth Gardiner wrote to Ella and Percy Grainger in May 1942:

I am actually doing some musical work, scoring a piece written by a boy in Oxford – most lovely harmonies & a good gift for melody, but weak in con-struction. It is like old times sitting at one's desk with music-paper in front of one. My many years' respite, with their theorising, have done me good, but I find myself woefully prone to fancies – one day I want a passage one way, and the next another. I shall get Dick (Austin) to play the piece over at a rehearsal and it will be a great excitement.

He took to this new challenge with surprising ease: 'I found I was ter-ribly rusty about scoring, not having done any for years, but in the end it came back to me, and after I had puzzled about a passage for a long time, all of a sudden the right solution would come to me, like a vision.' And some months later in March 1943:

I have had much enjoyment, the last few days, in gathering the crumbs that fall from a rich man's table, & putting together fragments from sketches for a slow movement of a piano concerto which he had rejected, & piecing them together for string IVtet! In one place I had to find an equivalent for heavy trombone chords & bravura piano passages above them. It took some doing!

His relationship with Blood, with their disparate ages, as well as reviving musical interests, injected a new lease of life into Gardiner who was captivated by the young man's charm and élan. Gardiner's friendship soon became rooted in a deep affection. Blood's music, passing through a phase of Delian chromaticism, found a sympathetic response. While the collaboration produced relatively little and nothing went as far as performance (despite one score being shown to Henry Wood in his last years and Bliss, then director of music at the BBC, holding out hopes for either a Prom performance or a broadcast), it brought much delight to Gardiner who took endless trouble in reshaping the sketches. Generosity went hand in hand. He gave Blood a cottage in Iwerne Minster, a short distance from Fontmell Magna, as well as many other gifts including money towards a car, and two mementos of the Delius years – a portrait of the composer by his wife Jelka and a miniature wax bust of him sculpted by Catherine Barjansky, wife of the famous Russian cellist. This very intimate friendship was interrupted when Blood left for America in 1947. 'Beech [Cottage] is sold, and I feel rather lonely without him', Gardiner wrote to Grainger on 29 November 1947.

Among the other undergraduates who had a brief acquaintance with Gardiner at Oxford was the composer Geoffrey Bush, a Nettleship scholar at Balliol. He and Blood wrote a blues and a tango for a revue about which the old man showed an irreverent curiosity. Gardiner's remarkable eye for assessing a musical score was always evident and Bush remembers his unusual way of judging a composition's worth: he would go straight to the cello part and if he found it to be above middle C he would know the piece was well scored. Bush also remembers Gardiner being appalled at the first performance of some composer's latest work and how he described it with equal horror: 'There they were, the orchestral players, row on row of them, triple woodwind, horns, brass, strings, harps and percussion, as far as the eye could reach. And what did the composer do? He began with a solo viola . . .'[17]

By now Gardiner had mellowed with age. He was still as unpredictable and outspoken as ever, but time had rubbed off much of the bitterness that stood between him and the world at large. His appearance more stooped than in former years, and dressed as was his custom (like his father) in thick Norfolk tweeds, he could sit back with a detached air, tinged with disenchantment and a hint of melancholia, proclaiming the world to be 'full of bosh and tosh'. Always the eccentric – in the true sense of the word – he cut an almost Pickwickian figure to his undergraduate circle. Once a term he would dine them on a rich Dorset goose and regale them with Frankfurt anecdotes. They in turn once even succeeded in dragging him off to a local cinema.

A close friend in Oxford for many years was Sir Thomas Armstrong, then organist of Christ Church and later principal of the Royal Academy of Music. He remembered how Gardiner believed

that music must be an intoxication. He wanted it to carry him out of this world into some world of beauty and power. He used to come up into the organ-loft at Christ Church when I was there and get me to extemporise, constantly urging me on: 'Build it up, Tom, build it up! Let's have a climax now! Build it up! Don't let it relax!' This was always what he felt about music.[18]

Gardiner attended some of Armstrong's choral and orchestral concerts and was particularly moved by a rare performance of *April* given in May 1944 by the Oxford Bach Choir. On another occasion an old irritation returned when a comment in a programme note caused him sufficient annoyance to walk out of the concert. He was generally happier when reading scores than hearing a performance. He did however attend a recital in Oxford given by Peter Pears and Benjamin Britten, and briefly met the composer afterwards. The name of Gardiner was certainly not unknown to Britten who as a nine-year-old had heard *News from Whydah* sung by the Lowestoft Choral Society and the work had made a great impression on the young boy.

With increasing years Gardiner's generosity reached extravagant proportions. Old friends he never forgot. From 1944 Frederic Austin, then on the staff of the RAM, annually received two hundred pounds under a seven-year deed of covenant. There were even more lavish arrangements for a trust through which Denis Blood would be paid annual sums for a twenty-year period following Gardiner's death. These sums, which were always to be paid anonymously into Blood's account, would vary from year to year and, indeed, in some years there was a nil payment. On expiry there came a lump sum with the accrued interest, the whole scheme bearing the imprint of Gardiner's astute hand. Other friends received equally liberal gifts – cash, war bonds, share certificates, ranging from comparatively small amounts to sums in four figures. A friendship at Oxford with a Slade student brought about further plentiful gifts of money, and when it became known that the art student had contracted tuberculosis, with typical concern Gardiner offered to pay the full cost for his treatment in a sanatorium.

During the war Gardiner's customary travels abroad had been restricted to Eire. The post-war years found him more immobile and tending to stay closer to home. In October 1946 he called on Cyril

Scott who was staying at Pevensey Bay in the cottage then belonging to Ella Grainger's niece and which had been lent to him for a while. Scott had for many years been interested in therapeutics and medicinal herbs, a favourite health cure being black-strap molasses which he would strongly recommend to his friends. On their holiday together in 1936 he had urged a course of All-Bran on Gardiner as a solution to his perennial ailments, and when Gardiner visited him with a friend for what was to be the last time they would see each other, they had hardly been together for two hours before Scott was once again recommending molasses to Gardiner and prescribing some pills for his companion. Of their mutual friend Roger Quilter there was sad news to impart: although he had recently come through a successful operation for the removal of the prostate gland, he was now suffering from mental illness for which he had periodically to be treated in a home.

Later that October in London Beecham mounted a second Delius Festival of seven concerts spread over as many weeks. But an old sore remained unhealed and Gardiner kept away from all the concerts, save one in which Richard Austin shared the conducting with Beecham. In December he wrote to Fenby:

I went to one of the Delius Festival concerts, but am glad to say I avoided seeing Beecham. You know how I dislike his conducting: part of Brigg Fair was so unrhythmical as to be unintelligible. I often think of the days at Grez, & it is sad to think that the life there is all blotted out, with hardly a trace remaining.

When a friend who went to hear *Sea Drift* at the Festival asked Gardiner about it he replied: 'It is too poignant and I can never bear to hear it again.'

It is hard to know exactly how Gardiner's conception of the Delius scores differed from Beecham's. Sometimes he complained that Beecham took them too fast, whereas Delius, who was always happy with Beecham's interpretations, would complain of conductors like Wood dragging his music. Reviews of concerts at which Gardiner conducted unfortunately make little if any comment on either his technique or interpretation. There is just one clue in the *Times* review of the *Polovtsian Dances* in March 1912: 'They might have made more effect if Mr Balfour Gardiner had not treated them with so rigid a beat, and if he had not let the strings become so prominent in places where they ought to fall into the background as a thrumming accompaniment.' Since rhythm plays such a prominent part in much of his own music, one might suspect him of wanting to emphasise it, even perhaps at the risk of making it too insistent. One certainly does not think of Beecham's Delius as being unrhythmical, even if the rhythm were not as pronounced as Gardiner may have wished it. With Beecham it was intuition, a case of art concealing art.

During the forties there came the deaths of two old friends. The first had been of Benjamin Dale whose longest and most elaborate orchestral work, *The Flowing Tide*, was premièred at the Proms on 6 August 1943. But Dale was not to hear the performance as a week earlier he died suddenly after attending its rehearsal in the Royal Albert Hall. And now over three years later, in February 1947, came the death of Adine O'Neill following a heart attack. That same month Gardiner slipped on some ice and broke four ribs in the fall, but he was somewhat cheered by the prospect of a visit by Grainger in June. After their forced separation during the war they were together again that month in Dorset. From Springhead in the post-war years Rolf Gardiner organised a series of concerts, generally held in Dorset churches, that became the high-point of the local musical life. On such occasions Balfour would normally withdraw to Oxford, but this time he made a rare exception by accompanying Grainger, breaking his rule for the added reason that his good friend Thomas Armstrong was to conduct.

Grainger came to England again the next year and appeared in a Promenade concert, but Gardiner found reasons for not attending either the rehearsal or the concert, and even stooped to so feeble an excuse as having to pay his foresters their wages on the morning of the rehearsal. Instead he listened in to the broadcast. Grainger, with his curious racial prejudices, had all his life idealised the 'cornfield hair and cornflower eyes' Nordic type and one of his current theories (that Delius once remarked that he was 'bunged up with') was that blue eyes were an indication of real creativity. To satisfy this notion he was collecting colour photographs of composers – Austin, Bax, Bliss, Quilter, Scott, Vaughan Williams and Walton. He even persuaded Gardiner to have his taken, and while it produced the warmest and most natural portrait of him the reluctant subject could only comment: 'I never thought much of my beauty, but am quite dismayed to find I am so hideous – that is, if any reliance is to be placed in Tunbridge [the photographer], and I can't help doubting it.'[19] Before Percy and Ella Grainger left England he was able to entertain them for the last time, first in Dorset and then shortly before their departure that November in Oxford.

Plans for holidays abroad had as always been passing through his mind. In June 1948 he had been able to travel to Ireland but his last years are a sad tale of failing health. At Christmas he wrote to Fenby: 'Work goes on in Dorset even better than it did before, owing to the excellence of my forester, but I myself am very lame and find it hard to walk in the plantation.' One of his great pleasures had been to walk the woodland rides, but now that sturdy tweed-clad figure with his stout stick became a less familiar sight. During 1949 he was busy transferring most of his property to Rolf. Then in the summer, not for the first time, he slipped on the Spanish-tiled stairs at Fontmell Hill, undoing all the good from his steady recuperation since the previous fall. In September he told Grainger: 'I am as lame, or even lamer, than before, & have pains in my left leg.' His doctor advised him to cut his activities down drastically. Fortunately he could have been in no more caring hands than Adams's. But more serious still was a mild stroke he had at the end of the year. He was eventually admitted to the Acland Home in Oxford. On 12 June 1950 the ever-faithful Adams wrote to Ella Grainger:

I am writing this for Mr Gardiner as he is too ill to bother about anything. He asked me to tell you he is so sorry he will not be able to entertain you this year when you visit England. I am sure you will quite understand. I am sorry to tell you but I don't think there is much chance for him to ever be able to get about again. He is gradually going downhill & every thing seems too much for him. He is in no pain & every thing has to be done for him. He is in a nursing home here & I stay up with him every night & I can assure you there's every thing possible done to give him all the comfort possible to have. He is getting very childish & at times is his old self & quite cheerful. It seems so very hard as he has always been so very kind & considerate to others . . .

He was now in a very feeble state, dreadfully confused for most of the time, utterly vague and quite incapable of carrying anything in his head for more than a few moments. But one thing was clear to him: he wanted to be back among his beloved woods. So on the morning of 28 June with Adams he left the Acland Home in an ambulance for Dorset. But the journey proved too much for him and before reaching Fontmell Hill he had another stroke and died in the Salisbury hospital. Adams passed on the sad news to friends who felt that, however great their personal loss, it was in some ways after all a blessing. Balfour Gardiner was always one wanting to enjoy life to the full and a lingering end of decrepitude and inability was something he would have hated.

He left an estate valued at nearly £313,000 and his various bequests were in keeping with his accustomed largesse, remembering friends and employees alike. His death went almost unnoticed in the musical press, perhaps understandably so for a person who for the past twenty-five years had effectively turned his back on music and lived a secluded, private life. Thus a gifted, albeit minor and limited, composer and his many deeds of patronage were forgotten. The funeral was a private family affair. At the end Gardiner truly came home to his woods, for his ashes were buried not far from his house at the junction of four woodland rides, among a thuya circle which he himself had set.

But clearly there was much more to be done. How could his friends pay their last respects to this remarkable man? Kennedy Scott was right when he wrote that the extent of Balfour Gardiner's generosity will never be known. Only each one knew the full debt they owed him and they repaid it in the only way they could. The Oriana Madrigal Society, which had been revived in 1947 after a war-time silence, held a special concert in March 1951 at which four of his part-songs were sung together with Delius's *On Craig Ddu*, an appropriate pairing. Then on 23 April friends and relatives gathered at the French Institute in London for a memorial concert of his works, arranged by Guy Warrack and Richard Austin. Both the String Quartet and the quintet *Movement for Strings* were played (with Leily Howell the cellist and May Harrison as first violin), Rowland Jones and Roderick Jones each sang a group of songs accompanied respectively by Arnold Bax and Richard Austin, Jean Hamilton played some piano solos, and the concert ended with Charles Kennedy Scott conducting the Oriana choir in five part-songs (and considerably elevating the standard of performance that until then had been, in the circumstances perhaps understandly, variable to say the least). In the absence of Vaughan Williams who was unable to be present,[20] Sir Steuart Wilson gave a short address. It was a fitting occasion. A man who had given so much to his friends was honoured at the end by his friends. Roger Quilter wrote afterwards that 'it was a very charming concert . . . It was almost as if Balfour were there in person with that unspeakable charm and glinting but kind and humorous glance of his.'[21]

Grainger was unable to attend the memorial concert but he had other ways of showing his gratitude. In September 1941, when war had raised doubts of them ever seeing each other again, he had written Gardiner an extraordinary letter from Oklahoma with an intensity that for a moment almost brushes aside the ludicrous eccentricities of Grainger's style:

We are both growing old & may not have so long a span to say things in. So while I still may, I want to tell you what your friendship & oversoulship (genius) have meant to me & also to state the ruths as well as the hopefulfilments I have felt in our friendship. Your tone-art (music) has *always* been hopefulfilling (satisfying) to me; but I will go into that later. On the other hand, I have always rued (regretted) that you & I have not been closer, as friends. I love a closeknit bond, a close-living wont, between men who are drawn together in the same life's-work & whose outlook upon that life's-work is same-deemy enough to make a dove-tailed living fruitful.

At times there is a touching frankness as he ranges nostalgically in ten pages over their years of loyal friendship:

For the shining sparkle of all-giftedness, lordliness, helpfulness & understandingness that you brought into my life I can never thank you enough. All I have seen of you, all I have known of you, has been a golden soul-gain in my life; but there has been too little of it; I have seen too little of you. I do not doubt that I have often been riling & boring to you – I talk too much & I am cursed with samishness. So it may well be that you saw enough of me, & have not gone hungry for me as I have gone hungry for you. But I have never seen enough of you, never could see enough of you.

And he closes this outpouring with repeated regrets:

I am always so grieved to leave you & I rue deeply every sway, duty, task that holds you & me so far apart – apart in miles, apart in life-paths, apart in the tone-world. I wish it could have been given to me to see much more of you, to have shared much more of life with you.

In 1932 Grainger had conceived the idea of a museum to be built in the grounds of the University of Melbourne, the city of his birth. The main purpose of his 'past hoard house' was, as he explained to Rolf Gardiner in July 1950, to 'keep a record of the creative (as distinguished from the executive) side of music and especially of the rise of English-speaking music to its pre-Bach heights during the period Australia has been in music consciously, roughly from 1870 on'. Not surprisingly the Frankfurt Group were the focal point of the scheme and an amazing mass of material was collected and housed in the Grainger Museum, as it became known. Contrary to Grainger's expectations, Gardiner proved most amenable to his requests, donating manuscripts of *News from Whydah*, *Noel*, and the *Movement for Strings*, as well as supplying copies of all his published works. At the time of Jelka Delius's death Grainger was in Australia from where he cabled to Gardiner, asking him to obtain those of Jelka's paintings that she had promised but unfortunately not bequeathed to him in her will. These Gardiner bought out of his own pocket and presented to the museum. In 1938 he lent Grainger £1,250, much needed financial assistance enabling the museum to be completed, for as Percy wrote himself 'the extensions to the Grainger Museum buildings would have been impossible without his noble help'.[22]

The project was not without its unusual aspects. Grainger had the bizarre desire to display 'dummies' of some of his Frankfurt friends dressed in characteristic clothing, preferably items previously worn by the subject of the model. He approached Quilter, Scott and Gardiner for samples of their old suits. Scott had long since discarded anything representative of their earlier days but was willing to have a suit specially made to the design of an old photograph of himself. However, when the suit was made and he tried it on, he took such a liking to it that he was reluctant to part with it. From Gardiner, Grainger asked for a full suit of clothes (underclothes, socks, shoes, as well as outer clothing), a request to which, he wrote, Gardiner responded more quickly and more fully than any other person he asked. At their last meeting Grainger went further to request that he set aside some of his typical working clothes for tree-planting as well as the hat and veil he used for bee-keeping. At the time Gardiner was not well enough to respond immediately but further 'exhibits' were collected when Grainger visited Fontmell after Gardiner's death. While this macabre plan was materialising, he wrote from New York to Rolf Gardiner on 2 October 1951:

This is an urgent SOS. You know I want to display Balf's clothes, hat, stick, shoes, on dummies that will stand close to the photos of Balf. in my museum.

Now I have found someone who can make papier-mâché likenesses, life-size, from photos and clothes, & I have till January to supervise the work. You know that I sent Balfour's clothes to the museum in Melbourne so I have none of B's clothes here, for the sculptress to get the dimensions from, & it would take too long to get a suit from Australia. If you have a suit of Balfour's still, would you be will[ing] to send it to me, here, quickly? I could return it to you afterwards. If you still have that brown tweed suit & would be willing to send it to me, would you be willing to let me keep it for the museum, & let me send you from the museum (when I get to Australia) a light suit in exchange? (I chose too many light suits, & should have taken *one* brown one.) If you don't favour this last plan, & just send me a suit (if you will) & let me return it to you afterwards. What I need is: 1. Balfour's height 2. Complete suit 3. Tie, collar, shirt, socks 4. Pair of shoes (underclothes not needed – I have them in Australia). *Try & help me with this if you can!* Folk go to waxworks & see royalty, criminals, movie stars, politicians. I want people to be able to go somewhere & see GENIUSES as they looked & were clothed. If we don't 'play up' genius it will not make its full effect.

Such were the extraordinary lengths to which Grainger went in pursuance of his museum project. The completed, dressed but headless papier-mâché dummies (not wax because of Grainger's fear of fire) of Scott, Quilter and Gardiner are housed within a glass display cabinet at the Grainger Museum in an arrangement clearly modelled on a photograph of Scott, Quilter and Grainger taken in July 1929 at the Harrogate Festival, with Gardiner taking Grainger's place. With the dummies adopting similar poses, the display lacks only the walking stick that Quilter is clutching in the photograph. Grainger got the museum curator to behead the figures when he was dissatisfied with their finished faces.

A far more valuable asset to the museum is the correspondence relating to the Frankfurt Group. With fortunate foresight and an unbounded magpie instinct Grainger meticulously preserved letters between himself and his friends, often copying out others in his own hand, and even going so far as to supply friends with transparent paper for their correspondence so that duplicate copies could be made in case of fire. So while Gardiner kept few letters himself, about two hundred and forty letters from Gardiner to Grainger now, thanks to Grainger's keen archival sense, rest in the Grainger Museum, Melbourne, about half of which have been transferred there from the Library of Congress, Washington.

Generously suggesting that without the 1912-13 Gardiner concerts he might never have been in a position to build a museum at all, Grainger wanted Gardiner to be represented in it as fully as possible. And this debt he repaid with the loving attention he gave to Gardiner's scores after the latter's death. His scheme was to have photostat negatives made of all the surviving manuscripts from which any number of 'positives' could then be printed, this process being considerably cheaper than having the works engraved. His museum would obviously benefit from a copy of each score, but there were other advantages to such a scheme, which he outlined to Rolf Gardiner in May 1952:

19 Display case at Grainger Museum,
Melbourne, containing clothes of
Scott, Quilter and Gardiner worn
by dummies modelled on the 1929
Harrogate photograph of Scott,
Quilter and Grainger (inset)

May I repeat or enlarge upon the advantages I see (from the standpoint of Balfour's posthumous fame & from the standpoint of the welfare of British music & World music) in having a printed edition of at least 100 copies of which a goodly number could be spread around in libraries such as the Central London Music Library, New York Public Library, the Australian, New Zealand & Scandinavian Broadcasting Libraries, British & American University Libraries, etc.? If I or anyone else writes to Basil Cameron or other conductors about 'April' it is very satisfactory & practical to be able to say 'There is a copy of the score in the Central London Music Library.' On the other hand it is very unsatisfactory & unpractical to have to refer the conductor to an only MS copy at Stainer & Bell's, the score might be out on hire & the conductor won't be able to consult it.

Rolf's brother John Gardiner undertook the making of the negatives through his own printing firm. Grainger visited Fontmell Hill early in September 1950, two months after Balfour's death, stayed at his house and, in Rolf's words,

sorted his music with scrupulous care. Percy's loyalty and passionate admiration for Balfour were extraordinarily touching. Until recently reminded, I had forgotten the enormous painstaking trouble to which he went to advise and inform me. Balfour's memory is nobly enshrined in numerous collections at the Grainger Museum of Melbourne University. Percy went to almost absurd lengths to assemble these relics and trophies of his friend . . .[23]

When he sailed for America on 21 September he was able to take with him the photostat negatives. On his return to New York and in between concert engagements he set about making copies of the scores as well as doing some minor editing necessary in the score of *April*. But progress was slow for, in addition to his public appearances, Grainger had other work of his own, notably experimenting with his 'Free Music' machines. Deteriorating health further delayed work. On 14 August 1957 he wrote to Rolf:

We are hoping to be back in England within a year. In the meanwhile, Ella & I are hoping to get ahead with the home-photographing of Balfour's scores, sketchbooks, etc. I am sorry that my various ailments the last 3 or 4 years have made us late with our home-music-printing. I will try & do better in future!

Sadly he never lived to see the project through to the end, though he was able to send two photocopies of each of the important works to Rolf Gardiner, but the dissemination of scores abroad remained a hope unfulfilled. Grainger's fondness for Gardiner's music had also tempted him in other directions. After editing the *Movement for Strings* (of which he secured two performances of the quintet version in Cincinnati a few weeks before Gardiner's death) he turned his hand to arranging more of his music, notably *The Joyful Homecoming* and an unfinished piece he called *Flowing Melody* that Gardiner had given him at the turn of the century. This last piece, together with *Shenadoah* and some other piano

216

pieces, he intended treating freely in a *Gardineriana Rhapsody* for piano and orchestra. Although none too keen on the idea at first, in April 1945 Gardiner gave his 'unwilling' consent, adding: 'Of course you will make it clear that the work is yours & not mine.' He saw some of the sketches in 1947 and offered suggestions and criticisms, but the work on this and similar arrangements advanced no further.

With friendship very much the cornerstone of Balfour Gardiner's life, it would be only right to allow his friends the last words. In a personal note of condolence to Rolf Gardiner, Patrick Hadley wrote on 3 May 1951:

How I do miss Balfour. I can think of no friend who has passed whom I do miss more. Some of the happiest times of my life were spent with him, at his homes, at mine, and abroad. He was very good to me, indeed he was.

Echoing the sentiments of one of Gardiner's employees who spoke of him as 'one of Nature's gentlemen', Arnold Bax wrote the previous month in his tribute:

By the death of Balfour Gardiner all who knew him have lost an affectionate open-handed and ever loyal friend. He was (as Arnold Bennett once said of me) 'a man of very rigid opinions' and of charming and amusing cantankerousness. As long as any of us remain alive his often startling obiter dicta will be appreciatively and wistfully quoted. His social manners were perfect: indeed he may be said to have embodied the beau ideal of an old-fashioned (very English) gentleman.[24]

Charles Kennedy Scott, who had shared a professional relationship with Gardiner, wrote an affectionate note to Rolf Gardiner in June 1950:

My life in one way or another . . . was closely bound with Balfour's. No name more than his comes so readily to my lips and to no-one do I owe more. He was so kind to me and illuminated my poor mind with his wit and wisdom as scarcely anyone else has done. There was only one Balfour in this world, his temper and quality were of the finest, an original splendid soul who did more good than he was aware of.

Frederic Austin touched on Gardiner's many and varied characteristics:

Strongly masculine in his ways and character of thought, in his sports he was, at the most active time of his life, a brilliant tennis-player, a great walker, and a dare-devil cyclist – often much to the dismay of his cycling friends! – and a motorist of a similar calibre, never so happy as when making his way over unknown and forbidden tracts of strange country.

Fun he had in plenty, but in all he thought and did, there was an almost terrifying admixture of common-sense. A keen brain and impeccable taste were evident at every turn of his thought and speech, making him the refreshing and invigorating companion that he was. Add to these attributes an openhanded generosity that, within his means can have had few equals, in public as well as in private affairs, and you have, although inadequate, something like a general picture of the rare type of man that he was.[25]

217

In his tribute Cyril Scott recalled their Frankfurt professor Iwan Knorr's high opinion of Gardiner as 'the most understanding pupil he had ever had', praise indeed 'from a German at a time when England was looked upon as an unmusical nation!' he added.[26] In his anecdotes Grainger summed up Gardiner by cataloguing a gamut of traits:

Balfour was a strangely queer mixture of not-to-be-expected-together things: heroic deedfulness, male harshness, womanly feelingfulness, fickleness, selfishness, endless benevolence, distressing self-criticism, unique politeness, secretiveness, down-rightness, compassion, surging enthusiasm . . .

Much impressed by Quilter's note printed in the memorial concert programme, Grainger wrote to him on 30 May 1951: 'I think your words about Balfour . . . were the cleverest and most penetrating of anyone's. Passion – that was the keynote of Balfour's charm and powers, & you were the only one to strike that note.'

Let Quilter's words then, in which he perceptively highlighted that fundamental part of Gardiner's make-up, stand as a final tribute:

Balfour Gardiner so often appeared to me to be 'up against' something, to have an almost fierce impatience with anything that seemed to prevent his getting at the truth, or as near to the truth as was possible. His was a passionate nature, and this quality of passion I found in his music, sane and genial as it so often was. English poets have generally been able to express passion quite naturally and spontaneously in their work. How little can one say the same for English composers: charm, grace, lightness, all these are there in abundance, but not great warmth or passion. Balfour's music to me seemed to possess these very qualities, and I have always admired and treasured them beyond words.[27]

Appendix A: Catalogue of works

The following list includes every work by Balfour Gardiner either known or thought to have been completed. As far as possible all important information relevant to each work is given, though for those which are no longer extant the entry is sometimes unavoidably brief. In such cases the manuscripts, thought to have been burnt by the composer, are entered as 'presumed lost/destroyed', and reference is made where possible to two useful lists of Gardiner's works which suggest the likelihood of their completion and existence at the time: the list which accompanied an article on the composer in the August 1912 issue of *The Musical Times*, and the entry in the British Music Society's 1920 Annual devoted to the works of British composers (abbreviated to MT 1912 and BMS Ann. 1920 respectively). Any enquiries about works in the possession of the executors of the Gardiner Estate should be addressed to John Eliot Gardiner, Gore Farm, Ashmore, near Salisbury, Wiltshire.

All the performances listed, unless otherwise stated, took place in London. The timings of works are approximate and are only intended to give some idea of a work's duration. Details of instrumentation are given in a standard form: thus 2(1) 2 + 1 2 2 / 4 3 3 1 / timp. (b-dr. tr.) / hp / strings denotes an orchestra requiring two flutes (one player doubling with piccolo), two oboes and a cor anglais, two clarinets, two bassoons, four horns, three trumpets, three trombones, one tuba, timpani, one player for both bass drum and triangle, harp and strings. A number appearing outside bracketed percussion instruments would similarly denote the number of players specified by the composer for those instruments.

The works have been arranged chronologically within the following groups:

1 Orchestral works
   (a) written originally for orchestra
   (b) orchestrations of piano pieces
2 Vocal with orchestra
3 Chamber works
4 Songs etc.
   (a) for solo voice
   (b) for mixed or unison voices
   (c) arrangements
5 Piano works
6 Works for the stage etc.
7 Additional
8 Arrangements made by others

219

1. Orchestral works

(a) Works written originally for orchestra

SYMPHONY [No. 1] (in four movements)
Composition Sketches of 1st Mvt Nov. 1900 and Feb. 1901. Slow Mvt and
        Scherzo Jan. 1901
MS Presumed lost/destroyed   *Unpublished*
First performance c. Aug. 1901 (Sondershausen/composer)
        No further performances traced
Revision Sketches for reworking 1st Mvt Sept. 1901

HEROIC OVERTURE
Composition Dec. 1900. Reworked Mar. 1901
MS Presumed lost/destroyed   *Unpublished*
First performance c. Aug. 1901 (Sondershausen)
        No further performances traced

ENGLISH DANCE
MS Whereabouts of original MS unknown. Lithographed full score by D. Blyth
    & Co. in copyist's hand and photostat copies prepared by Grainger in posses-
    sion of executors
    65 pages of full score, including three-page appendix of a revised opening
Unpublished
Scoring 3(1) 2 + 1 3 3(1) / 4 3 3 1 / timp. tr. cym. b-dr. glock. bell / 2hps / strings
Duration 9 minutes
Dedication To Percy Grainger who first taught me 'The English Dance'
First performance 21 Oct. 1904 (Queen's Hall Proms/Henry Wood). No further
        performances traced
Revision Attempts at reworking in 1925 and 1928
        Thematically related to *In Maytime* (see below)
Other versions Arranged for two pianos by Grainger (see section 8)

SUITE IN A MAJOR
1. Andante – Allegro   2. Adagio – più mosso   3. Prestissimo – meno mosso
4. Moderato ma con moto – allegro molto
Composition Extensive reworking of *Summer Suite* from Sept. 1901 and
        throughout 1902. No later sketches extant
MS Presumed lost/destroyed   *Unpublished*
Scoring For 'large' orchestra, probably four horns and triple woodwind
Duration 10 minutes
First Performance 9 Mar. 1905 (RCM Patron's Fund/composer)
        Other known performance 29 April 1909 (Bournemouth/
        composer)
Further reference Composer's programme note with twelve music examples for
        first performance. Listed in BMS Ann. 1920

OVERTURE TO A COMEDY (Original version)
MS Whereabouts unknown. Presumed lost/destroyed
Unpublished
First performance 28 Nov. 1906 (Queen's Hall/LSO/Ronald)
        No further performances of this version traced
Revision See below

FANTASY (Original version)
MS Presumed lost/destroyed   *Unpublished*
First performance 13 June 1908 (Queen's Hall/NSO/Beecham)
                    No further performances of this version traced
Revision See below

SYMPHONY [No. 2] (in three movements)
1. Poco adagio – andante non troppo – allegro animato – più lento – andante
2. Andante molto moderato; leading to   3. Con anima – moderato
Composition Begun June 1904. Revised and completed 1908
MS Presumed lost/destroyed   *Unpublished*
Duration 26 minutes
Scoring For 'large' orchestra, including two harps
First performance 27 Aug. 1908 (Queen's Hall Proms/Henry Wood)
                    No further performances traced
Further reference Prom programme note by Rosa Newmarch. Select reviews:
                    The Yorkshire Post 28 Aug. 1908, *The Observer* 30 Aug. 1908,
                    The Times 29 Aug. 1908. Listed in BMS Ann. 1920

OVERTURE TO A COMEDY (Revised version)
MS Whereabouts unknown   *Published* Novello 1913
Scoring 2222/4231/timp. tr. cym. glock./hp/strings
Duration 8¼ minutes   *Dedication* To York Bowen
First performance 2 May 1911 (Queen's Hall/NSO/composer)

SHEPHERD FENNEL'S DANCE (after Hardy)
Composition Christmas 1910
MS Whereabouts unknown   *Published* Boosey & Hawkes 1912
Scoring 2+1 2+1 2 2+1 / 4231 (timp. tamb. tr. cym. s-dr. cast.) 6 / 2 hps / strings
Duration 5½ minutes   *Dedication* To Sir Henry Wood
First performance 6 Sept. 1911 (Queen's Hall Proms/Henry Wood)
Other versions   Piano solo (see section 5)
                    Arranged for reduced orchestra by C. Woodhouse (see section 8)
                    Arranged for military band by F. Winterbottom (see section 8)
                    Arranged for viola and piano (see Discography), unpublished
Note This work was intended to form part of the unfinished one-act opera based
    on Thomas Hardy's *The Three Strangers*

A BERKSHIRE IDYLL
Composition Completed 28 July 1913 Ashampstead
MS 52 pages full score, photostat copies prepared by Grainger and parts in pos-
    session of executors
Unpublished
Scoring 2 1+1 2 2 / 4231 / timp. tr. glock. cel. b-dr. / hp / strings
Dedication None *Duration* 15½ minutes
First performance 6 April 1955 (RFH/LSO/Richard Austin)
Note Second performance 6 Nov. 1977 (St John's, Smith Square/Monteverdi
    O/ John Eliot Gardiner)

IN MAYTIME
MS Presumed lost/destroyed   *Unpublished*
Scoring For 'large' orchestra including bass clarinet, double-bassoon and piano

Duration 8 minutes
First performance 3 Oct. 1914 (Queen's Hall Proms/Henry Wood)
No further performances traced
Further reference Prom programme note by Rosa Newmarch. Select review: *The Daily Telegraph* 5 Oct. 1914
Note Listed in BMS Ann. 1920

FANTASY (Revised version)
MS Presumed lost/destroyed   *Unpublished*
First performance 15 Nov. 1915 (Queen's Hall/RPS/Beecham)
Only other known performances 25 Nov. 1915 and 29 Jan. 1916 (Manchester/Hallé/Beecham)
Note Listed in BMS Ann. 1920
Further reference Composer's programme note with six music examples in RPS programme

'SMALL PIECE IN IV'
MS Dated 9 Aug. 1915 Ashampstead. 11 pages of full score, in pencil and probably not completed, in possession of executors
Unpublished
Scoring 2 1 + 1 2 2 / 4200 / hp / strings
Performance None known
Note The title would appear to be a temporary one, pending completion; 'in IV' probably refers to music sketchbook number four

BALLAD
Composition At intervals between 1915 and 1919
MS Presumed lost/destroyed   *Unpublished*
First performance 27 Feb. 1920 (RCM Patron's Fund rehearsal/LSO/composer or Boult)
Note Score and parts are listed in a diary entry for 3 June 1918. A brief incomplete run-through was given by Geoffrey Toye at an RPS rehearsal in spring 1919. After the first listed above no other performances known. The work is listed in BMS Ann. 1920. It seems unlikely, though not impossible, that it relates to the *'Small Piece in IV'*

CAFE MILANI '95
Composition Begun 20 Oct. 1925, scoring completed by 14 Nov. 1925
MS Presumed lost/destroyed. Only sketches have survived.
Unpublished   *Performance* None
Note The above title is the one Gardiner considered giving in the sketches to this concert waltz. Arrangement for piano duet also sketched (see pp 168-9)

(b) Orchestrations of piano pieces

HUMORESQUE
MS Presumed lost/destroyed
Scoring For small orchestra
Note Presumably an orchestration of the piano piece of the same name (section 5), it was listed in MT 1912 and BMS Ann. 1920. A letter from W.J. Drewe (Forsyth Brothers) to Rolf Gardiner 9 April 1951 lists the MS as being held

by Forsyth Brothers. The present whereabouts of the score and parts not known

PRELUDE

Note Listed thus as being for 'full orchestra' with MS held by Forsyth Brothers (letter 9 April 1951, see above). Present whereabouts of score and parts not known. No further mention found

NOEL

MS Forsyth Brothers. Full score and parts on hire
Unpublished
Scoring 2 2 + 1 2 2 / 4231 / timp. cym. cel. / strings

GAVOTTE

MS Forsyth Brothers. Full score and parts on hire
Unpublished
Scoring For string orchestra *Duration* 1½ minutes
Note This is an orchestration of the fifth of *Five Pieces* for piano (see section 5)

LONDON BRIDGE

Note Listed as being for 'full orchestra' with MS held by Forsyth Brothers (letter 9 April 1951, see above). Present whereabouts of score and parts not known. No further mention found. See also arrangement by Grainger (section 8)

THE JOYFUL HOMECOMING

Composition June 1919 *MS* presumed lost/destroyed
Unpublished
Scoring For 'large' orchestra, with bells
Dedication To Percy Grainger *Duration* 3 minutes
First performance 16 Aug. 1919 (Queen's Hall Proms/composer)
                  No performances traced after 1919
Other versions For piano solo (see section 5)
                  Incomplete arrangement for strings and 'tuneful percussion' by Grainger (see section 8)

SHENADOAH

Note Version for string orchestra listed in BBC orchestral catalogue as being on hire from Forsyth Brothers. MS listed by them in letter 9 April 1951 to Rolf Gardiner. Present whereabouts of score and parts not known. This presumably relates to the fourth of *Shenadoah (and other pieces)* for piano (see section 5)

JESMOND

Note Listed as being for 'full orchestra' with MS held by Forsyth Brothers (letter 9 April 1951, see above). Present whereabouts of score and parts not known. No further mention found. Presumably an orchestration of the first of the *Shenadoah* set of piano pieces (see section 5)

2. Vocal with orchestra

DREAM-TRYST (Francis Thompson) for baritone and orchestra (First version)
MS Dated 30 June 1902 Brushwood. 23 pages full score in possession of executors
Unpublished
Scoring 2222/4200/timp./hp/strings
Performance None traced
Note In June 1904 HBG attempted to rework *Dream-Tryst* for a tenor voice, but
    eventually he made instead an entirely new setting, again for baritone, in
    1909 (see below)

TWO LOVE SONGS FROM 'THE SONG OF SOLOMON'
Composition The few existing sketches date from April 1905
MS Presumed lost/destroyed   *Unpublished*
Performance None traced
Note Presumably a setting for two soloists and orchestra, this work is listed in
    MT 1912 and BMS Ann. 1920. No further mention found

WHEN THE LAD FOR LONGING SIGHS (Housman) for baritone and
    orchestra
MS Presumed lost/destroyed   *Unpublished*
First performance 3 July 1906 (Queen's Hall/F. Austin/composer)
Note Last performance traced 14 June 1911 (Queen's Hall/F. Austin/composer).
    Listed in BMS Ann. 1920

THE RECRUIT (Housman) for baritone and orchestra
MS Presumed lost/destroyed   *Unpublished*
First performance 3 July 1906 (Queen's Hall/F. Austin/composer)
Other versions For baritone and piano (see section 4a). Reorchestrated by David
           Owen Norris for Gardiner Centenary concert (see section 8)
Note A note on the piano version states that 'the Orchestral parts & Score
    can be hired or purchased from the Publishers'. Unfortunately these do not
    appear to have survived. Listed in BMS Ann. 1920

THE GOLDEN VANITY (Hampshire folk-song) for bass-baritone and
    orchestra
MS Boosey & Hawkes. '7 Pembroke Villas' not dated. 13 pages full score
Unpublished Score and parts on hire
Scoring 2022/4000/timp./strings (8.8.6.6.5)
Dedication 'Scored in B maj. for Plunket Greene'
Other version For voice and piano (see section 4c)
Note This version is in most respects similar to the version in C with piano except
    for the 2½ bars orchestral introduction

DREAM-TRYST (Francis Thompson) for baritone and orchestra (Second
    version)
MS Dated 31 Oct. 1909, Ashampstead and London (7 Pembroke Villas). 33
    pages full score and photostat copies prepared by Grainger in possession of
    executors
Unpublished
Scoring 2(1) 2 2 2 / 4231 / timp. tr. / hp / strings

Performance None traced

Note This setting is entirely different from the first version. MT 1912 and BMS Ann. 1920 list only one version

A CORYMBUS FOR AUTUMN (Francis Thompson) for soprano, chorus and orchestra

Composition Existing sketches date from May 1908 to about Nov. 1910

MS Presumed lost/destroyed   *Unpublished*

Performance None traced

Note Listed in MT 1912 but not in BMS Ann. 1920

NEWS FROM WHYDAH (Masefield) ballad for chorus and orchestra

Composition Completed Oct. 1911

MS Whereabouts of original MS unknown. A copy in the composer's hand made in 1919 presented by him to the Grainger Museum, Melbourne

Published Novello 1912. Vocal scores in both standard and Tonic Sol-Fa notation

Scoring 2 + 1 2 + 1 2 + 1 2 + 1 / 4 3 2 + 1 2 / timp. (s-dr. tr. cym. b-dr.) / 3 hps / strings (14.12.8.8.6)

Dedication To Arnold Bax   *Duration* 4¼ minutes

First performance 13 Mar. 1912 (Queen's Hall Gardiner Concerts/London Choral Soc./NSO/composer)

Other version With reduced scoring prepared by Holst (see section 8)

Note A German translation, unpublished, was prepared by the composer. See also *Whydah Variations* by Geoffrey Bush (section 8)

APRIL (Edward Carpenter) for chorus and orchestra

Composition MS dated Ashampstead 17 May 1912, 20 May 1913 & 16 Sept. 1913

MS Original MS, in the keeping of Stainer & Bell, is missing. A copy in the composer's hand and photostat copies prepared by Grainger (with minor editing) in possession of executors. 43 pages full score.

Published Stainer & Bell (Vocal score) 1913

Scoring 2(1) 2(1) 2 2(1) / 4231 / 3 timps. (b-dr. tr.) (gong cym. glock. cel.) 2 / 2 hps / strings

Dedication To Arthur Fagge   *Duration* 8½ minutes

First performance 3 Dec. 1913 (Queen's Hall/London Choral Soc./LSO/ composer)

PHILOMELA (Matthew Arnold) for tenor, women's voices and orchestra

Composition Probably begun before First World War. Existing sketches are dated 10 Sept. 1922 Lesjaskog, 2 Oct. 1922 Ashampstead, Aug. & Sept. 1923. Finished 18 Sept. 1923 then transposed down a semitone. MS dated 30 Sept. 1923 Ashampstead 'after many years'

MS Original and transposed versions, the former marked 'transposed a semitone lower & altered considerably', with photostat copies prepared by Grainger, in possession of executors. 40 pages full score

Unpublished

Scoring 2 2 + 1 2 2 / 4231 / timp. (b-dr. glock.) / hp / strings

Dedication None   *Duration* 8 minutes

First performance 4/5 May 1955 (Argo recording/artists as below). 6 May 1955 (RFH/A. Young/Goldsmiths' Choral Union/LSO/Austin)

SIR EGLAMORE for solo, mixed or unison voices and string orchestra
MS Whereabouts of original MS unknown. 3 full scores in copyist's hand and parts on hire from Novello & Co. (1924)
Other versions For other versions and the source of words and tune see section 4c

3. Chamber works

STRING QUINTET IN C MINOR

    1. Allegro non troppo   2. Presto con brio
    3. Adagio espressivo   4. Moderato – presto

Composition c. 1901-3 though possibly begun as early as 1899
MS Presumed lost/destroyed   *Unpublished*
Scoring String quartet with second viola
First performance 5 Nov. 1903 (St James's Hall/Cathie Quartet with Alfred Ballin)
           No further performances traced
Revision 'The score . . . bears many and varied dates of working, ranging from 1903 to 1907, revealing the enormous care and pains which have been bestowed upon it' (*Musical Opinion* Aug. 1912). Last movement later rewritten as *Movement for Strings* (see below)
Note Listed in MT 1912 and BMS Ann. 1920
Further reference Descriptive note by Robin Legge in the Broadwood Concert programme

STRING QUARTET IN B♭ (in one movement)
Composition Begun about 1903. Completed Feb. 1905
MS Whereabouts unknown
Published Breitkopf and Härtel (Avison Edition) 1907
First performance 28 Feb. 1905 (Aeolian Hall/Cathie Quartet)
Duration 8 minutes

MOVEMENT FOR STRINGS IN C MINOR
Composition Recommenced around 1932. Completed in Oxford 11 Nov. 1936. Minor alterations in 1939 and 1947
MSS Grainger Museum, Melbourne. One is a 'working' MS, the other a fair copy of the first dated '11 Nov. 1936 Oxford (begun about 1899)'. Published score states 'composed about 1901, but was added to and altered about 1936'
Published (edited Grainger) Schott 1949
Scoring String quartet with second viola (but see note below)
Dedication For Percy Grainger   *Duration* 9¼ minutes
Note This is an extensive reworking of the last movement of the 1903 String Quartet (see above). Grainger edited the revised movement, making it playable by any numbers up to full string orchestra, adding a double-bass part. It was published in this edition as a facsimile full score with a detailed explanatory preface. Five of the eight staves are the original quintet parts left unaltered, with three other staves in smaller script (marked Violin III, Cello II and Double-Bass) for when more strings are used

Found among Gardiner's scores was a MS of uncertain authorship, not in his hand and both undated and unsigned, of a *Romance in G major* for cello and piano, inscribed 'For Silvia'. This could conceivably have been a student work, 84 bars in length

4. Songs etc.

(a) For solo voice and pianoforte

THE BANKS OF CALM BENDEMEER (from Thomas Moore's *Lalla Rookh*)
MS Dated 20 Jan. 1893, 6 pages, in possession of executors
Unpublished

HOW SWEET I ROAMED FROM FIELD TO FIELD
MS Dated 28 Sept. 1895, 4 pages, in possession of executors
Unpublished
Note Text, unacknowledged, from William Blake's *Poetical Sketches*

AH, SWEET THOSE EYES THAT USED TO BE SO TENDER
MS Dated 7 Nov. 1895, 3½ pages, in possession of executors
Unpublished
Revision Written out again 2 Mar. 1932 with different accompaniment and
        slight alterations to the vocal line: 'The above is only approximate. I
        got tired thinking out the exact harmonies and disposition of the
        accompaniment & had better return to it later.' No further sketches
First known performance 13 May 1977 (Purcell Room/David Wilson-Johnson
        acc. by David Owen Norris)

D'UN VANNEUR DU BLÉ AUX VENTS (Joachim du Bellay 1522-60)
MS Dated 17 April 1896, 'Paroles par Joachim du Bellay Musique H. Balfour
    Gardiner', 3 pages, in possession of executors
Unpublished

LIGHTLY WE MET IN THE MORN
MS Dated 1 June (no year), 4 pages, in possession of executors
Unpublished
First known performance 6 Feb. 1977 (Purcell Room/David Wilson-Johnson
        acc. by David Owen Norris)
Note Year of composition unspecified on MS but probably about 1897.

THREE SONGS

1. FEAR NO MORE THE HEAT O'THE SUN (Song out of *Cymbeline*)
   MS Dated 17 Dec. 1897, 3¼ pages, in possession of executors
   Unpublished
   Revision Later revised and published as *Fidele* (1908) with alterations chiefly
           to the accompaniment

2. DIRGE - ROUGH WIND THAT MOANEST LOUD (Shelley)
   MS Dated 17 Dec. 1897, 1½ pages, in possession of executors
   Unpublished

3. MUSIC WHEN SOFT VOICES DIE (Shelley)
   MS Dated 19 Dec. 1897, 2 pages, in possession of executors
   Unpublished
   Revision Later revised and published as No. 1 of *Two Lyrics* (1908) with
           alterations to the accompaniment

FULL FATHOM FIVE (from *The Tempest*)
Composition Sketches dated 7 July 1898
MS Dated 26 Aug. 1898, 2 pages, in possession of executors
Unpublished
Note Written at the end of MS: 'Knorr saw this Sept. 3rd '98: I cannot write a
    song yet; I have no sense of detail & build every slight composition on a
    disproportionately large scheme. H.B.G.'

THE STRANGER'S SONG (Hardy)
MS Whereabouts unknown   *Published* Boosey 1903
Earliest known performance 25 May 1904 (St James's Hall/W. Higley)
Note Printed on score: 'Sung by Mr Frederic Austin'.
    Also known as *The Hangman's Song*, it was intended to be incorporated in
    the one-act Hardy opera *The Three Strangers*. It is not known if this was
    orchestrated at any stage; a 1907 Prom performance may well have had
    piano accompaniment only

THE RECRUIT (Housman)
MS Whereabouts unknown   *Published* Goodwin & Tabb 1906
Dedication To S. Ernest Palmer Esq. Founder of the Royal College of Music
    Patron's Fund
Other version With orchestra (see section 2)
Note The score states that 'the pianoforte accompaniment is an adaptation from
    the Orchestral Score, by the composer'. Also printed on the score: 'Sung
    by Mr Frederic Austin, Mr Albert Garcia, Mr Kennerley Rumford'

TWO LYRICS
1. MUSIC WHEN SOFT VOICES DIE (Shelley)
2. WHEN I WAS ONE-AND-TWENTY (Housman)
MSS Whereabouts unknown   *Published* Goodwin & Tabb 1908
Note The first is a revision of the version from 1897. On the printed score: 'Sung
    by Mr William Higley'

FIDELE (from *Cymbeline*)
MS Whereabouts unknown   *Published* Goodwin & Tabb 1908
Dedication To William Higley
Note A revision from 1897, there are two versions – for tenor or baritone – in F
    and E♭. A note in HBG's 1913 diary reads: 'Orchestral acc. Fidele for
    Goodwin & Tabb one guinea'. It is not known if an orchestral version was
    made

ROADWAYS (Masefield)
Composition Sketches date from 21 Sept. 1908
MS Whereabouts unknown   *Published* Forsyth Brothers 1908
Dedication To Frederic Austin
Other version Orchestral version by G. Stacey (see section 8)

THE WANDERER'S EVENSONG (Goethe, translated by Edward Carpenter)
MS Dated 9 Dec. 1908, 7 Pembroke Villas. 1½ pages, in possession of executors
Unpublished

First known performance 13 May 1977 (Purcell Room/David Wilson-Johnson acc. by David Owen Norris)
Revision Minor pencilled alteration to penultimate bar dated 20 Aug. 1919

WINTER – WHEN ICICLES HANG BY THE WALL (from *Love's Labours Lost*)
MS Whereabouts unknown
Published Novello (Avison Edition) 1912; Carey & Co. 1921
Note On printed edition: 'Sung by Gervase Elwes'

ON CHELSEA EMBANKMENT (E.L. Darton) for alto
MS Dated 15 Feb. 1915 Ashampstead 24 April 1938 Fontmell Hill. 4 pages, in possession of executors
Unpublished   *Dedication* H.B.G. for F.A.
Note Words ('It is a night of sighs') from *Pall Mall Gazette* of 15 Dec. 1914

RYBBESDALE (words adapted from an Old English Poem by Clifford Bax)
Composition Started 5 Nov. 1920, alterations 3 April 1922
MS (E♭version) Dated 16 April 1922, British Library Add. MS 54404
Published Augener 1922
Earliest known performance 23 Jan. 1923 (Chelsea Town Hall/J. Coates)
Note Two published versions, in C and E♭

THE QUIET GARDEN (Frank Prewett)
Composition Sketches dated 23 Oct. 1922
MS Dated Nov. 1922, British Library Add. MS 54404
Published Augener 1923
Dedication To John Coates
First performance 23 Jan. 1923 (Chelsea Town Hall/J. Coates)

(b) For mixed or unison voices

TE LUCIS ANTE TERMINUM (EVENING HYMN) for SATB with organ
Composition Early attempts at setting this text date from June 1900, July 1902 and later. This existing version probably dates from late 1907/ early 1908
MS Whereabouts unknown *Published* 1908 Novello Anthem 1127. Included in *King of Glory* collection of anthems 1975 Novello
Dedication To E.T. Sweeting
Note English/Latin text
Other version Specially orchestrated for Gardiner Centenary Concert (see section 8)

THE STAGE COACH (4-part song with words from William Barnes's *Poems of Rural Life in the Dorset Dialect)* for SATB unacc.
MS Whereabouts unknown *Published* 1912 Novello PSB1237. Tonic Sol-Fa 2198
First performance 17 April 1912 (Queen's Hall Gardiner Concert/Oriana Madrigal Soc./C.K. Scott)

EVENEN IN THE VILLAGE (William Barnes, as above) for SATB unacc.
MS Whereabouts unknown   *Published* 1912 Novello PSB1236
First performance 18 June 1912 (Westminster Cathedral Hall/Oriana Madrigal
          Soc./C.K. Scott)

PROUD MAISIE (Sir Walter Scott) for SATB unacc.
MS Whereabouts unknown
Published 1912 Novello MT No. 829. Tonic Sol-Fa 2288

CARGOES (Masefield) for SATB unacc.
MS Whereabouts unknown
Published 1912 Novello PSB1251. Tonic Sol-Fa 2073
Other versions For men's voices 1920 Novello *The Orpheus* No. 564
          For unison voices and piano 1934 Novello School Songs No. 1711
          Orchestral version by J.W. Ivimey for small school orchestra
          (see section 8)

A SONG FOR SUPPER NIGHT for unison voices and piano
Composition 1915
MS Whereabouts unknown, 17 bars, four verses with chorus
Unpublished
Note Written for Ludgrove School ('Tis the end of term') and duplicated for use
          on prize-giving day. Copies at Ludgrove.

AN OLD SONG RE-SUNG (Masefield) for SATB unacc.
MS Whereabouts unknown
Published 1920 Novello PSB 1387. Tonic Sol-Fa 2336
First performance 20 Nov. 1920 (Newcastle Bach Choir/W.G. Whittaker)

THE SILVER BIRCH (Eric Ennion) for three-part treble voices
Composition Sketches from 23 Dec. 1920
MS Whereabouts unknown
Published 1921 Edward Arnold Series of Singing Class Music No. 207

CAVALIER (Masefield) for unison voices and piano
Composition Sketches from 16 Jan. 1921 and 19 Jan. 1921
MS Whereabouts unknown
Published 1921 Edward Arnold Series of English Class Music No. 44

ON EASTNOR KNOLL (Masefield) for SATB unacc.
MS Dated 29 Dec. 1923 and 1 Nov. 1924, 7 pages, in possession of executors
Unpublished

(c) Arrangements

THE GOLDEN VANITY (Hampshire folk-song) for bass voice and piano
Composition Probably during 1907
MS Whereabouts unknown   *Published* 1908 Goodwin & Tabb
Dedication To G.B. Gardiner Esq.
Earliest known performance 14 Sep. 1908 (Queen's Hall Proms/F. Austin)
Note On printed score: 'Sung by Mr Frederic Austin, Mr William Higley, Mr
          Albert Garcia'

Composer's note: 'The tune and words of this folksong were taken down from the singing of Moses Blake, Emery Down, Lyndhurst, by J.F. Guyer, L.R.A.M., and G.B. Gardiner, D. Sc., respectively. I have adhered to the singer's original as far as possible; but some minor alterations were unavoidable, both in the words and in the music.'
Other version For orchestra (see section 2)

HAMPSHIRE FOLK-SONG SETTINGS
Note Gardiner made at least four other folk-song settings at the same time as *The Golden Vanity*, including one of *Swansea Town*, but these have not been found

BULLEY IN THE ALLEY (trad. sea-chanty) for three-part bass chorus
MS Whereabouts unknown. Copy in possession of executors
Unpublished
Possible first performance 11 Mar. 1915 (Westminster Cathedral Hall/Oriana Madrigal Soc./C.K. Scott)
Note The programme note does not attribute the arrangement to Gardiner, but he made this version for the Oriana Madrigal Society. The sea-chanty appeared in their programmes on 11 Mar. 1915 and 13 July 1915

AND HOW SHOULD I YOUR TRUE LOVE KNOW (Old English melody) for solo and SSA unacc.
MS Whereabouts unknown   *Published* 1915 Novello Trios No. 456
Possible first performance 11 Mar. 1915 (Westminster Cathedral Hall/Oriana Madrigal Soc./C.K. Scott)

GOD SAVE THE KING for SATB acc. or unacc.
MS Whereabouts unknown
Publication 1915 Curwen Choral Handbook No. 1061
Dedication For the Oriana Madrigal Society
First performance 15 June 1915 (Aeolian Hall/Oriana Madrigal Soc./C.K. Scott)
Note The National Anthem was programmed by the Oriana Madrigal Society on 11 Mar. 1915 but not attributed to Gardiner

HEAVE HO! (trad. sea-chanty)
Composition About 1915
MS Whereabouts unknown   *Unpublished*
Note Written for Ludgrove School. No copy located at present

THE THREE RAVENS (THERE WERE THREE RAVENS) (from *Melismata* published by T. Ravenscroft in 1611) for SATB unacc.
MS Whereabouts unknown   *Published* 1919 Curwen 61095
First performance 21 Dec. 1915 (Aeolian Hall/Oriana Madrigal Soc./C.K.Scott)
Note Programmed on 21 Dec. 1915 for 4 soli. Performance on 10 April 1919 also announced as first performance, possibly sung by full choir.

SIR EGLAMORE (words from *The Melancholy Knight* 1615, tune from Playford's *Pleasant Musical Companions* 1687)
MS Whereabouts unknown   *Published* 1917 Novello
Various versions For treble chorus and piano 1917 Novello, for female voices Novello No. 454; for unacc. male voice quartet or unacc. male

231

chorus 1917 Novello *The Orpheus* No. 555 Tonic Sol-Fa 2327; for SATB and piano 1917 Novello PSB1321 Tonic Sol-Fa 2293; for solo and SATB 1917 Novello; unison song 1923 Novello School Songs No. 1099a Tonic Sol-Fa 1099b; with string orchestra (arr. composer, see section 2) 1924 Novello

THE HUNT IS UP (words and tune *c.* 1540 reprinted in Chappell's *Popular Music of the Olden Time*) for SATB unacc.
MS Whereabouts unknown   *Published* 1919 Curwen 61096
First performance 10 April 1919 (Aeolian Hall/Oriana Madrigal Soc./C.K. Scott)

SONG OF THE VOLGA BOATMEN (words by W.G. Rothery)
MS Whereabouts unknown   *Published* 1927 Novello
Various versions For unacc. SATB Novello PSB1433 Tonic Sol-Fa 2552; for unacc. TTBB Novello *The Orpheus* No. 605 Tonic Sol-Fa 2553

5. Piano works

THE COMPLETE PIANO MUSIC
At the time of writing, a complete edition of Balfour Gardiner's piano music is being planned for publication during 1984 by Forsyth Brothers Ltd, of 126-8 Deansgate, Manchester. This single volume will include those works never previously published

FOUR STUDIES IN SMALL FORM
  1. Sonatina   2. Valse   3. Scherzo and trio
  4. Variations on an 8-bar theme
Composition Sketches dated 29 Sep. 1899
MS In possession of executors   *Unpublished*

HUMORESQUE
MS Whereabouts unknown
Published Forsyth Brothers 1905, G. Schirmer (USA) 1923
Dedication To Evelyn Suart
First performance (Original version) 15 June 1904 (Bechstein Hall/E. Suart).
                    (Revised version) 25 Nov. 1905 (Bechstein Hall/E. Suart)
Other version For small orchestra, now lost (see section 1b)
Note The revised version is the one published. In the absence of the original the extent of the alterations is not known. The early Forsyth edition was entitled 'Humoreske', changed to 'Humoresque' in later issues. The American edition was edited by Grainger, with reference chiefly to the pedalling

MERE
MS Whereabouts unknown   *Published* Forsyth Brothers 1905
Dedication To Percy Grainger

PRELUDE (DE PROFUNDIS)
MS Whereabouts unknown

Published Forsyth Brothers 1905, G. Schirmer (USA) 1923
Dedication To Evelyn Suart
First performance 9 May 1905 (Bechstein Hall/Suart)
Other versions An American edn edited by Grainger has copious study notes (see
        section 8); possible orchestral version untraced (see section 1b)

NOEL
MS Grainger Museum, Melbourne
Published Forsyth Brothers 1908, G. Schirmer (USA) 1923
Dedication To Arthur Newstead
Earliest performance traced 16 June 1908 (Aeolian Hall/Grainger)
Other versions Arranged for two pianos (see below). For orchestra (see
        section 1b)

CHRISTMAS GREETINGS
Composition Completed Christmas Day 1908
MS RCM Parry Room MS4499, 24 bars   *Unpublished*
Dedication Christmas Greetings to Evelyn [Suart]

FIVE PIECES
    1. Molto allegro   2. Adagio non troppo
    3. *London Bridge* Allegretto   4. Andante con moto
    5. *Gavotte* Tempo di Gavotta allegro assai
MS Whereabouts unknown
Published Forsyth Brothers 1911, G. Schirmer (USA) 1923
Dedication None
Note For separate publication in America the first two pieces were named
        Pembroke and *Clun* respectively. The *Gavotte* was also published separate-
        ly in both England and America
Other versions The *Gavotte* exists in a version for string orchestra (see section 1b).
        London Bridge may also have been orchestrated by the composer
        but it is not extant in that version (see section 1b). Grainger
        arranged *London Bridge* in a version incorporating 'tuneful per-
        cussion' (see section 8)

SHEPHERD FENNEL'S DANCE (after Hardy)
MS Whereabouts unknown   *Published* Forsyth Brothers 1911
Dedication To Sir Henry J. Wood
Note 'This pianoforte version is a free arrangement from the orchestral score,
        made by the composer.'
Other versions For orchestra (see sections 1 and 8) and military band (see
        section 8)

THE JOYFUL HOMECOMING
Composition June 1919
MS Whereabouts unknown
Published Forsyth Brothers 1919, G. Schirmer (USA) 1919
Dedication To Percy Grainger
Other versions For orchestra (see sections 1 and 8)

233

SALAMANCA
Composition Begun 25 Feb. 1920
MS Whereabouts unknown   *Published* Forsyth Brothers 1920
Dedication None
Note Sketches showing the work's origin exist in the possession of the executors

SECOND PRELUDE
MS Whereabouts unknown
Composition Diary entry *c.* Oct. 1918: 'Ashampstead piano piece for
         Ascherberg'
Published Ascherberg 1920 (Repertoire Series of Pianoforte Music by Modern
         British Composers No. 15). Also included in *The Music Lovers' Port-
         folio of the World's Best Music* No. 10, edited by Landon Ronald
         (George Newnes Ltd.)
Dedication None

SHENADOAH (AND OTHER PIECES)
     1. Con brio   2. Allegretto   3. Molto allegro e vivace
     4. *Shenadoah* Andante   5. Allegro giusto
Composition Nov. 1921 – July 1922
MS Whereabouts unknown
Published Forsyth Brothers 1922, G. Schirmer (USA) 1924
Dedication To W.G. Whittaker
Note For separate publication in America the first two pieces were named
         Jesmond and *Melcombe* respectively. The fourth piece also saw separate
         American publication. The spelling of the set's title differs from that of the
         well-known sea-chanty *Shenandoah.*
Other versions Possible orchestrations of *Jesmond* and *Shenadoah* (see sec-
         tion 1b)

A SAILORS' PIECE
Composition July 1922
MS Whereabouts unknown
Published Forsyth Brothers 1922, G. Schirmer (USA) 1924
Dedication To Roger Quilter

THE IRONIC BARCAROLLE
Composition Begun 15 Oct. 1921 Completed Ashampstead 18 Oct. 1922
MS 3 pages, in possession of executors   *Unpublished*

MICHAELCHURCH
Composition Sketches 2 Mar. 1920 and at intervals, Sept. 1921 until Jan. 1923
MS Whereabouts unknown   *Published* Forsyth Brothers 1923
Dedication To Percy Grainger

FANTASIA
Composition Begun 7 Oct. 1921 Completed Feb. 1925
MS Douglas Fox   *Published* Forsyth Brothers 1925
Dedication To D.G.A. Fox
Note 'This piece was originally written for the left hand only, and can still be so
         played if desired.'

NOEL for two pianos
MS Whereabouts unknown
Published Forsyth Brothers 1935
Dedication To Ethel Bartlett and Rae Robertson
Other versions For piano solo (see above). For orchestra (see section 1b)

6. Works for the stage etc.

THE PAGEANT OF LONDON
 1. The Plague of London
 2. Fire of London
 3. Lord Mayor's Show, including a 'Clothworkers' song
Composition Sketches from April 1910
MS Presumed lost/destroyed   *Unpublished*
Scoring For enlarged military band with stringed basses
Frist performance June 1911 (Crystal Palace/W.H. Bell)
Note Gardiner was one of many composers commissioned to write music for this
    Coronation spectacular. The existing sketches include a march tune 'to be
    developed symphonically for military band . . . like the Huldigungsmarsch'
    (of Wagner)
Further reference The Musical Times, June 1911, pp. 384-5

OLD KING COLE – music for a children's play by Clifford Bax
Composition Mostly done in short score during Dec. 1920 with some scoring the
    same month and Feb. 1921 Ashampstead
MS Piano score only in possession of the executors. Orchestration not completed
Note 'The music is set for: the various characters in the play that sing, including
    a chorus of children, two fiddles (Dick and Harry) violin and viola respec-
    tively; and an orchestra composed as follows –
    2 vlns vla cello d-bass, flute clar. trumpet horn bassoon, drums & percus-
    sion (one player)
    The orchestral part is here arranged for piano.'
    In three acts – Act One Overture and nine songs
                    Act Two Eleven songs
                    Act Three Twelve songs
    Throughout the score the composer makes much use of traditional tunes

7. Additional

Hampshire folk-songs

95 tunes noted down by Balfour Gardiner between 1905 and 1907 at the request of
G.B. Gardiner. MSS and microfilm copies at Cecil Sharp House, London. H
denotes Hampshire in the G.B. Gardiner collection, and the first line of the song
is given in brackets where it differs from the title. Alternative titles are also given
where they exist.
*denotes the folk-songs that Gardiner possibly set but are no longer extant.

Sung by John Carter, Twyford, Hants., June 1905
 H49   The Green Mossy Banks of the Lea (When first in this country a
       stranger)
 H50   Rap-a-tap-tap! (Oh! my master's gone to market)

H51   The Sweet Primeroses (*sic*) (As I walked out one midsummer's morning)

*H52   Eggs in Her Basket (Two sailors walked out one morning)

H53   The Bonny Scots/Scotch Lad (It's of a regiment of soldiers you soon will hear)

H54   The Garden Gate (The day was spent)

H55   Rosemary Lane (When I dwelt in service in Rosemary Lane)

H56   Hark Shepherd How the Angels Sing

H57   God Bless the Master of this House (Christmas Mummers' Carol – 2 versions)

Sung by William Smith, Twyford, Hants., June 1905

H59   Who Is A-Tapping at My Window?

H60   Green Bushes (As I was a-walking one morning in spring)

H61   The (Slave's) Dream (I had a dream, a happy dream)

Sung by William Randall, Hursley, Hants., June 1905

*H67   Swansea Town (Oh farewell to you, my Nancy)

H69   Hunting Song (On a bright and rosy morning)

H71   Come Arise My Good Fellow – We're All Jolly Fellows That Follow the Plough ('Twas early one morning)

H72   The Bold Princess Royal (On the fourteenth of February)

H73   The Game on All Fours (As I was a-walking one fine summer's morning)

H74   Johnson – Three Jolly Butchers ('Twas of a jolly butcher boy)

H75   The Isle of France (The sun was fallen, the clouds advance)

H79   Bold Tanner – Robin Hood and the Tanner ('Twas of a bold tanner in old Devonshire)

Sung by Richard Hall, Itchen Abbas, Hants., 1905

H83   The Parson (Now winter is coming on)

H84   Lord Paget (In quarters we lay)

H85   Summerswell (Come all you warlike seamen bold)

H86   Poor Little Sweep (On a cold winter's morning)

H87   I Am a Brisk Young Sailor

H88   Buttercup Joe (I am a jolly sort of chap)

H89   My Father's Servant Boy (You lovers all both great and small)

H90   In Fair Gosport City

H91   The Labouring Man [Hall supplied no text – found in *Folk Music Journal*, Vol. 1, p. 198]

H92   The Painful Plough (Come all you jolly ploughmen)

H93   Avington Pond (Come gentlemen all and a song you shall hear)

H94   The Ploughboy and the Cockney [Sung by Hall to a text furnished by John Jackson, Old Alresford, Hants.]

*H95   The Female Highwayman (It's of a maiden, a maid so gay)

H96   Seventeen Come Sunday [Sung to a text in *Folk Music Journal*, Vol. 1, p. 92]

H97   Adieu to Old England, Adieu (It was once of the bread I did eat)

H98   (Pretty) Caroline (It was early in the month of May)

H99   Fair Susan (I left)

H100   (My) Bonny, Bonny Boy (I once loved a boy)

Sung by John Jackson, Old Alresford, Hants., 1905

H102   Polly Oliver (One night as Polly Oliver laid musing abed)

H103   The Hole in the Stocking ('Twas in Alresford city, as I have heard say)

Sung by William Brown, Cheriton, Hants., 1905
H104   The Moon Shines Bright (Carol)
H105   The Miners – Six Jolly Miners (It's of six jolly miners)
H106   Nancy and William (So abroad as I was walking)
H107   The Jolly Ploughboy (There were two brothers)
H108   The Streams of Lovely Nancy
H109   Our Ship She Lays/Lies in Harbour (There lays a ship in the harbour)
H110   The Deserter (As I was a-walking up Ratcliffe Highway)

Sung by Charles Mills, Cheriton, Hants., 1905
*H112   The Seeds of Love [Mills only knew a fragment of text]
H113   The Jolly Shilling [Text uncertain]
H114   The Saucy Sailor Boy [Text uncertain]

Sung by Charles Clark, Ropley, Hants., 1905
H115   Young Edwin in the Lowlands Low (Come all you wild young people)
H116   Erin's Green Shore (One evening so late as I strayed)
H117   The Daughter in the Dungeon (It's of a damsel both fair and handsome)

Sung by Henry Lee (aged 68), Whitchurch, Hants., 28 May 1906
H346   The Wild Rover (I've been a wild rover)
H347   The Crocodile (Come landsmen, list you all to me)
H348   The Merry Haymaker – Haymaking Song ('Twas in the merry month of May)
H349   Just As the Tide Was Flowing (One morning in the month of May)

Sung by Stephen Phillimore (aged 75), Andover, Hants., Aug. 1906
H613   Captain Ward (Come all you British seamen)
H614   The Fox (Old Beau Reynolds walked out) [Tune missing]
H615   The Lowlands of Holland (As I walked out one May morning)

Sung by Charles Wiltshire (aged 76), Andover, Hants., Aug. 1906
H616   Erin's Lovely Home [Text not noted – referred to H430]

Sung by William Winter (aged 85), Andover, Hants., July 1906
H617   The Pleasant Month of May (Now the merry month of May)
H618   Long Looked for Come at Last (Abroad as I was walking)

Sung by Robert Guyat, Andover, Hants.
H619   In All the Care and Misery [Tune 'got' but missing]

Sung by Charles Bell (aged 66), Andover, Hants., Aug. 1906
H620   The Unquiet Grave (So cold the wintry winds do blow)

Sung by Mrs Esther Newman (aged 90), Andover, Hants., Aug. 1906
H621   Marlborough (Ye generals all and champions bold)

Sung by William Stratton (aged c. 70), Easton, Winchester, Hants., Nov. 1906
H629   Nobleman and Thresher (Oh! the nobleman met the threshman one day)
H630   The Indian Lass (As I was a-walking)
H631   The Molecatcher (In Wellington town)

Sung by William Mason (aged c. 60), Easton, Winchester, Hants., Nov. 1906
H632   The Everlasting Circle (Down in yonders [sic] green meadow)
H633   (Sing) Ivy (My father gave me an acre of land)

Sung by Benjamin Arnold (aged 78), Easton, Winchester, Hants., Nov. 1906

H634   The (Bold) Fisherman (As I walked out one May morning)
H635   As I Sailed out of Glasgow
H636   'Twas Early, Early All in the Spring (As I walked out so early)
H637   The Gallant Poachers – Upon Van Dieman's Land (Here's poor Tom Brown from Nottingham town)
H638   My Jolly Sailor Boy – Tarry Trousers (As I walked out one fine summer's morning)
H639   The Green Bed (A story, a story, a story was one)
H641   The Maid and the Box – The Beautiful Damsel – The Undaunted Female ('Tis of a fair damsel) [No text noted]
H643   As I Walked out the Other Day
H644   Come, All You Young Men
*H645   The Bold Grenadier (As I was a-walking one morning in May)
H646   The Squire/Knight and the Shepherd's Daughter
H647   The Shepherd's Song (Shepherds are the cleverest lads)
H648   My Old Father Was a Good Old Man
H649   Poacher's Song – It's My Delight of a Shiny Night (When I was bound apprentice)
H651   John Barleycorn (There was three men come from the North)
H652   The Jolly Ploughman ('Twas early one morning at the break of the day)

Sung by Mr Rolf, Kingsclere Workhouse, May 1907

H668   The Spotted Cow [No text]
H669   The Rose in June [No text]
H670   Banks of Sweet/Green Willow – The Sea Captain [No text]
H671   Master's Health – Harvest Song [No text]

Sung by Charles Taylor (aged 67), Kingsclere Workhouse, May 1907

H672   Jimmy/Jamie Raeburn (My name is Jamie Raeburn)
H673   It's of an Ancient Farmer [No text]
H674   Long Lost Child – The Little Chimney Sweeper (It is of a little boy)

Orchestration and rescoring of Denis Blood's material

All MSS in Gardiner's hand and a music notebook 36×27 cm in possession of executors

L'INUTILITÉ (DB 1935)
MS 3pp. piano score. 'An alteration made 21.11.42 in another copy sent to Denis 10 Aug. 1943' (HBG)

BRADFIELD TUNE (DB March 1938)
'Set for string quartet by Balfour Gardiner using Denis Blood's sketches for a piano concerto', Mar. 1943. 74 bars, parts and two copies of full score, incomplete in short score

ORGAN SONATA IN C (in two movements)
MS 18pp. Begun by DB Sep. 1938, completed autumn 1939. 'In January 1940 first movement was altered and provided with a new second subject but the result was not more satisfactory formally than the previous version' (HBG)

ORGAN MOVEMENT IN C
MS 10pp. dated 28 Mar. 1940. 'Composed by H. Balfour Gardiner from material by Denis Blood'

SHADOW RHAPSODY
Piano score completed by DB Oct. 1940, copy made by HBG Dec. 1940, 7 pp. Sketches for orchestration Jan. 1941

OUTGATE HILL for orchestra
MS 33pp. scored by HBG June 1942, altered Feb. 1943. Also a 'rough arrangement for piano from score MS made by HBG June 1942', 9pp.

SOLDIER FROM THE WAR(S) RETURNING (Housman) for chorus and orchestra
MS full score, 13pp., copy made by HBG at the end of 1945

Frederick Delius: 'A Mass of Life'

Introduction to the words and music by Dr Hans Haym. English translation from the German by HBG (unattributed). Universal Edition No. 8256 (1925)

Frederick Delius: 'A Poem of Life and Love'

Tone-poem (1918) for full orchestra, arranged for two pianos by Balfour Gardiner and Eric Fenby (1928). MS in possession of the Delius Trust. (See Rachel Lowe, *Catalogue,* pp. 96-101, and Robert Threlfall, *Catalogue,* p. 154, with illustrations on pp. 156-7)

Frederick Delius

1. General note about the phrasing of string passages in Delius's works
2. A note on the irregularities in Delius's work
3. Metronome markings and notes on *The Song of the High Hills*
4. Tempi of Delius's Cello Concerto sanctioned by Delius

14pp. sent by HBG from Ashampstead on 26 Aug. 1925 to Philip Heseltine as 'copy' for his book on Delius, and acknowledging Grainger as the source of much information in items 3 & 4. Additional information from Grainger was included in a letter from Gardiner to Heseltine dated 3 Sept. 1925

Gardiner's Music Notebooks

Six small notebooks 17 × 10.5 cm and two 16 × 9.5 cm (all made in Leipzig) containing sketches from 1898 to 1909
Two notebooks 23 × 11 cm from 1909 to 1912
Three large music-books 35.5 × 27.5 cm numbered VII, VIII and IX containing sketches from 1920 onwards

Gardiner's Pocket Notebooks

52 small notebooks, generally ruled but otherwise blank, varying in size from

5.5 × 10.5 cm to 8 × 12.5 cm, used from 1900 to 1945 as jotters or for memoranda. In possession of executors

8. Arrangements made by others

(Listed in the order in which the original works appear in the preceding sections)

ENGLISH DANCE, arr. Grainger for two pianos, four hands
MS British Library Add. MS 50885, 12 pp. inscribed 'S.S. "De
  Grasse" Atlantic Ocean 8-11 Aug. 1925'
Unpublished

SHEPHERD FENNEL'S DANCE, with reduced scoring by C. Woodhouse
Published Hawkes 1937
Scoring 2(1)222/4231/timp. perc./hp/strings

SHEPHERD FENNEL'S DANCE, arr. for military band by F. Winterbottom
Published Hawkes 1913 Military Band Edition 389

THE RECRUIT (Housman), orchestrated by David Owen Norris
MS Dated 7 Aug. 1977, with parts, in possession of executors
Scoring 2222/4210/timp. s-dr. cym./organ/strings
Duration 4 minutes
Note In the absence of the composer's orchestration, this version was prepared
  for the Gardiner Centenary Concert given on 6 Nov. 1977 by the composer's great-nephew, John Eliot Gardiner, with David Wilson-Johnson
  and the Monteverdi Orchestra

NEWS FROM WHYDAH (Masefield), with reduced scoring by Holst
Published Novello 1913, manuscript material on hire. Whereabouts of original
  MS full score unknown
Scoring 2121/2210/timp./strings

WHYDAH VARIATIONS, by Geoffrey Bush for two pianos
Published Novello 1966
Note Originally for solo piano; the work was rewritten for two pianos

MOVEMENT FOR STRINGS IN C MINOR, arr. Grainger for string orchestra
See under section 3

ROADWAYS (Masefield), arr. for orchestra by G. Stacey
Scoring 1121/0230/perc./pfte hp/strings
Note Listed as such in BBC Orchestral Catalogue with MS on hire from Forsyth
  Brothers. Present whereabouts of MS not known

EVENING HYMN, arr. for choir and orchestra by David Owen Norris
MS Dated 24 Oct. 1977, with parts, in possession of executors
Scoring 2 2(1) 2 2 /4100/timp./strings *Duration* 6½ minutes
Note Orchestrated for the Gardiner Centenary Concert on 6 Nov. 1977 (St
  John's, Smith Square/Monteverdi Choir and Orchestra/John Eliot
  Gardiner)

CARGOES (Masefield), arr. for choir and orchestra by J.W. Ivimey
Published On hire from Novello & Co. *Duration* 2 minutes
Scoring Arranged for choir and small school orchestra consisting of flute, 2
   cornets in B♭, bass drum, side drum, timpani and cymbals, and strings,
   with optional parts for oboe, B♭ clarinet, and horn in F

PRELUDE (DE PROFUNDIS), edited, pedalled and with study hints by Percy
   Grainger
Published G. Schirmer 1927 (Percy Grainger Guide to Virtuosity No. 1)

LONDON BRIDGE, arr. Grainger
Scoring 2 pianos, harmonium, 'tuneful percussion' and double-bass
MS Sept.–Nov. 1935, Grainger Museum, Melbourne. Published edition (No. 3 of
   Five Pieces) for Piano 1 and a set of six MS parts for Piano 2 (3 players,
   28 Oct. 1935), harmonium, metal marimba (2 players, 31 October),
   glockenspiel (30 October), chime bells (2 players, 30 October), and
   double-bass

THE JOYFUL HOMECOMING, arr. Grainger
Note Incomplete. Intended by Grainger to be scored for strings and 'tuneful
   percussion'. Instrumental parts eleven bars long written out for 'sound
   trial, Montreal, Nov. 1946'. String parts, dated 22 Nov. 1946, at the
   Grainger Library Society, New York, and the wind, brass and percussion
   parts (2222/4331/timp. cym. s-dr. b-dr.) at the Grainger Museum,
   Melbourne

FLOWING MELODY, sketches only, arr. Grainger
MS 2 pp. dated 14-21 Jan. 1947, Grainger Library Society, NY
Note Written on MS: 'P.A. Grainger's sketch for completing H. Balfour
   Gardiner's unfinished "Flowing Melody" (given by HBG to PAG around
   1900–04, for the latter to finish as best he might) – Gardiner's material in-
   accurately remembered by Grainger – BG's MS not being available at the
   moment.'

GARDINERIANA RHAPSODY, sketches only, arr. Grainger
MS 3 pp. dated 18–19 Feb. 1947, Grainger Library Society, NY
Note Written on MS: 'P.A. Grainger's sketches for last lap of *Gardineriana
   Rhapsody* for piano & small orchestra (piano pieces & other tone-stuffs by
   H. Balfour Gardiner freely treated by P.A. Grainger). (These sketches
   were tone-wrought Jan. [20–30] 1947, White Plains.) The whole "Gard-
   ineriana Rhapsody" will likely begin with Gardiner's "Shenadoah". After
   wandering thru lots of other Gardiner tone-thoughts (amongst which the
   "Flowing Melody") the rhapsody may be brought to an end by a last-lap
   using the following tone-stuffs:'

Appendix B: Programmes for the Balfour Gardiner concerts

First Concert 13 March 1912

BAX   *Enchanted Summer*
                 (soloists: Caroline Hatchard, Carrie Tubb)
                 f.p. conducted Gardiner

DELIUS   *Dance Rhapsody (No. 1)*
                 conducted Gardiner

GRAINGER *Irish Tune from County Derry* (for unacc. mixed wordless voices)
                 conducted Grainger
                 Faeroe Isles Dance: Father and Daughter
                 f.p. conducted Grainger

GARDINER *News from Whydah*
                 f.p. conducted Gardiner

GRAINGER *Morning Song in the Jungle*
                 f.p. conducted Fagge
                 Tiger! Tiger!
                 f.p. conducted Fagge
                 We Have Fed Our Seas for a Thousand Years
                 f.p. conducted Fagge

W.H. BELL   *The Baron of Brackley*
                 f.p. conducted Fagge

      London Choral Society
      New Symphony Orchestra

Second Concert 27 March 1912

BAX   *Festival Overture*
                           f.p. conducted Gardiner

BORODIN   *Prince Igor: Polovtsian Dances*
                           conducted Gardiner

TCHAIKOVSKY   Piano Concerto in B♭ minor
                           (soloist: Percy Grainger)
                           conducted Gardiner

ELGAR   Symphony No. 2
                           conducted Elgar
          New Symphony Orchestra

Third Concert 17 April 1912

AUSTIN   *Rhapsody 'Spring'*
                           conducted Austin

BENET   Madrigal: *All Creatures Now Are Merry-Minded*

BATESON	Madrigals: *Phyllis, Farewell!* *Down the Hills Corina Trips*

LAWES	Round: *She Weepeth Sore in the Night*
	  (Soloists: Maude Willby, Mrs Gordon Pillans, Jessie Epps,
	  Kathleen Peck)

BYRD	Round: *Hey Ho! to the Greenwood*
FORD	Ayre: *Since First I Saw Your Face*

WEELKES	Madrigal: *Lo, Countrie Sports*
	  Oriana Madrigal Society
	  Charles Kennedy Scott

GRAINGER	*Mock Morris* (for seven-part string orchestra) f.p. conducted Grainger
GARDINER	*Shepherd Fennel's Dance* conducted Gardiner

GRIEG	Psalms from Op. 74: *My Jesus Sets Me Free*
	  My Heavenly Home
	  (soloist: Ernest Groom)

STANFORD	Part-songs: *The Witch* *Chillingham*

GARDINER	Part-song: *The Stage Coach*
	  f.p.
	  Oriana Madrigal Society
	  Charles Kennedy Scott

VAUGHAN
WILLIAMS
	Norfolk Rhapsodies Nos. 2 & 3
	  f.p. in London
	  conducted Gardiner

New Symphony Orchestra

Fourth Concert 1 May 1912

HARTY	*With the Wild Geese* conducted Harty

SCOTT	*English Dance No. 1*
	  conducted Gardiner
	Helen of Kirkconnel
	  (soloist: Frederic Austin)
	  conducted Gardiner

HOLST	*Beni-Mora* f.p. conducted Holst
GARDINER	*Shepherd Fennel's Dance* (repeated by general request) conducted Gardiner

O'NEILL	*La belle dame sans merci*
	  (soloist: Frederic Austin)
	  conducted O'Neill

GRAINGER	*English Dance* conducted Grainger

New Symphony Orchestra

Fifth Concert 11 February 1913

PARRY   Symphony in Four Linked Movements (No. 5)
     conducted Parry
GIBBONS   Anthem: *Hosanna to the Son of David*
WILBYE   Madrigal: *Happy, O Happy He*
BYRD   Psalm: *Come, Let Us Rejoice*
PURCELL   Canon: *Miserere mei, O Jesu*
     (soloists: Beatrice Hughes-Pope, Winifred Williamson, Alonzo Thorogood, J.K. McLean)
WHYTE   Psalm: *O Praise God*
     Oriana Madrigal Society
     Charles Kennedy Scott
VAUGHAN   *Fantasia on a Theme by Thomas Tallis*
WILLIAMS   f.p. in London
     conducted Vaughan Williams
DALE   *Before the Paling of the Stars*
     f.p. conducted C.K. Scott
DOWLAND   Ayres: *Fine Knacks for Ladies*
     Weep You No More, Sad Fountains
GRAINGER   *The Inuit*
     f.p.
HOLST   *Two Eastern Pictures*
     f.p. in London
C. WOOD   Part-song: *Haymakers, Rakers*
     Oriana Madrigal Society
     Charles Kennedy Scott
GRAINGER   *Green Bushes*
     conducted Grainger

New Symphony Orchestra

Sixth Concert 25 February 1913

BELL   *The Shepherd* (revised version)
     conducted Gardiner
HOLST   *The Mystic Trumpeter*
     (soloist: Cicely Gleeson-White)
     f.p. revised version
     conducted Holst
GRAINGER   *Hill-Song* (for 15 wind, 8 brass and 5 percussion)
     f.p. conducted Grainger
     Molly on the Shore
     conducted Grainger
     Colonial Song
     (soloists: Cicely Gleeson-White and Gervase Elwes, John Cockerill (harp))
     f.p. conducted Grainger
DELIUS   *Lebenstanz*
     f.p. in England (revised version)
     conducted Gardiner

QUILTER	Two Songs from *To Julia*: *To Daisies*
	The Nightpiece
POLDOWSKI	Songs: *Cortège*
	Le faune
	Dansons la gigue
	(soloist: Gervase Elwes)
O'NEILL	*Introduction, Mazurka and Finale*
	conducted O'Neill

New Symphony Orchestra

Seventh Concert 4 March 1913

VAUGHAN	*Fantasia on Christmas Carols*
WILLIAMS	(soloist: J. Campbell McInnes)
	f.p. in London
	conducted Vaughan Williams
BAX	*Christmas Eve on the Mountains*
	f.p. conducted Gardiner
GRAINGER	*Irish Tune from County Derry* (for unacc. mixed wordless
	voices)
	conducted Grainger
	Sir Eglamore
	f.p. conducted Grainger
HOLST	*The Cloud Messenger*
	f.p. conducted Holst
McEWEN	*Grey Galloway*
	conducted Gardiner

London Choral Society
New Symphony Orchestra

Eighth Concert 18 March 1913

BANTOCK	*Fifine at the Fair*
	f.p. in London
BAX	*In the Faery Hills*
DELIUS	Piano Concerto
	(soloist: Evelyn Suart)
AUSTIN	Symphony in E major
	f.p.
GARDINER	*Shepherd Fennel's Dance*

New Symphony Orchestra
Balfour Gardiner

Notes

1. One of the 'Frankfurt Group' 1877-1901

1. Fenby, *Delius As I Knew Him*, p. 27
2. Letter from Arnold Bax to H. Balfour Gardiner, 11 July 1930 (see above p.184)
3. Letter from Charles Kennedy Scott to Rolf Gardiner, June 1950 (see above p.217)
4. Margaret Gardiner, '[My Uncle, Balfour Gardiner]', pp. 3-4
5. *A Short History of Bradbury Greatorex & Co. Ltd*, [p. 3] (his name is consistently mis-spelt as 'Gardner')
6. 'H. Balfour Gardiner', *The Musical Times*, 53 (1912), 501
7. *The Carthusian*, 1952, quoted in Ursula Vaughan Williams, *RVW: a Biography of Ralph Vaughan Williams,* p. 26
8. Litzmann (ed.), *Letters of Clara Schumann and Johannes Brahms*, 2, p.84
9. *Ibid.*, 2, p. 87
10. *Ibid.*, 2, pp. 91-2
11. Scott, *Bone of Contention*, p. 42
12. *Ibid.*, p. 65, and Scott, *My Years of Indiscretion*, p. 14
13. Cahn, 'Percy Grainger's Frankfurt Years', *Studies in Music*, 12 (1978), 108
14. Scott, *My Years of Indiscretion*, p. 20, and *Bone of Contention*, pp. 42, 144
15. Hudson, *Norman O'Neill: a Life of Music*, p. 22
16. Scott, *Bone of Contention*, p. 11
17. Bantock, *Granville Bantock: a Personal Portrait*, p. 134
18. Grainger, '[The Balfour Gardiner Concerts]', legend for display in Grainger Museum, Melbourne
19. Bird, *Percy Grainger*, p. 29
20. Letter from Percy Grainger to Cyril Scott, 26-28 February 1930
21. Percy Grainger, 'English-Speaking Leadership in Tone-Art', 21 September 1944 in Slattery, *Percy Grainger: the Inveterate Innovator*, p. 270
22. Cahn, p. 108
23. Armstrong, 'Delius Today', in *Delius*, souvenir programme, p. 18
24. Bird, p. 146
25. Armstrong, 'The Frankfort Group', *PRMA*, 85 (1959), 12-13
26. Slattery, p. 269
27. Scott, 'The Late Balfour Gardiner', *The Music Teacher & Piano Student*, September 1950, 396
28. Litzmann, 2, p. 78
29. Scott, 'The Late Balfour Gardiner', *The Music Teacher & Piano Student,* September 1950, 396
30. Church, *The Voyage Home*, p. 60
31. Quoted in an undated and unsigned typescript found among Balfour Gardiner's papers

2. 'A Civilised Being . . .' 1902-1903

1. Scott, *Bone of Contention*, p. 73
2. Scott, 'The Late Balfour Gardiner', p. 396
3. *Ibid.*
4. Hudson, *Norman O'Neill*, p. 110
5. Scott, *My Years of Indiscretion,* p. 38
6. Bird, *Percy Grainger*, p. 40
7. 'Grainger's Anecdotes'
8. Irving, *Cue for Music*, p. 94
9. Scott, 'The Late Balfour Gardiner', p. 396
10. Letter from Cyril Scott to H. Balfour Gardiner, n.d.
11. Scott, *My Years of Indiscretion*, p. 86
12. Winefride and Richard Elwes, *Gervase Elwes: the Story of His Life*, pp. 156–8

3. Hampshire folk-song collecting 1903-1906

1. Scott, 'The Late Balfour Gardiner', p. 396
2. Programme note, 1 May 1912
3. *British Music Society Bulletin*, 4, No. 11 November 1922
4. Programme note for 25 August 1903 quoted in *The Times* 26 August 1903
5. Orr, 'Elgar and the Public', *The Musical Times*, 72 (1931), 17-18
6. Introduction to Sharp (ed.), *Folk-Songs of England: Book III*
7. Undated and unidentified newspaper cutting (1906?)
8. Purslow, 'The George Gardiner Folk-Song Collection', *Folk Music Journal*, 1, No. 3 (1967), 131
9. Lucas, *London Lavender*, p. 140
10. Letter from Cecil Sharp to H. Balfour Gardiner, 20 October 1907
11. *Ibid.*, 27 October 1907
12. Bird, *Percy Grainger*, p. 110
13. Quinlan, 'A.E. Housman and British Composers', *The Musical Times*, 100 (1959), 138
14. *Ibid.*
15. Information imparted to the author by Guy Warrack

4. Delius, Beecham and Hardy 1907-1909

1. In Warlock (revised Foss), *Frederick Delius*, p. 155, Quilter is quoted as meeting 'Delius for the first time with Percy Grainger in London'.
2. Letter from H. Balfour Gardiner to Frederick Delius, 7 March 1908
3. Letter from H. Balfour Gardiner to Frederick Delius, 30 November 1908
4. Scott, *Bone of Contention*, p. 73
5. Letter from H. Balfour Gardiner to Frederick Delius, 24 July 1908
6. Letter from H. Balfour Gardiner to Frederick Delius, 14 June 1908
7. 'Grainger's Anecdotes'
8. Grainger, 'Henry Balfour Gardiner: Champion of British Music'

5. '. . . a place of enchantment' 1909-1911

1. Beecham, *Frederick Delius*, p. 147

2. *The Musical Times*, 52 (1911), 385
3. Fenby, *Delius As I Knew Him*, p. 27
4. Bashford, *Lodgings for Twelve*, pp. 222-3
5. *Ibid.*, pp. 210-11
6. Godfrey, *Memories and Music*, p. 50
7. *Ibid.*, p. 143

6. 'Oriana will sing for me . . .' 1912-1913

1. Ralph Vaughan Williams, 'Who Wants the English Composer?', *RCM Magazine*, 9, No. 1 (Christmas 1912), reprinted in Foss, *Ralph Vaughan Williams*, p. 197
2. Scott, 'A Tribute to Josef Holbrooke', *The Musical Times*, 99 (1958), 425
3. Grainger, '[The Balfour Gardiner Concerts]', museum legend
4. Arnold Bax, *Farewell, My Youth*, p. 92
5. *Ibid.*, p. 93
6. Grainger, 'English Pianism and Harold Bauer', quoted in Bird, *Percy Grainger*, p. 29
7. Warlock, revised Foss, *Frederick Delius*, pp. 157-8
8. Scott-Sutherland, *Arnold Bax*, pp. 38-9
9. Letter from H. Balfour Gardiner to Percy Grainger, 7 February 1915
10. Grainger, 'Henry Balfour Gardiner: Champion of British Music'
11. *The Daily Telegraph*, 14 March 1912
12. Grainger, '[The Balfour Gardiner Concerts]'
13. *The Times*, 28 March 1912
14. *Collected Poems of John Masefield*, p. 3
15. Letter from H. Balfour Gardiner to Percy Grainger, 31 March 1919
16. Holst, *A Thematic Catalogue of Gustav Holst's Music*, p. 244
17. See Beecham, *A Mingled Chime*, p. 80
18. Two flutes and a piccolo, two oboes, cor anglais, three clarinets, E♭ and bass clarinet, two bassoons and a contra-bassoon, six horns, three cornets, three trombones, euphonium, tuba, timpani, glockenspiel, strings. The work was rescored much later and parts for piano(s) and organ added
19. Heseltine, 'Introduction: XVIII E.J. Moeran', *BMS Bulletin*, 6 (1924), 172
20. Moeran, 'Folk-songs and Some Traditional Singers in East Anglia', *The Countrygoer (in the Autumn)*, 7 (1946), 31
21. See Beecham, *A Mingled Chime*, pp. 75-7, and Arnold Bax, *Farewell, My Youth*, pp. 90-1
22. Eastaugh, *Havergal Brian: the Making of a Composer*, p. 101
23. Arnold Bax, *Farewell, My Youth*, pp. 80-8
24. Cohen, *A Bundle of Time*, p. 30
25. pp. 92-3

7. 'Full of unexpected harmonies . . .' 1912-1914

1. Newmarch, *Jean Sibelius*, p. 32. To his wife Jelka, Delius wrote on 2 October: 'Sibelius interested me much more [than Elgar's *The Music Makers*], he is trying to do something new & has a fine feeling for Nature & he is also unconventional – sometimes a bit sketchy & ragged, but I should like to hear the work again.'
2. Letter from Philip Heseltine to Colin Taylor, quoted in part (n.d.) in Cecil Gray, *Peter Warlock*, p. 49

3. *The Daily Telegraph*, 26 February 1913
4. 21(?) October 1912
5. Margaret Gardiner, '[My uncle, Balfour Gardiner]', p. 3
6. Arnold Bax to Rosalind Thorneycroft, n.d.
7. Clifford Bax, 'Recollections of Gustav Holst', *Music & Letters*, 20 (1939), 2 (although in her autobiography of her father, Imogen Holst writes that 'Astrology had begun to interest him before the Spanish holiday, and since meeting Clifford Bax he had learnt a great deal more about it', *Gustav Holst*, p. 43)
8. Holst, *Gustav Holst*, p. 41
9. pp. 211–44
10. This person has not been identified with any certainty
11. Tomlinson, *A Peter Warlock Handbook 1*, p. 41
12. Sleeve-notes to Argo recording RG69
13. Armstrong, 'Delius Today', p. 16
14. Letter from Philip Heseltine to Viva Smith, 14 February 1914, quoted in Tomlinson, *Warlock and Delius*, p. 17
15. See also Gray, *Peter Warlock*, p. 96

8. 'The wasted years . . .' 1914–1919

1. Arnold Bax, *Farewell, My Youth*, p. 80
2. Clifford Bax, *Inland Far*, pp. 242–3
3. *The Daily Telegraph*, 16 November 1915
4. *The Musical Times*, 59 (1918), 470
5. Elkin, *Queen's Hall 1893–1941*, p. 29
6. Letter from Frederick Delius to Philip Heseltine, 6 November 1916, in Gray, *Peter Warlock*, p. 136
7. Letter of 18 December 1917, in Short (ed.), *Gustav Holst: Letters to W.G. Whittaker*, p. 35
8. Boult, *My Own Trumpet*, p. 35
9. Letter of September 1918, in Short, *Letters*, p. 44
10. Letter of 18 April 1919, in Holst, *Gustav Holst*, pp. 74–5
11. Letter of June 1919, Constantinople, in Holst, *Gustav Holst*, p. 77
12. Quoted in a 'Round Letter' from Percy Grainger to friends, 17 February 1947
13. Holst, *Gustav Holst*, p. 78, and Short, *Letters*, p. 47
14. Short, *Letters*, p. 50
15. 'Charles Kennedy Scott', *The Musical Times*, 61 (1920), 661

9. Philharmonic patronage 1919–1922

1. Elkin, *Royal Philharmonic*, pp. 108–9
2. Taylor, 'Charles Kennedy Scott', *The Musical Times*, 92 (1951), 493–4
3 Warlock (revised Foss), *Frederick Delius*, p. 176
4. Lowe, *Delius Collection of the Grainger Museum*, p.69
5. Letter from Jelka Delius to Sydney Schiff, 25 March 1924
6. Letter (dictated to Jelka Delius) from Frederick Delius to Norman O'Neill, 20 August 1922, in Hudson, *Norman O'Neill*, p.71
7. Letter from Frederick Delius to Charles Kennedy Scott, 31 May 1928, in Warlock (revised Foss), *Frederick Delius*, p.169
8. *The Times* and *The Morning Post* 28 February 1920

9. Letter from Frederick Delius to Sydney Schiff, 9 March 1920
10. Short, *Letters,* p. 56
11. Winefride and Richard Elwes, *Gervase Elwes,* p. 281
12. *Ibid.,* p. 285
13. Goossens, *Overture and Beginners,* p. 168
14. *Ibid.,* p. 170

10. 'None shall revive the flame that perisheth . . .' 1922–1924

1. Slattery, *Percy Grainger,* p. 101
2. Grainger, 'English-Speaking Leadership in Tone-Art', 21 September 1944, in Slattery, *Percy Grainger,* p. 271
3. 'Grainger's Anecdotes'
4. *Ibid.*
5 Letter from Percy Grainger to Henry Rolf Gardiner, 10 July 1950
6. Letter from Arnold Bax to Clifford Bax, November 1925
7. Evans, 'Modern British Composers: III – Benjamin Dale', *The Musical Times,* 60 (1919), 205
8. Maine, *Twang with Our Music,* pp. 113–14
9. Fenby, *Delius As I Knew Him,* p. 27
10. 'Grainger's Anecdotes'

11. 'My substituted occupation . . .' 1919–1927

1. 'Upper Lambourne', *John Betjeman's Collected Poems,* p. 56
2. Letter from Jelka Delius to Sydney Schiff, 2 August 1924
3. Warlock (revised Foss), *Frederick Delius,* p. 163
4. Barjansky, *Portraits with Backgrounds,* pp. 103–4
5. Delius, *Frederick Delius: Memories of My Brother,* p. 257
6. Warlock (revised Foss), *Frederick Delius,* p. 164
7. Letter to the author, 27 June 1976
8. 27 December 1927, in Lowe, *Delius Collection of the Grainger Museum,* p. 76
9. In 1977 Eric Fenby revised Buths' arrangement of *Paris* in line with the later alterations, and this version was first performed on 12 December 1977 at the Queen Elizabeth Hall, London, in a Balfour Gardiner Centenary concert promoted by the Redcliffe Concerts Society

12. 'If I might have two rows of trees . . .' 1927–1933

1. Hardy, *Tess of the d'Urbevilles,* London, Macmillan, 1957 p. 47
2. Holst, *Gustav Holst,* p. 103 (though Adams is not mentioned by name)
3. Helen Bainton, *Remembered on Waking,* p. 56. In references to Gardiner elsewhere in her memoirs, there are two facts open to question. She states that in the early days of their friendship Gardiner and her father 'met on examination tours'. While Bainton travelled with his educational work, the implication is that Gardiner was similarly occupied, but this has not been substantiated. She also erroneously states that Gardiner inherited the Dorset estates on his father's death
4. Fenby, *Delius As I Knew Him,* pp. 44–5
5. *Ibid.,* p. 27

6. Jelka Delius's postscript to a dictated letter from Frederick Delius to Norman O'Neill, 24 April 1929, in Hudson, *Norman O'Neill*, p. 73
7. 11 January 1913, in Gray, *Peter Warlock*, p. 53
8. pp. 92–4
9. Sir Thomas Armstrong, in conversation with the author
10. Hudson, *Norman O'Neill*, p. 116
11. *Ibid.*, p. 117
12. Cohen, *A Bundle of Time*, p. 206

13. 'This is a terrible time . . .' 1934–1936

1. Letter from H.Balfour Gardiner to Percy Grainger, 6 November 1947
2. p. 223
3. 'Grainger's Anecdotes', dated 8 October 1949
4. 'Round Letter' from Percy Grainger to friends, 17 October 1947, quoted in Bird, *Percy Grainger*, p. 223
5. Letter from H.Balfour Gardiner to Percy Grainger, 31 March 1919
6. 'Round Letter' from Percy Grainger to friends, 17 October 1947
7. Letter from H.Balfour Gardiner to Eric Fenby, 26 October 1936
8. Reid, *Thomas Beecham: an Independent Biography*, p. 49

14. 'We are growing old . . .' 1937–1950

1. Olsen, *Percy Grainger*, English translation by Bent Vanberg, p. 22
2. 'Grainger's Anecdotes'
3. 10 November 1949
4. Information supplied to the author by Guy Warrack
5. 'Grainger's Anecdotes' dated 19 October 1949 and 8 September 1952
6. Information supplied by Richard Austin in a letter to the author, 3 March 1976
7. Letter from Frederick Delius to Philip Heseltine, 24 September 1912
8. Clifford Bax, *Inland Far*, p. 211
9. *Ibid.* pp. 236–7
10. Information supplied to the author by Guy Warrack
11. Margaret Gardiner, '[My Uncle, Balfour Gardiner]', p. 7
12. 'Grainger's Anecdotes'
13. *Ibid.*
14. Margaret Gardiner, '[My Uncle, Balfour Gardiner]', p. 3
15. From Joy Finzi's journal, dated 25 September 1940, giving Gerald Finzi's reactions. Information supplied in a letter from Joy Finzi to the author, 9 June 1976
16. Information supplied by Richard Austin in a letter to the author, 3 March 1976
17. Bush, 'When I Was Young and Twenty', *Performing Right*, No. 45, November 1967, 15
18. BBC broadcast, 23 October 1977
19. Letter from H. Balfour Gardiner to Percy Grainger, 15 June 1949
20. At the time Vaughan Williams was much concerned with rehearsals prior to the first performance of his morality *The Pilgrim's Progress* at Covent Garden three days later

21. Quoted in a letter from Percy Grainger to Henry Rolf Gardiner, 30 May 1951
22. Grainger, '[The Balfour Gardiner Concerts]', museum legend
23. Henry Rolf Gardiner, 'Percy Aldridge Grainger'
24. Enclosed with letter to Rolf Gardiner, 14 April 1951, and written for inclusion in the Memorial Concert programme in which it appeared slightly abbreviated
25. Printed in the Memorial Concert programme
26. *Ibid.*
27. Sent for inclusion in the Memorial Concert programme to Rolf Gardiner on 14 April 1951

Bibliography

Armstrong, Sir Thomas, 'Gardiner, Henry Balfour', *Dictionary of National Biography* 1941–50, p. 288

'The Frankfort Group', *Proceedings of the Royal Musical Association*, 85 (1959), 1–16

'Delius Today', in *Delius*, souvenir programme for Delius Centenary Festival, Bradford, 1962, pp. 16–19

Bainton, Edgar L., 'Some British Composers', No. 11 'H. Balfour Gardiner', *Musical Opinion & Music Trade Review*, 35 (1912), 765–6

Bainton, Helen, *Remembered on Waking*, Sydney, Currawong Publishing Co., 1960

Balough, Teresa, *A Complete Catalogue of the Works of Percy Grainger*, Nedlands, University of Western Australia, 1975

Bantock, Myrrha, *Granville Bantock: a Personal Portrait*, London, Dent, 1972

Barjansky, Catherine, *Portraits with Backgrounds*, London, Bles, 1948

Bashford, H.H., *Lodgings for Twelve*, London, Constable, 1935

Bauer, Prof. Dr M., *Iwan Knorr: ein Gedenkblatt*, Frankfurt, Retiz und Koehler, 1916

Bax, Arnold, *Farewell, My Youth*, London, Longmans, Green & Co., 1943

Bax, Clifford, *Inland Far*, London, Heinemann, 1925, Lovat Dickson, 1933

'Recollections of Gustav Holst', *Music & Letters*, 20 (1939), 1–6

Bayliss, Stanley, 'Henry Balfour Gardiner', *The Choir*, 46 (1955), No. 1

Beecham, Sir Thomas, *A Mingled Chime: Leaves from an Autobiography*, London, Hutchinson, 1944

Frederick Delius, London, Hutchinson, 1959

Best, Andrew (ed.), *Water Springing from the Ground: an Anthology of the Writings of Rolf Gardiner*, Shaftesbury, Trustees of the Gardiner Estate, 1972

Betjeman, John, *John Betjeman's Collected Poems*, London, John Murray, 1958

Bird, John, *Percy Grainger*, London, Paul Elek, 1976

Boult, Sir Adrian, *My Own Trumpet*, London, Hamish Hamilton, 1973

A Short History of Bradbury Greatorex and Co. Ltd, John Hampden Press, Nottingham, n.d.

Bray, Trevor, *Bantock*, London, Triad Press, 1973

'British Music Society 1920 Annual', a catalogue of composers' works, London

Bush, Geoffrey, 'When I Was Young and Twenty', *Performing Right*, No. 45, November 1967, 14-15

Cahn, Peter, 'Percy Grainger's Frankfurt Years', *Studies in Music*, 12 (1978), 101–13

Church, Richard, *The Voyage Home*, London, Heinemann, 1964

Cobbett, W.W., *Cyclopaedic Survey of Chamber Music*, London, OUP, 1929

Cohen, Harriet, *A Bundle of Time: the Memoirs of Harriet Cohen*, London, Faber, 1969

Delius, Clare, *Frederick Delius: Memories of My Brother*, London, Ivor Nicholson & Watson, 1935

Dreyfus, Kay, *Music by Percy Aldridge Grainger*, Percy Grainger Music Collection Part One, Parkville, University of Melbourne, 1978

Eastaugh, Kenneth, *Havergal Brian: the Making of a Composer*, London, Harrap, 1976

Elkin, Robert, *Queen's Hall 1893–1941*, London, Rider & Co., 1944

Royal Philharmonic, London, Rider & Co., 1947

Elwes, Winefride and Richard, *Gervase Elwes: the Story of His Life*, London, Grayson & Grayson, 1935

Evans, Edwin, 'Modern British Composers: III – Benjamin Dale', *The Musical Times*, 60 (1919), 201–5

Fenby, Eric, *Delius As I Knew Him*, London, Bell, 1936

Delius, The Great Composers Series, London, Faber & Faber, 1971

Foss, Hubert, *Ralph Vaughan Williams*, London, Harrap, 1950

Gardiner, Betty, *Notes on the Gardiner Family with Special Reference to the Family of the Late Henry Gardiner Esq. of Essendene, Caterham, Surrey*, London, printed for private circulation, 1915

'Mr H. Balfour Gardiner: British Musicians No. 15' *The Gentlewoman*, 1 September 1906

'H. Balfour Gardiner', *The Musical Times*, 53 (1912), 501–3

Gardiner, Henry Rolf, 'Mr H. Balfour Gardiner: Music and Forestry', unpublished typescript, July 1950, 1 p.

'Percy Aldridge Grainger', unpublished typescript, n.d., 1 p.

Gardiner, Margaret, '[My Uncle, Balfour Gardiner]', unpublished typescript, 1980, 17 pp.

Godfrey, Sir Dan, *Memories and Music*, London, Hutchinson, 1924

Goossens, Eugene, *Overture and Beginners*, London, Methuen, 1951

Grainger, Percy, '[The Balfour Gardiner Concerts]', legend for display in the Grainger Museum, Melbourne, unpublished, 5 December 1938

'Grainger's Anecdotes', unpublished, Grainger Archives, White Plains, New York, 1949–54

'Henry Balfour Gardiner: Champion of British Music', unpublished typescript, Grainger Museum, Melbourne, 9–11 April 1951, 3 pp.

Gray, Cecil, *Peter Warlock: a Memoir of Philip Heseltine*, London, Cape, 1934

Hardy, Florence Emily, *The Life of Thomas Hardy 1840–1928*, London, Macmillan, 1962

Hardy, Thomas, *Tess of the d'Urbevilles*, London, Macmillan, 1902

Wessex Tales, London, Macmillan, 1903

Hassall, Christopher, *Rupert Brooke*, London, Faber, 1964

Havergal, Henry, 'Quilter, Roger Cuthbert', *Dictionary of National Biography 1951–60*, pp. 830–1

Heseltine, Philip, 'Introduction: XVIII E.J. Moeran', *British Music Society Bulletin*, 6 (1924), 170–5

(see also under Warlock, Peter)

Holbrooke, Josef, *Contemporary British Composers*, London, Cecil Palmer, 1925

Holst, Imogen, *Gustav Holst: a Biography*, London, OUP, 1938

Holst, The Great Composers Series, London, Faber & Faber, 1974

A Thematic Catalogue of Gustav Holst's Music, London, Faber Music, 1974

Hudson, Derek, *Norman O'Neill: a Life of Music*, London, Quality Press, 1945

Hull, A.Eaglefield,*Cyril Scott: the Man and His Music*, London, Kegan Paul, Trench, Trubner & Co., 1918

Irving, Ernest, *Cue for Music*, London, Dobson, 1959

Kennedy, Michael, *The Works of Ralph Vaughan Williams*, London, OUP, 1964

Keynes, Sir Geoffrey (ed.), *The Letters of Rupert Brooke*, London, Faber, 1968

Lamond, Frederic, *The Memoirs of Frederic Lamond*, Glasgow, Maclellan, 1949

Litzmann, Dr Berthold (ed.), *Letters of Clara Schumann and Johannes Brahms*, 2 vols., New York, Longmans, Green & Co., 1927

Lloyd, Stephen, *H. Balfour Gardiner 1877-1950: Composer – Patron – Forester*, programme for Centenary concert, Monteverdi Choir and Orchestra, St John's, Smith Square, London, 6 November 1977

    [H. Balfour Gardiner], script for BBC Radio 3 Gardiner Centenary broadcast, 7 November 1977

    'Balfour Gardiner 1877-1950', *Music and Musicians*, December 1977, 22-5

    Balfour Gardiner: Composer, patron and forester, programme for Centenary concert, Redcliffe Concerts of British Music, Queen Elizabeth Hall, London, 12 December 1977

    'The Ghost of a Smile' [Cyril Scott Centenary assessment], *Music and Musicians*, September 1979, 20-2

    'Grainger "In a Nutshell"' in Lewis Foreman (ed.), *The Percy Grainger Companion*, London, Thames Publishing, 1981, pp. 15-22

    'Grainger's Original Compositions', *Studies in Music*, Percy Grainger Centennial volume, 16 (1982), 11-21

    'Grainger and the "Frankfurt Group"', *Studies in Music*, Percy Grainger Centennial volume, 16 (1982), 111-18

Longmire, John, *John Ireland: Portrait of a Friend*, London, John Baker, 1969

Lowe, Rachel, *Frederick Delius: a Catalogue of the Music Archive of the Delius Trust*, London, Delius Trust, 1974

    A Descriptive Catalogue with Checklists of the Letters and Related Documents in the Delius Collection of the Grainger Museum, London, Delius Trust, 1981

Lucas, E.V., *London Lavender*, London, Methuen, 1912

Maine, Basil, *Twang with Our Music*, London, Epworth Press, 1957

Masefield, John, *The Collected Poems of John Masefield*, London, Heinemann, 1926

Moeran, E.J., 'Folk-Songs and Some Traditional Singers in East Anglia', *The Countrygoer* (*in the Autumn*), 7 (1946), 31-5

Newmarch, Rosa, *Jean Sibelius*, London, Goodwin & Tabb, 1944

Olsen, Sparre, *Percy Grainger*, Oslo, Norske Samlaget, 1963, with separate English translation by Bent Vanberg, edited by Stewart Manville, from Grainger Library Society, New York

Orr, C.W., 'Elgar and the Public', *The Musical Times*, 72 (1931), 17–18

Purslow, Frank, 'The George Gardiner Folk-Song Collection', *Folk Music Journal*, 1, No.3 (1967), 129-57

Quinlan, John, 'A.E. Housman and British Composers', *The Musical Times*, 100 (1959), 137-8

Reid, Charles, *Thomas Beecham: an Independent Biography*, London, Gollancz, 1961

    John Barbirolli, London, Hamish Hamilton, 1971

'Charles Kennedy Scott', *The Musical Times*, 61 (1920), 659-62

'Profile: Kennedy Scott', *The Observer*, 11 November 1951

Scott, Cyril, 'Iwan Knorr 1853–1916', *The Monthly Musical Record*, 46 (1916), 240–2

My Years of Indiscretion, London, Mills & Boon, 1924

'The Late Balfour Gardiner and Our Student Days', *The Music Teacher & Piano Student*, September 1950, pp. 396 & 427

'A Tribute to Josef Holbrooke', *The Musical Times*, 99 (1958), 425–6

Bone of Contention: Life Story and Confessions, London, The Aquarian Press, 1969

Scott-Sutherland, Colin, *Arnold Bax*, London, Dent, 1973

Sharp, C.J. (ed.), *Folk-Songs of England: Book III*, London, Novello, 1909

Short, Michael (ed.), *Gustav Holst: Letters to W.G. Whittaker*, University of Glasgow, 1974

Slattery, Thomas C., *Percy Grainger: the Inveterate Innovator*, Evanston, Illinois, The Instrumentalist Co., 1974

Taylor, Stainton de B., 'Charles Kennedy Scott', *The Musical Times*, 92 (1951), 492–6

Threlfall, Robert, *A Catalogue of the Compositions of Frederick Delius*, London, Delius Trust, 1977

Tomlinson, Fred, *A Peter Warlock Handbook*, vols. 1 & 2, London, Triad Press, 1974 & 1977

Warlock and Delius, London, Thames Publishing, 1976

Warlock and van Dieren, London, Thames Publishing, 1978

Treves, Sir Frederick, *Highways and Byways in Dorset*, London, Macmillan, 1935

Vaughan Williams, Ralph, *National Music and Other Essays*, London, OUP, 1963

Vaughan Williams, Ursula, *RVW: a Biography of Ralph Vaughan Williams,* London, OUP, 1964

Warlock, Peter (Philip Heseltine), *Frederick Delius*, reprinted with additions, annotations and comments by Hubert Foss, London, The Bodley Head, 1952

Wood, Henry J., *My Life of Music*, London, Gollancz, 1938

256

Discography

The following list contains all known recordings up to January 1983 of Balfour Gardiner's music. In compiling this list the author wishes to acknowledge the invaluable assistance of Lewis Foreman, Eric Hughes and Malcolm Walker. Italicised record numbers indicate recordings issued at 78 or 80 r.p.m. Of the commercial releases included, the majority are no longer available for purchase, but most of the works may be heard either at the National Sound Archive (formerly the British Institute of Recorded Sound), 29 Exhibition Road, London SW7 (to which application should first be made), or at The British Music Information Centre, 10 Stratford Place, London W1.

APRIL
Goldsmiths' Choral Union, London Symphony Orchestra, Austin   Argo RG69[1]

CARGOES
Glasgow Orpheus Choir, Roberton (rec. Oct. 1925)   *HMV E407*
                                                      in EMI MRS5175
John Barrow (bar.), Wilfrid Parry (pf.)   BBC Trans. 131340

EVENING HYMN
Philharmonic Choir & organ, Charles Kennedy Scott   HMV D1304[2]
King's College Choir & organ, Willcocks   HMV CSD3752
                                                     Q4-CSD3752
                                                     ④TC-CSD3752
Worcester Cathedral Choir, Robinson   Polydor 2460 250
                                                         ④ 3170 241
Marlborough College Choir & organ, Wilkinson   Wealden WS137
Guildford Cathedral Choir & organ, Moore   Abbey LPB771
Peterborough Cathedral Choir & organ, Vann   Abbey LPB658
Exeter Cathedral Choir & organ, Dakers   Pilgrim JLP154
                                                         JLPS154
Holy Trinity Choir & organ, Cayless   Holy Trinity HT1
Bishop's Stortford Parish Church Choir & organ,   Strobe 128
    Banton
Norwich Cathedral Choir & organ, Nicholas   Vista VPS1084
Queen's College Cambridge Choir & organ,   QCR 8818[3]
    Armstrong
Liverpool Metropolitan Cathedral Choir & organ   Abbey LPB816

FIVE PIECES
3,5   York Bowen (pf.)   *Vocalion K-05259*
1,2,3,5 Jean Hamilton (pf.)   Private recording[4]

257

HUMORESQUE
Stephen Fisher (pf.)   *Beltona 465*
Maurice Cole (pf.)   *Aco G15351*
Percy Grainger (piano roll rec. 1928)   Duo-Art 6415

JOYFUL HOMECOMING, THE
Jean Hamilton (pf.)   Private recording[4]

MICHAELCHURCH
Jean Hamilton (pf.)   Private recording[4]

MOVEMENT FOR STRINGS IN C MINOR
Quintet ensemble   BBC Trans. 141971[5]

NOEL
Performer unknown   Artona Music Rolls 6306

OVERTURE TO A COMEDY
BBC Symphony Orchestra, Raybould   *BBC Trans. 16201/3*
London Symphony Orchestra, Austin   Argo RG69[1]

PHILOMELA
Alexander Young (tenor), Goldsmiths' Choral   Argo RG69[1]
   Union, London Symphony Orchestra, Austin

QUIET GARDEN, THE
Peter Pears (tenor), Roger Vignoles (pf.)   BBC Trans. 141971[5]

SALAMANCA
Jean Hamilton (pf.)   Private recording[4]

SHENADOAH (AND OTHER PIECES)
4 Jean Hamilton (pf.)   Private recording[4]

SHEPHERD FENNEL'S DANCE
New Queen's Hall Orchestra, Wood   *Columbia L1033*[6]
Royal Albert Hall Orchestra, Ronald   *HMV D159*[7]
Royal Opera Covent Garden Orchestra, Collingwood   *HMV C1469*
Liverpool Philharmonic Orchestra, Sargent   *Columbia DX1393*
BBC Symphony Orchestra 'A', Boult   *BBC Trans. 25152/3*
   (rec. 23 September 1944)
Hamburg Philharmonia Orchestra, Walther   *MSB 78152*
    MGM 3143
New Symphony Orchestra, Collins   Decca LW5297
    ACL108
    DPA627/8
London Symphony Orchestra, Austin   Argo RG69[1]
Light Music Society Orchestra, Dunn   EMI TW0295
   (arr. for viola and piano, excerpt only)
Frederick Riddle (vla), Malcolm Sargent (pf.)   Decca LXT5573[8]
    SXL2199
    ECS2102

STRING QUARTET IN B♭
Kutcher Quartet   *Edison Bell X563*[9]

WINTER
Peter Pears (tenor), Roger Vignoles (pf.)   BBC Trans. 141971[5]

NOTES

1. Argo recording, partly financed by the Gardiner family, made on 4 and 5 May 1955, prior to the Royal Festival Hall concert on 6 May when, in addition to the four works recorded, Richard Austin conducted the London Symphony Orchestra in the first performance of *A Berkshire Idyll*. The concert opened with Wagner's overture to *Die Meistersinger* and ended (ironically) with Beethoven's Piano Concerto No. 5. By November 1959 record sales totalled 300 copies.
2. Slightly abridged version, sung in English, with cuts of eighteen bars chiefly in the organ linking passages.
3. Two-record set, 'A Theatre Records Production', recorded on 15 and 16 July 1979.
4. A private recording commissioned by the Gardiner family and made on 1-3 December 1958. On receiving a copy, Grainger wrote to Rolf Gardiner on 23 April 1959: 'It was awfully nice of you to send me the recording of Balfour's piano pieces so delightfully played by Jean Hamilton. If you would be kind enough to let me have her title (Mrs Miss?) I would be most happy to write and congratulate her on her splendid playing.'
5. Recording made by the BBC Transcription Unit at the 30th Aldeburgh Festival. The quintet ensemble consisted of Malcolm Layfield and Theresa Ward (violins), Sally Beamish and Anne Rycroft (violas), and Carmel Russill (cello).
6. Cuts from ②-⑤ and ⑪ - ⑭ .
7. Much abridged version. The first eight bars are played, then a cut to page 17 one bar before ⑦; from ⑧ there is another cut to page 19, after which the music is played complete to the end.
8. 21 bars only: the middle section from ⑦, slightly abridged.
9. Barbirolli played in this quartet for a while *c.*1924 and performed this work with them, including an early broadcast. It is unlikely, however, that he is playing in this recording.

BBC TRANSCRIPTION UNIT

Further recordings were made at the time of the Gardiner Centenary. A recital entirely of his songs was recorded by David Wilson-Johnson (baritone) and David Owen Norris (piano) on 27 June 1977 and broadcast on the day of the Centenary. The following were recorded (P1230BW):

> *Lightly We Met in the Morn*
> *The Stranger's Song*
> *Fidele*
> *The Recruit*
> *When I Was One-and-Twenty*
> *The Wanderer's Evensong*
> *The Golden Vanity*
> *Roadways*
> *Winter*
> *Rybbesdale*
> *The Quiet Garden*

The Unit also recorded a concert of works by Gardiner and his friends at St John's, Smith

Square, given on 6 November 1977 by the Monteverdi Choir and Orchestra under their conductor John Eliot Gardiner. Gardiner's works recorded (CN3119/SQ) were:

Movement for Strings, arr. Grainger
News from Whydah
A Berkshire Idyll
Evening Hymn (orch. Norris)

Index

9 780521 619226